California White Water

California
White Water

A GUIDE TO THE RIVERS

Jim Cassady
Fryar Calhoun

©Copyright 1984 Jim Cassady and Fryar Calhoun
Printed in the United States of America
Published by Jim Cassady and Fryar Calhoun
Text by Jim Cassady and Fryar Calhoun
River maps by Audre Newman
Back cover map by Mary Robertson
Typesetting by Jana Janus
Printing by Kingsport Press

ISBN 0-9613650-0-5

First printing September 1984
Second printing July 1985

Portions of the text are reprinted with the permission of *California Magazine* and *Sacramento Magazine*.

Cover: Middle Fork American, Tunnel Chute
Photo: *Whitewater Voyages*

For our parents

Table of Contents

                                                                        Page

Preface xiii

Acknowledgments xv

Introduction 1

   How To Use This Guide 2

Rivers of the Southern Sierra Nevada

Kern 13

   1. Forks of the Kern 15

   2. Upper Kern 21

   3. Lower Kern 29

   4. Rio Bravo Run 35

Kaweah 39

   5. East Fork Confluence to Main Kaweah 39

Kings 43

   6. Upper Kings 44

   7. Garnet Dike Campground to Kirch Flat Campground 49

Rivers of the Central and Northern Sierra Nevada

Merced 54

   8. Red Bud to Bagby 54

Tuolumne 59

   9. Upper Tuolumne: Cherry Creek Run 62

   10. Meral's Pool to Ward's Ferry 69

Stanislaus 76

   11. Lower Stanislaus: Goodwin Dam to Knight's Ferry 78

Mokelumne 82

   12. Electra Run 82

Cosumnes 86

   13. Highway 49 to Highway 16 86

Carson 90

    14. Upper East Fork 91

    15. East Fork: Wilderness Run 94

American 96

    16. South Fork: Chili Bar and Gorge Runs 98

    17. Middle Fork 105

    18. North Fork: Giant Gap Run 111

    19. North Fork: Chamberlain Falls and Big Bend Runs 115

Truckee 119

    20. River Ranch to Floriston 119

Yuba 123

    21. North Fork: Downieville and Goodyears Bar Runs 123

Feather 127

    22. Middle Fork Gorge 128

Deer Creek 133

    23. Ishi Caves Run 133

Rivers of the Coast Ranges

Russian 139

    24. Squaw Rock Run 139

Cache Creek 143

    25. Rumsey Run 143

Rancheria Creek 147

    26. Mountain View Road to Hendy Woods State Park 147

Stony Creek 151

    27. Fouts Springs Run 151

Eel 155

    28. Main Eel: Pillsbury Run 158

    29. Main Eel: Dos Rios to Alderpoint 161

    30. North Fork 166

    31. Middle Fork 168

    32. South Fork 173

Redwood Creek 179

   33. Tall Trees Run 179

Sacramento 184

   34. Upper Sacramento: Box Canyon Dam to Shasta Reservoir. 184

Trinity 189

   35. Main Trinity: North Fork Confluence to China Slide 191

   36. Burnt Ranch Gorge 194

   37. Lower Trinity: Hawkins Bar to Weitchpec 198

   38. South Fork 202

Salmon 208

   39. Methodist Creek to Klamath River Confluence 208

Scott 213

   40. Canyon Run 213

Klamath 217

   41. Upper Klamath 219

   42. Main Klamath: Sarah Totten Campground to Weitchpec. 224

Smith 233

   43. North Fork 234

   44. Main Smith: Gasquet to South Fork Confluence 237

   45. South Fork 240

More California Rivers 243

   • San Joaquin • West Walker • North Fork Stanislaus • North Fork Mokelumne • South Fork American (Kyburz to Riverton) • Bear • South Fork Yuba • McCloud • San Lorenzo • Noyo • Rivers of the Central Coast •

The Lay of the Land 248

   Geology of California River Country

What's That on the Bank? 253

   Plant Communities of the River Canyons

Try the Top of the Eddy 260
    Fishing on California White Water Rivers
Water Follies 265
    A Guide to California Water Politics
Whose Rivers Are They? 272
    Legal Problems of River Running and River Access
Where To Get It and How To Do It 275
    White Water Equipment, Instruction, and Publications
Easy White Water 277
Index of Featured Rivers 279
About the Authors 283
Index of First-Person Stories 284

Preface

White water river running is a young sport changing fast. Nowhere have those changes been more dramatic than in California, where there are more rivers and more boaters than in any other state. Fifteen or twenty years ago, a small number of kayakers and rafters had the streams to themselves. Commercial outfitters were few and far between, and the Chili Bar run and the Stanislaus impressed most river runners as very difficult. The Tuolumne was the prime test of technical boating in California, perhaps in the western United States.

Things are different today. The Stanislaus, sad to say, has been drowned by the dam builders, and the Tuolumne is in danger. But in the meantime, white water sport has exploded. Every year 100,000 people run the South Fork American, the second most popular white water river in the country. The traditional Tuolumne run beginning at Meral's Pool gets so much traffic that the Forest Service has instituted a strict permit system for non-commercial as well as commercial boaters. And as techniques and equipment have evolved, kayakers and rafters have stretched the upper limits of boating. River runners looking for really tough rapids on the "T" now put in on Cherry Creek, miles upstream from Meral's Pool. Commercial outfitters even offer guided raft trips on Class V rivers that remained unexplored until the end of the sixties or later—rivers like the Upper Tuolumne, the Forks of the Kern, and Burnt Ranch Gorge of the Trinity.

Though California has more than 1200 dams, many fine boating streams remain in the vast expanses of the state's mountain ranges. Short one-day trips and longer wilderness floats may be found from the Kern in the southern Sierra Nevada to the Smith in the far northwest. White water runs featured in this book range from easy Class II stretches that can be navigated in open canoes (at low water) to remote, extremely difficult Class V wilderness runs known only to a few experts. For 45 of the state's best runs we provide maps, mile by mile guides, and other information most boaters like to have before they set out for the river. There are briefer notes on other runs in the chapter *More California Rivers*. For quick reference, see the list of more than twenty *Easy White Water* runs as well as the general *Index of Featured Rivers* at the back of the book. Our goal has been to put together a guide worthy of California's fine rivers. We hope our readers enjoy it and find it useful.

Jim Cassady
Fryar Calhoun
Richmond and Berkeley
June 1984

Acknowledgments

If this book proves to be useful, it will be largely due to the aid and advice of friends and fellow river lovers almost too numerous to name— but we're going to try. For information on California rivers we turned to boaters from one end of the state to the other, among them John Adams, Koll Buer, Jeb Butchert, Bill Center, Brian Clark, David Dickson, Ann Dwyer, Sam Fortner, Jake Green, Don Harriman, Mark Helmus, Moss Henry, Tom Hoeck, Marty McDonnell, Dean Munroe, Monte Osborne, Dan Patterson, Gary Peebles, Bob Porter, Royal Robbins, John Sweetzer, Chuck Stanley, Cindy Wall, David Wallace, Bryce Whitmore, and the Whitewater Voyages staff.

We learned a lot about river running, river lore, and the history of white water boating in California from Bill Carlson, Bob Carlson, Doug Carson, Reg Lake, Jerry Meral, Marty McDonnell, Bill McGinnis, Spreck Rosekrans, and Carl Trost. And we never stopped referring to the pioneering guide books by Charles Martin and Dick Schwind.

Ann Dwyer, Ted Kearn, Reg Lake, Keith Miller, and Chuck Stanley helped with questions concerning kayakers and canoeists. Our understanding of rivers in their various contexts—geological, ecological, historical, political, and economic—was enriched by conversations with John Amodio, Betty Andrews, Bill Cross, Nancy Dagle, Dodge Ely, Richard Ely, Fred Fisher, Tom Graff, Bob Hackamack, Jerry Meral, Michael McIntyre, Bill Resneck, Dick Roos-Collins, and Michael Storper. A few of these experts wrote or collaborated on particular chapters.

Erick Pinkham, Ed Manegold, and Andy Ross generously allowed us to write this book on their IBM computers. Julie Anjos, Bill Cross, Polly Greist, Erick Pinkham, Rick Batts, and a number of other friends took the time to read and check our manuscript and proofs at various stages. We are grateful to the boaters who shared river stories with our readers and us. We were fortunate to find available the work of some fine photographers, all of whom are credited individually in these pages except for Steve Givant, who took most of the photos credited to Whitewater Voyages. Our special thanks to consultants on photography and art, Brian Fessenden and Steve Kowalski, and to Audre Neuman for her maps and Jana Janus for her typesetting and page design. Diana Clardy and Kathy Springmeyer also provided valuable help with typesetting and cover design.

For the book's merits, much of the credit goes to these collaborators, friends, and advisors. Blame the authors for its shortcomings.★

★And tell us about them. We would appreciate comments, criticism, corrections, and suggestions. Please write us at PO Box 3580, Berkeley, CA 94703.

California White Water

Introduction

From the southern Sierra Nevada to the Oregon border, California offers boaters the widest variety of quality white water runs in the country. This book is a guide to the state's best rivers, not an instruction manual on how to run them. A guide book can no more teach you how to run a rapid than a road map can teach you how to drive.

On the river, you are responsible for your own safety. Reading this book is no substitute for experience, prudence, common sense, and first-hand observation. We have tried to be accurate, but we may have made mistakes in locating, rating, or describing rapids, or conditions may have altered. Trust your eyes first and the book second.

Don't make the mistake of running a white water river without knowing what you are doing. Seek advice and instruction first. (For references see the end of the book.) Meanwhile, here are some principles of safe river running:

- Be sure your white water skills and experience are equal to the river and the conditions. Never boat alone.
- Wear a life jacket at all times when you are in or near the river. High-flotation jackets are best. Know how to float in a white water river: feet first, in the deepest channel, never just ahead of a boat. Know when and how to swim for an eddy. Protect your feet by wearing shoes that won't come off in the river.
- Helmets are a must for kayakers all the time, and for rafters in Class V water.
- Be prepared for extremes in weather, especially cold. Know about the dangers of hypothermia and how to deal with it. When air and water temperature add up to 120° or less, hypothermia is a high risk. Wear a wet suit and booties throughout the rainy season and into early summer, at least until high water is over—and always on Class V rivers.
- Beware of high water. Most California rivers undergo a profound and dangerous change when their flows rise. Never run a river at or near flood stage.
- Brush and trees in or across the river are deadly hazards. Stay clear.
- Use sturdy equipment in good repair. Carry toss bags, safety lines, spare oars or paddles, repair kits, a pump (rafts), and a safely sheathed knife. Rig gear securely and pad hard objects.
- Carry a first-aid kit and know how to use it. Learn or review first aid and CPR. Avoid rattlesnakes and poison oak, but know how to deal with emergencies if someone is unlucky.
- Know how to recognize and react to river hazards such as holes, snags, wrap rocks, undercut boulders and walls, rock sieves, and horizon lines across the river.

- Never run a rapid unless you see a clear path through it or an eddy you can catch. Watch out for new snags after winter and spring floods.
- Allow the craft ahead of you to pass through the rapid before you enter it. This will avoid a double disaster if the leading boat blocks the channel.
- When in doubt, stop and scout. Still in doubt? Portage.
- Tell someone where you are going, when you expect to return, and where to call if you don't (see river chapters for emergency telephone numbers).

How to Use This Guide

This guide book features 45 of the best white water runs in California. Contiguous runs are separated only when they vary dramatically in difficulty. In many cases these runs can be extended, or there are other runnable stretches elsewhere on the river. See the essays and mile by mile guides, as well as the chapter "More California Rivers."

Difficulty

Rating the difficulty of a river is a tricky business. No simple system can adequately convey a river's unique combination of potential difficulties—especially when complicating factors such as degree of risk, variations in flow, season, weather, and water temperature are considered. Remember:

- Slight fluctuations in the water level can change a rapid dramatically.
- Some rapids change from year to year—particularly on Coast Range rivers—and there is always the potential problem of a new snag or a fallen tree.
- As any qualified boater knows, most rivers become more difficult at high flows, and mistakes are more likely to have serious consequences. The South Fork American between Chili Bar and Salmon Falls is a Class III river, but at higher flows (3000–4000 cfs and up) boaters should have Class IV skills before they attempt it.
- Is there a recovery pool after the rapid, or does it lead to more white water with little chance to stop? Would a swimmer* be in danger, or could he make it to shore?

*"Swimming" is a white water euphemism for floating in a life jacket. Nothing remotely resembling swimming takes place until the usually unwilling victim is through the rapid itself.

2

- Is there a road out? A trail? Emergency help? Remote rivers through isolated wilderness should be approached with caution, since aid is difficult or impossible to obtain in case of accident.
- The danger of hypothermia increases at high water; during spring snow melt, when the river is cold; at high elevations; and in the rainy season, when days are short and air temperatures are even lower than water temperatures.

Rivers in this guide are rated by the international scale of I to VI.* (See below, **Rating the Rapids**.) Rivers, or portions of rivers, are classified according to their most difficult typical rapids. The main Tuolumne is rated Class IV+, though of course it has numerous Class I, II, and III rapids as well.

We split the rating when the same run includes sections of contrasting difficulty. For example, though most of the Middle Fork Eel is Class II, its rating of Class II–IV$_6$ indicates that there is also a Class IV section, with at least one even bigger Class VI rapid. In cases like this one, the presence of one or two uncharacteristically tough rapids is indicated by a subscript, in Arabic numerals instead of Roman. A "p" indicates one or more portages, as in the Middle Fork American (Class II–Vp).

*A few U.S. rivers, notably the Grand Canyon of the Colorado, are often still rated by the old western American system of 1 to 10. Lava Falls and Crystal, the Grand Canyon's biggest rapids, rate 10 on that scale, V on the international scale.

Rating the Rapids

In this book we attempt to rate rapids realistically, in terms that reflect the accomplishments of modern white water sport. That means, among other things, that we don't overrate rapids to protect boaters. But we don't downgrade rapids simply because more people are running them these days. Clavey Falls on the Tuolumne is still a Class V rapid, but more and more boaters are learning to handle it (most of the time, anyway). Still, it may be true that the concept of Class V has been stretched at its upper limit—first by kayakers, more recently by rafters. As anyone who has run the Upper Tuolumne, the Forks of the Kern, or Burnt Ranch Gorge can testify, there are rapids that should be rated not only V but V+ or V–VI. We have also made a stab at distinguishing between Class VI rapids, which are runnable only by teams of experts taking considerable risks, and Class "U" (unrunnable) passages, which we feel should never be attempted by anyone. But such decisions are relevant only to experts. For most boaters these questions should never arise, except perhaps around the campfire.

Most rapids change in difficulty with the flow. Some are easier at high water, some at low. In particularly well-known instances—but by no means in all—we have shown a rapid's rating as III–IV, IV–V, and so on. In theory, rapids rated III–IV or IV–V vary more with the flow than rapids rated simply III+ or IV+. An extreme example is Table Rock Rapid (IV–VI) in Burnt Ranch Gorge of the Trinity. At low flows boats can reach a safe channel, but at higher flows they are swept toward a dangerous undercut rock.

Class I rapids are merely riffles—small waves and no obstacles.

Class II rapids have bigger waves but no major obstructions. Most open canoeists should never tackle anything tougher than Class II.

Class III rapids are longer and rougher than Class II, and they have considerably bigger hydraulics (waves, holes, and currents). Route-finding is sometimes necessary, though Class III rapids generally require no more than a few maneuvers. Advanced and expert boaters can usually "read and run" them, but less experienced river runners should scout. Class III rapids may seem easy to passengers who have been guided by experts—for example, on a commercial raft trip—but intermediate and even advanced boaters sometimes run into trouble on Class III rapids. Only expert open canoeists should attempt Class III rivers, and only at low flows.

Class IV rapids are generally steeper, longer, and more heavily obstructed than Class III rapids. They are often "technical" runs requiring a number of turns and lateral moves. Preliminary scouting of all Class IV rapids is definitely recommended unless the boater is highly skilled and knows the river intimately. Few want to, but when they must, boaters can usually "swim" Class IV rapids without high risk of major injury.

Class V. Even to the uninitiated, a Class V rapid looks different—and bigger. In addition to strong currents, big waves, boulders, and holes powerful enough to hold or flip boats, Class V rapids usually have one or more major vertical drops. Everyone scouts Class V rapids, even experts. Many are routinely portaged even though they are runnable at certain water levels. An accident in a Class V rapid risks injury to boaters as well as damage or loss of equipment.

Class VI rapids—magnified versions of Class V, with additional problems and hazards—are usually considered unrunnable. For most boaters they are. But at certain water levels, teams of experts taking all precautions can and have run Class VI rapids. Nevertheless, even in the best of circumstances, risks may include not only injury but loss of life. Definitely not recommended.

Class U rapids (unrunnable) are usually falls and should never be attempted. This judgment, like any classification of rapids, is subjective to a degree. In fact, a few which we label "U" have been run. Nevertheless, we consider them unsafe at any flow.

4

Skill Levels Necessary for Boaters

	Rafts and Kayaks		Open Canoes
Difficulty	Low and Moderate Flows	High Flows	Low Flows Only
I	Novices	Novices	Novices/Intermediates
II	Novices	Intermediates	Intermediates/Advanced
III	Intermediates	Advanced	Experts
IV	Advanced	Experts	Experts at Risk
V	Experts	Experts at Risk	Unrunnable
VI	Experts at Risk	Unrunnable	Unrunnable
U	Unrunnable	Unrunnable	Unrunnable

Length

This guide shows total river miles from put-in to take-out for each run. If alternate access points make longer or shorter floats possible, we say so.

Gradient

The average gradient of each run, or portions of each run, is shown in vertical feet of drop per river mile. Usually, the steeper the gradient, the more difficult the river. California rivers with average drops of 50 feet per mile and more are usually Class V; 30 to 50 feet per mile, Class IV; 15 to 30, Class III; and below 15, Class II.

But this rough generalization applies to pool-and-drop rivers, which should be distinguished from rivers with a more continuous gradient. The latter are typically less difficult than a pool-and-drop river with a similar gradient. For example, the lower Stanislaus above Knight's Ferry has an overall gradient of only 30 feet per mile, but this short stretch contains several steep, difficult Class V drops which punctuate long, flat pools. In contrast, the Upper East Fork Carson above Hangman's Bridge drops at 65 feet per mile, but the decline is spread fairly evenly over the run, whose most difficult rapids are only Class III.

5

Drainage

Size of the watershed drained by the river and its tributaries at or near some point along the run. Generally, the larger the watershed, the bigger the stream bed and the higher the river's potential peak flow — though of course the location of the watershed and the amount and type of precipitation are also key factors. Rivers with larger watersheds and stream beds tend to have higher minimum and maximum runnable flows than rivers with smaller drainages.

Elevation at Put-in

In California most runnable stretches of white water are at elevations below 3000'. There are exceptions, particularly eastern slope rivers like the Truckee and the Carson, where the put-ins are above 6000', as well as the Forks of the Kern (4680'). Prudent boaters restrict their winter and early spring runs to lower-elevation stretches, where temperatures are warmer and the danger of hypothermia is less acute.

Season

We have tried to indicate the boating season for each run in a year of "average" precipitation and weather. In fact, rain, snow, and the timing and duration of spring snow melt vary considerably from year to year. In the very wet year of 1983, rafts were still running the undammed Forks of the Kern and Upper Kern in September. But in the drought year of 1977 the river was runnable for only a few days in May. Tough-hided boaters may feel that we have started the seasons too late both for rain-fed and snow melt rivers. True, if you don't mind the cold, you can run rivers in December, January, and February as well as in the spring months we tend to indicate. But beware of hypothermia. Generally, we have started seasons later for higher elevation rivers and earlier for those at lower altitudes. Overnight trips and floats on difficult rivers should be scheduled later in the season, when days are longer and the weather is better.

California rarely has "average" years, so information on a river's boating season should be taken as only a rough indication of what a given year may hold in store — especially for undammed rivers. Dam-controlled flows have widely varying impacts. Sometimes they ruin a downstream run, sometimes they extend its boating season.

Most dam releases vary from year to year, month to month, and day to day depending on factors ranging from demand for electrical power to how much water upstream reservoirs are holding. Most were very low in 1977, the second year of the most recent drought. One way to keep informed about what kind of season to expect is to subscribe to the free reports on water conditions in California published by the state Department of Water Resources, PO Box 388, Sacramento, CA 95802.

Runnable Levels

Flows are given in cubic feet per second (cfs)—for example, 400/700 –6000 cfs. The first figure (400) is the minimum flow for kayaks. The second figure (700) is the minimum for **small** rafts (10 to 12 feet in length). The minimum runnable level is literally that: just enough water to scrape down the river. (The minimum flow is not the optimum flow. Optimum flow is a matter of personal preference, but it is usually at least two to three times the minimum flow.) The last figure (6000) is the maximum recommended flow for both kayaks and **large** rafts (15 to 18 feet).

Warning: Upper levels given here are for advanced or expert boaters only. Most rafters and kayakers should set their own maximum levels considerably lower. For example, we say the main Tuolumne is runnable up to 8000 cfs; in fact, it has been run at much higher levels. But most commercial outfitters cancel their trips when the river is at or near 8000 cfs, and anyone who knows the river can confirm that difficult high-water runs begin around 4000 cfs.

Flow Information

California boaters and fishermen are well served by the state Department of Water Resources, which maintains two taped phone messages (updated several times a week) giving flows on a number of the state's rivers. Most of the best-known runs are included on the main number, (916) 322-3327. Some of the North Coast rivers are mentioned only on the North Coast number, (707) 443-9305. But there are some rivers for which there is no reliable source of flow information. In these cases, we sometimes offer ways to make an educated guess. No guarantees.

Special Hazards

Don't assume that this book can warn you of all the hazards on a river. In addition to our inadvertent mistakes and omissions, there are always new problems to watch out for—including rearranged rapids and trees and snags in the channel. Be particularly alert for changes made by high water in the winter and spring. (See the chapter on Redwood Creek for this book's most dramatic example of this situation.)

Water

Except for the few high-elevation runs, most boatable California rivers have water temperatures ranging from the low 40's to the low 50's during the rainy season and during heavy snow melt. That means prudent boaters wear wet suits well into June, and all summer when they run Class IV and V rivers where long "swims" are a possibility.

As for water quality, readers of this guide are advised that we take no legal responsibility for the accuracy of the information we offer, though we have made every effort to present the best available judgment. Personally, we often drink from white water rivers, especially in the upper sections of Sierra streams, and especially at high and moderate flows. But the Forest Service and other government agencies routinely warn hikers, campers, and boaters to purify all drinking water taken from rivers and streams. Sometimes side streams are polluted by fecal coliform bacteria, especially when cows graze in the watershed. Recently, giardia has been reported on some rivers.

Maps

We list U.S. Geological Service 15-minute and 7.5-minute topographical maps, national forest maps where appropriate, and AAA maps, which are helpful for getting to and from the river area and for finding shuttle roads. The authors of this book have also published detailed maps and guides to five of the state's most popular rivers: the South Fork American, Tuolumne, Forks of the Kern, Upper Kern and Lower Kern. See page 283 for more information.

Auto Shuttle

Mileages and estimated driving times are given one way, from put-in to take-out.

Logistics

How to get to the river area and find shuttle roads, plus special problems. We tried to get all these instructions right, but we probably blew a few. Sorry.

Mile by Mile Guide

The chief purpose of the mile guide is to give boaters an idea of what to expect on the river, when to stop and scout a rapid, and how to recognize it. Descriptions of individual rapids are not intended as instructions for running them. Nor do we pretend to have included anything like a comprehensive list of rapids. Those rated Class III and below are left out of mile guides to Class IV runs, and Class IV rapids appear only infrequently in mile guides to Class V runs. Better-known rivers are described in more detail than those where only a few experts have ventured—like the Upper Kings, Middle Fork Feather Gorge, and Deer Creek. Boaters on Class V rivers like these should be prepared to do plenty of scouting and to portage wherever necessary. In cases like these we rarely mention specific portages and sometimes list no individual rapids at all.

River miles start at the put-in. The location of rapids and other important features by mile is always approximate, though on well-known rivers like the South Fork American our guide should be pretty close. On the less frequently run rivers, however, readers are urged to take mileage as only a rough indication. Don't blunder into a big rapid just because you expect it to be half a mile downstream.

If it were up to us, rapids would be named whenever possible for prominent topographical features such as a nearby creek. But in this guide we have usually stuck to accepted names, even though too many ended up sounding like "Dick's Demise," "Satan's Dragon's Chipped Tooth," and "Foaming Death." Why so much fascination with devil and death in such a good sport with so few fatalities?

Forks of the Kern, between Vortex and The Gauntlet.   *Whitewater Voyages*

Rivers of the Southern Sierra Nevada

1. Forks of the Kern
2. Upper Kern
3. Lower Kern
4. Kern: Rio Bravo Run
5. Kaweah
6. Upper Kings
7. Kings

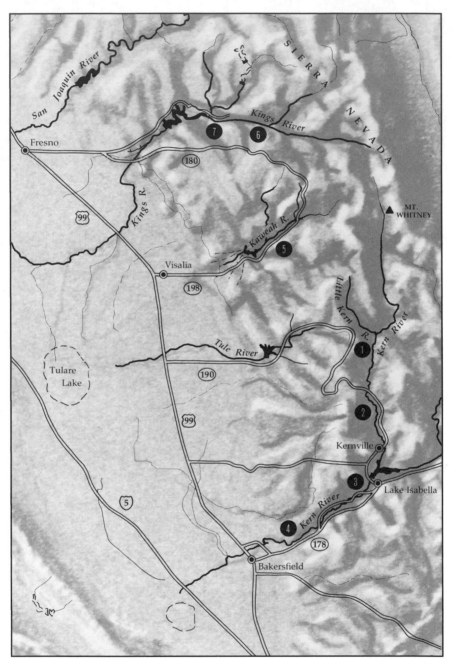

Rivers of the Southern Sierra Nevada

12

Kern River

The Kern is a mountain river on the edge of the desert. The scorched wastes of Death Valley lie only 50 miles to the east of its headwaters, which drain the western slopes of California's tallest peak, Mount Whitney (14,495'), and the Mojave Desert is less than 60 miles from Bakersfield, where the lower Kern empties from the mouth of its massive canyon onto the sun-baked valley floor.

This is one of the oldest rivers in California. The north-south patterns of the Kern and its South Fork—unusual in the Sierra Nevada —were established more than 80 million years ago, when the Sierra was a volcanic range. The Kern's deep gorge, cut into the uplifted granite bedrock of the southern Sierra, is parallel to and a couple of miles west of the great geological rift known as the Kern Canyon Fault. Before it reaches civilization at the Johnsondale Bridge, the Kern flows nearly straight south through more than 60 miles of untouched wilderness. Twenty miles downstream, its confluence with the South Fork is now under the warm, shallow waters of Isabella Reservoir. Here the river turns southwest through the Greenhorn Mountains toward the valley and its final destination, Buena Vista Lake.

The Kern is south of the main winter storm tracks and within the partial rain shadow created by the upthrust peaks of the Great Western Divide. But its watershed is both the largest in the Sierra and so high that the river is amply fed by melting snow until early July in years of average precipitation. In the very wet year of 1983, rafts were still floating the undammed Forks and Upper Kern runs in September. Below the dam at Isabella, irrigation releases to valley farms provide the Lower Kern and Rio Bravo runs with sufficient flows for boating throughout the summer. Kern County agriculture now consumes most of the river's water, as well as a considerable portion of the water shipped south from the Sacramento Delta via the California Aqueduct.

The river is the longest in the Sierra Nevada, and for white water boaters it is perhaps the most versatile. There are, however, only a couple of easy stretches: the short Powerhouse run on the Upper Kern and the last two miles of the Rio Bravo run on the valley floor, though the latter can be extended for ten more miles of Class I and II water. The other sections add up to more than 50 miles and range from Class III to Class V and VI.

The jewel in the Kern's crown is the dazzling wilderness run known as the Forks of the Kern, whose pristine mountain scenery and pounding rapids make it one of the finest rivers anywhere. Below the Johnsondale Bridge, where the Upper Kern begins, a road is usually nearby but the white water remains excellent. Both the Upper and Lower Kern are studded with very difficult rapids—some of which should be portaged—and dangerous brush.

Downstream, between Democrat Hot Springs and the mouth of the canyon, the river plummets at a rate of more than 100 feet per mile over awesome cataracts. Their sight alone should be enough to scare off anyone, yet over the years foolish swimmers and inner-tubers have been swept over their brinks, and imprudent fishermen and hikers have slipped on the banks and drowned in the falls. The story has been the same upstream. More people have died on the Kern than on any other white water river in the state, but few if any of the victims were wearing life jackets. The advent of organized boating on the Kern, with examples of good gear and correct safety measures, has helped to reduce a death rate that sometimes exceeded twenty per year.

The Kern has long been recognized as a dangerous river. The Spanish called it the Rio Bravo because it was so difficult to cross, and the flamboyant explorer John C. Fremont named the river in 1845 for his expedition's geographer, Edward Kern, who almost drowned trying to ford it.

Forks of the Kern

Little Kern Confluence to Johnsondale Bridge

Difficulty: V.   **Length:** 17 miles; 1–3 days.
Gradient: 60 ft./mi.   **Drainage:** 846 sq. mi. at take-out.
Season: May–July.   **Elevation at Put-in:** 4680′.
Runnable Levels: 300/600–4000 cfs.
Flow Information: (916) 322-3327. Flow at Kernville less 5 per cent.
Scenery: Excellent.   **Solitude:** Excellent.
Rafts: Experts only. Self-bailing rafts preferred at higher flows. Travel light. Not only are there possible portages, but you will probably want to hire pack animals to carry your gear down the trail to the put-in. The horses and mules can carry rafts, but frames and oars must break down. Allow an entire day for the put-in. For details contact Golden Trout Wilderness Pack Trains, PO Box 756, Springerville, CA 93265; phone (209) 539-2744 or 542-2816. In winter only the first number is in service.
Kayaks: Experts only. Kayakers can avoid the hassle and expense of pack animals if they're up to carrying their gear down the two-mile put-in trail. You can run the river in one day if you put in very early and resist the temptation to stop and play in the rapids.
Open Canoes: Absolutely not recommended—although we hear that an expert ran the Forks at low water in late 1983.
Special Hazards: Depending on the water level, boats may have to be portaged around or lined through several rapids, particularly Vortex (mile 11.4) and Carson Falls (mile 16.3). Long, nasty swims are possible at many points. Wet suits mandatory, even in mid-summer. Remote wilderness makes rescue difficult.
Permits: Required for private boaters. Apply to Forest Service (address below).
Commercial Raft Trips: Two- and three-day trips. Expensive because of the complex and costly logistics, but worth the money if you have it. Only one commercial trip per day. For a list of outfitters, contact Cannell Ranger District, Sequoia National Forest, Burlando Road and Whitley Road, Kernville CA 93238; phone below.
Water: Cold, clear, and delicious. Almost certainly drinkable. Purify to be sure.
Camping: Superb sites along the river.

Maps: Hockett Peak, Kernville (USGS 15'); Sequoia National Forest; Sequoia (AAA); Forks of the Kern (Cassady and Calhoun).

Auto Shuttle: 25 miles; 1 hour.

Emergency Telephone Numbers:
Tulare County Sheriff (Porterville): (209) 784-4670.
Kern County Sheriff (Lake Isabella): (619) 379-2641. If no answer, ask the operator for Zenith 9-9908.
Forest Service (Kernville): (619) 376-3781.

Logistics: The take-out at the Johnsondale Bridge is 20 miles north of Kernville on Sierra Way (Mountain Road 99). To reach the put-in, continue beyond the bridge. Just past the abandoned logging town of Johnsondale, turn right onto a paved road heading north toward Lloyd's Meadow. Follow this road for 15 miles, then turn right onto a dirt road marked by a sign reading "Fork of the Kern 4." The road ends two miles ahead, at the top of a well-maintained two-mile trail leading down into the canyon.

The Forks of the Kern is one of the finest stretches of expert white water on earth. Few rivers in this state are runnable at such a high elevation. Part of the magic—and the danger—of this run lies in its remote location, high in the southern Sierra where few trails penetrate. Hiking down to the put-in, boaters pass a sign marking the Golden Trout Wilderness, home of California's official state fish. The pristine mountain scenery is unsurpassed. Near the put-in, 4 million-year-old basaltic lava flows are draped over the walls of the inner gorge, indicating how slowly the landscape changes in the southern Sierra. Pine forests line the ridge tops and great slabs of granite form the sides of the canyon as the Kern pounds through some 80 major rapids.

The name "Forks of the Kern" is fairly recent. Before white water boaters arrived, this section of river was known to locals as Durrwood Canyon, and the confluence of the Kern and the Little Kern was referred to as the "fork" of the Kern. Apparently, early kayakers mistakenly called it "Forks of the Kern," and the name stuck. Pioneering kayakers on this run include Doug Carson and Dennis Johnson. In 1980 Jim Cassady and Bill McGinnis of Whitewater Voyages (El Sobrante) were the first rafters to run all the rapids on the Forks and to prove to the Forest Service that the river could be floated by commercial outfitters.

The seventeen-mile run includes many Class IV rapids, most unnamed; a number of long Class IV+ passages; and half a dozen Class V's, two of which are rated VI at certain flows. The guide below lists only the toughest spots, yet it would be hard to find a half mile of this run that contains no significant threat to rafts and kayaks alike. Crew members on rafts—including guests on commercial trips—should be fit, vigorous, experienced, and at least a little bit brave.

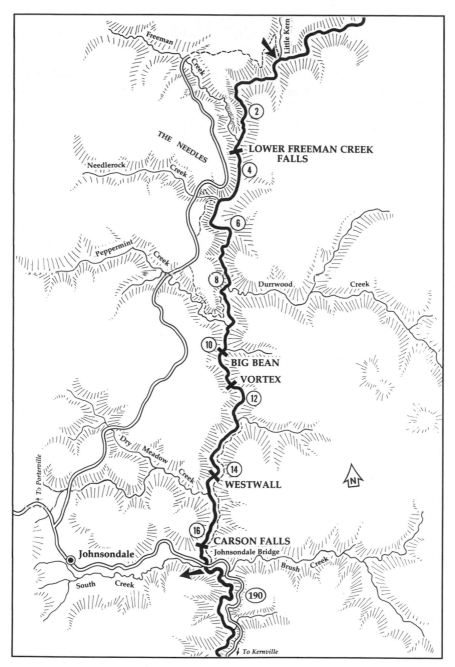

Forks of the Kern

Mile by Mile Guide

0   Put in on the right bank of the Kern just below the Little Kern confluence, or just upstream on the right bank of the Little Kern.

0–3.4   Class III and IV rapids.

3.5   Freeman Creek enters on the right. A hundred yards up the creek, water falls twenty feet into a lovely swimming hole. Eddy up above the mouth of the creek; a major rapid begins just downstream.

3.6   **UPPER FREEMAN CREEK FALLS (IV+).** Look for a runnable chute against the right bank.

3.8   **LOWER FREEMAN CREEK FALLS (V).** The river crashes through some big boulders, then turns sharply left into a large hole.

4.2   **WRAPID (IV+).** An S-turn through huge boulders. Difficult scout on the left.

5.5   **NEEDLEROCK FALLS (IV+).** Boaters usually choose a steep, narrow chute on the far right. Just below the rapid, Needlerock Creek cascades dramatically into the river. A crude emergency trail leads up to the road from the right bank. Needle Campsite is across the river, on the left.

5.6   **DOWNHILL (IV+).** After a short pool, the river races down a long, breathless boulder slalom laced with sharp drops.

6.1   **SLALOM (IV+).** If you can, eddy up on the left below Downhill to look at this, a shorter version of the same rapid. At high flows rapids are more or less continuous from Needlerock Falls to Slalom.

8   Poker Flats Camp (left bank) offers a fine view of the Needles, granite pinnacles towering 3000 feet above the upstream right bank.

8.3   Durrwood Creek enters on the left.

8.5   Durrwood Lodge was once a wilderness outpost for hunters. In recent years it has been cared for by a friendly prospector, Ed Alexander, who packs in his provisions on foot. Ask permission before looking around. Two trails (one upstream, one downstream) lead up to Rincon Trail from the left bank, and another leads from the right bank downstream to Peppermint Creek and then out of the canyon.

9.5   Peppermint Creek enters on the right. Good campsite. A trail up the creek provides a possible emergency exit.

10.1   **LITTLE BEAN (IV).** Difficult route-finding through a boulder garden. Hike down the right bank all the way to the campsite at the bottom of the rapid to plan your exit. Big Bean Rapid begins just a few yards downstream.

10.2   Bean Camp (right bank) is one of the last good campsites for nearly three miles.

10.3   **BIG BEAN (V).** The canyon walls steepen, the gradient increases, and the really big rapids begin here. This one is a long, violent run through a series of powerful holes and sharp drops.

11.4   ♦ *POSSIBLE PORTAGE* ♦
VORTEX (V–VI). Recognition: A large granite dome on the right with fallen debris at its base. Stop well upstream and scout on the right. There is a campsite just above the rapid. **The rapid:** Above 1300 cfs a runnable route on the right offers a way over the intimidating big drop at the top. Below 1300 cfs, when the right chute becomes too shallow and the middle chute drops into a dangerous keeper hole, both rafters and kayakers should portage on the left. After the first drop, more than 200 yards of continuous Class V drops —referred to as **The Gauntlet**— lie downstream.

12.8   Though many difficult rapids lie ahead, some comfort is provided by an excellent hiking trail which follows the the left bank to the Johnsondale Bridge.

12.8   **FOUR MILE RAPID (IV +).** The river bends right into a rocky rapid with big, unavoidable holes toward the bottom.

13–13.7   **RINCON AISLE (IV +).** Three continuous Class IV + rapids (**Rincon, Metamorphosis,** and **Basalt**) make up a very tough stretch at high flows. Layers of volcanic basalt can be seen at the top of the ridge above the right bank, and the folded rocks near the Kern Canyon Fault are visible upstream. After the river bends left, half a mile of Class III–III + rapids follow.

14.3   **WESTWALL (V).** The river bends back to the right and plunges down a spectacular rapid a quarter mile in length. Several hundred yards of boulder dodging, if properly executed, will bring you into position for an eight-foot vertical drop with a wrap rock lurking below. Take plenty of time to scout the rapid and memorize your route. Station rescue parties downstream.

14.8   Dry Meadow Creek falls fifteen feet into the river on the right. A difficult scramble up the creek leads to nearly a dozen different waterfalls and pools. At one point the creek flows under a natural granite bridge. Dry Meadow Creek is one of the most beautiful spots in the Sierra Nevada—or anywhere.

15.2   **RESPECT (IV +).** Big boulders block the river. Boaters must negotiate several treacherous drops and holes. At the bottom right, Maytag Hole has held rafts in its churning grip for more than five minutes.

16.3   ◆ *POSSIBLE PORTAGE* ◆
       CARSON FALLS (V–VI). Recognition: Abandoned mine on the right bank well above river level. **The rapid:** A short rock garden leads to a twelve-foot vertical drop. If running waterfalls isn't your idea of fun, consider portaging or lining on the left. Neither task will be easy.

16.8   *TAKE-OUT.* Johnsondale Bridge. Take out on either bank, or float two more miles of Class IV–V white water to an easier take-out above Fairview Dam. (This is the Limestone Run of the Upper Kern.)

The raft rocked slowly in the eddy while I leaned on the oars and caught my breath. I had just rowed the most difficult rapid in my six years of river running, and I knew a worse one was downstream. "What's between here and Carson Falls?" I called to the trip leader.

"Nothing," he grinned as he muscled his raft back into the current. "Just follow me."

Thirty seconds later his boat was upside down, its three occupants were bobbing in the cold, swift current, and I was desperately trying to keep my own raft from flipping at the same spot. White water boating is full of surprises, I thought.

That run down the Forks of the Kern in June 1982, my first time on a true Class V river, was a real eye-opener. After more than a dozen floats on the Tuolumne and a trip down the Grand Canyon, I still wasn't prepared for the intensity and the fury of the rapids on the Forks. Part of the problem was that the river was high—nearly 4000 cfs—but the intrepid journalists for whom we had planned the trip hadn't been interested when I proposed a less intimidating river. Judging by an article she wrote later, one of them changed her mind right away.

As it turned out, we were lucky. We suffered some anxious moments, with one raft flipped, another swamped, and a third stuck in a reversal and shedding passengers for five minutes. Somehow, though, we gathered everyone up without injury and lost only a few oars. But by the time we reached Carson Falls late in the afternoon and stared at the huge vertical drop, most of us had lost our nerve as well. The passengers hiked the short distance to the Johnsondale Bridge while the other two boatmen, Jim Cassady and Andy Sninsky, took turns running all three rafts over the falls—successfully. That was the first time I ever refused to take my own boat down a rapid someone else was willing to float. It probably won't be the last.   —Fryar Calhoun

Upper Kern River

Overall Difficulty: II–Vp.   **Elevation:** 3740′ at Johnsondale Bridge.

Total Length: 19 miles.   **Drainage:** 1009 sq. mi. at Kernville.

Season: April–July or August. See individual runs for details.

Flow Information: (916) 322-3327. Flow at Kernville; if unavailable, take 80 per cent of inflow into Isabella Reservoir.

Scenery: Good.

Solitude: Fair; good in Chamise Gorge, where the road leaves the river.

Rafts: Experts and beginners alike will find white water to suit them on the Upper Kern. Easy access from the road compensates for the shortness of the runs.

Kayaks: Except in dry years, kayakers can run Limestone and Powerhouse year round. Powerhouse is an excellent training run for novices and intermediates.

Open Canoes: Experts can run the Powerhouse section at low flows. No other stretches of the Upper Kern are suitable for canoes.

Special Hazards: (1) Fairview Dam, just below the take-out for the Limestone run; (2) Salmon Falls, half a mile of Class VI rapids between the Chamise Gorge and Gold Ledge runs.

Permits: Required for private boaters. Contact Forest Service in Kernville.

Commercial Raft Trips: Range in length from two days to one-hour "Lickety Split" floats down the easy Powerhouse section, which can sometimes be booked on the spot in Kernville. For a list of outfitters, contact the Forest Service in Kernville (for address and phone, see Forks of the Kern).

Water: Probably OK, but purify river water to be sure. Drinking water is available in the campgrounds along the road.

Camping: The Forest Service has six developed campgrounds and eight primitive sites along this stretch of river. Two private campgrounds just north of Kernville offer hot showers and other amenities: Camp James, (619) 376-6119; and Rivernook, (619) 376-2705.

Maps: Kernville (USGS 15′); Sequoia National Forest; Sequoia (AAA); Upper Kern River (Cassady and Calhoun).

Logistics: Easy auto shuttles along the road (Sierra Way/Mountain 99) that leads north from Kernville to the Johnsondale Bridge.

Emergency Telephone Numbers: See Forks of the Kern.

From its first contact with civilization at the Johnsondale Bridge to Isabella Reservoir twenty miles downstream, the Kern drops more than 1100 feet through a canyon surrounded by 8000-foot granite peaks. The Upper Kern provides southern Californians with their most convenient look at a wide range of white water. Kernville is only 54 miles east of Bakersfield and about three hours from Los Angeles, and all but a few rapids can be seen from the road (Sierra Way/Mountain 99) that follows the river upstream from the town.

Most of the Upper Kern is about as tough as any boater could want. Commercial outfitters train guides for the Forks of the Kern on the Upper Kern's most difficult segments, the Class IV–V Limestone and Chamise Gorge runs and the Class V Gold Ledge section. On the other hand, the short Powerhouse run just above Kernville is a traditional training stretch for beginning and novice kayakers and rafters.

We have split the Upper Kern into six separate runs divided either by a dramatic change in difficulty, by unrunnable rapids, or by man-made obstructions like a dam and a powerhouse. Because 500 cfs are diverted at Fairview Dam and returned to the river at the powerhouse, the first and last sections have longer seasons than the four middle runs. In wet years, Limestone and Powerhouse may be raftable into August and runnable in kayaks all year; in dry years, only into June. In wet years, the other runs can be boated from April to mid-July; in dry years, they may never be runnable at all. Be sure to scout each stretch carefully from the road, and be able to identify your take-out from the river. Beware of high water.

1. Limestone Run

Johnsondale Bridge to Fairview Dam

Difficulty: IV; V above 4000 cfs. **Length:** 2.4 miles.
Season: April–July. **Gradient:** 45 ft./mi.
Runnable Levels: 300/600–5000 cfs.

This is the favorite run for advanced rafters and kayakers on the Upper Kern because of its powerful rapids, longer season, and striking scenery. The river cuts through a narrow, dramatic canyon with large limestone outcroppings in its granite walls. The Limestone run is particularly dangerous at higher flows.

Mile by Mile Guide

0	A new put-in on the right bank at the foot of the bridge has replaced the old site, a turnout on the left bank just downstream.
0.7	Brush Creek enters on the left at a Class III rapid.
1	**LIMESTONE (IV; V above 4000 cfs).** At Limestone Campground the river drops sharply right, then turns left and pours into a big hole that becomes a monster at higher flows. Scout this rapid—a dangerous one at high water—from the campground before you put in, and station rescue parties downstream. The next big rapid is just around the corner.
1.2	**JOE'S DINER (IV; V above 4000 cfs).** A boat-stopping hole against the right bank can be avoided by running left at lower flows. At higher flows holes appear everywhere.
2.4	*TAKE-OUT.* A turnout beside the road a few hundred yards upstream from the dam. Parking space is limited, so don't linger or block vehicle access.

2. Fairview Run ("Calkins Flat Run")

Fairview Dam to Calkins Flat Primitive Camping Area

Difficulty: III. **Length:** 2.8 miles.
Season: May–June. **Gradient:** 35 ft./mi.
Runnable Levels: 1000/1500–6000 cfs at Kernville. The flow between the dam and the powerhouse (runs 2 through 5) is actually 500 cfs less.

This pretty stretch of river is considerably less difficult than those just upstream and downstream. It constitutes a good warm-up for the demanding Chamise Gorge run, which follows immediately.

Mile by Mile Guide

0	Put in at a turnout where the river and the road bend sharply left, 0.4 miles below Fairview Dam. Put in just below **Bombs Away**, the Class V rapid just downstream from the dam.
1.3	Fairview Campground (left bank).
1.6	Foot bridge over the river.
2.8	*TAKE-OUT.* Calkins Flat (left bank). If you miss the take-out, you face much tougher rapids right around the corner.

3. Chamise Gorge

Calkins Flat to above Salmon Falls

Difficulty: IV–V. **Length:** 2.2 miles.
Season: May–June. **Gradient:** 60 ft./mi.
Runnable Levels: 1000/1500–3500 cfs at Kernville. Flow is actually 500 cfs less here.

Here, the river turns away from the road and flows through a short gorge of striking beauty. The problem is finding the time to look away from the continuous rapids, which begin immediately. The three listed below are very big. Be sure your river skills can meet the test. Stay away at high flows. Before you put in, scout the take-out. Just below it is dangerous Salmon Falls, half a mile of sharp Class VI drops through menacing boulder fields. Most boaters combine this run with the Fairview Run beginning a couple of miles upstream.

Mile by Mile Guide

0	Calkins Flat Primitive Camping Area.
0.2	**ENTRANCE RAPID (IV–V).** A long, difficult boulder slalom.
1.8	**SATAN'S SLOT (IV–V).** Scout from the left where the road returns to a position near the river. The river crashes through two narrow channels; maneuvering is difficult above and below them.
2	*TAKE-OUT.* Pool just below Satan's Slot. Take out on the left.
2.2	*ALTERNATE TAKE-OUT* ◆ *HAZARD* ◆ Last chance to take out (left bank) before **Salmon Falls (Class VI)**.

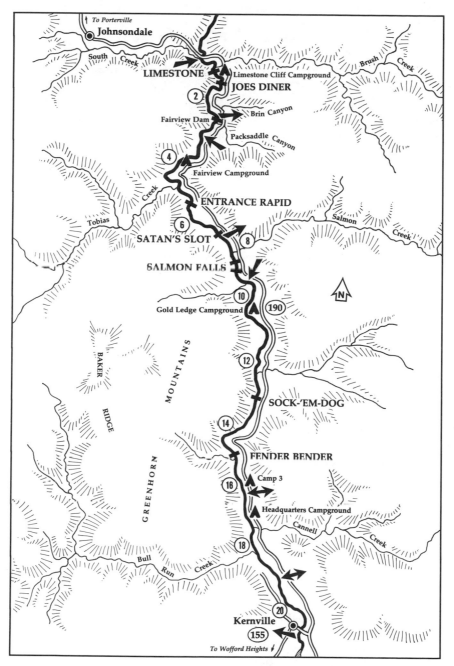

Upper Kern River

4. Gold Ledge Run

Ant Canyon to Camp 3 Campground

Difficulty: V.   **Length:** 7.2 miles.
Season: May–June.   **Gradient:** 65 ft./mi.
Runnable Levels: 1000/1500–3000 cfs at Kernville. Flow here is 500 cfs less.

This experts-only run is by far the most difficult on the Upper Kern. Even experts should avoid it at high flows. Scout the entire stretch carefully from the road before you put in. This guide lists only the biggest rapids; there are plenty of difficult, unnamed, and unmentioned passages throughout the run. Access from the road is good, so put in where it's convenient and take out when you've had enough. Survivors can combine this stretch with the Camp 3 and Powerhouse runs downstream for a total of 11.6 miles to Riverside Park in Kernville.

Mile by Mile Guide

0	Ant Canyon Primitive Camping Area, about a mile above Gold Ledge Campground, is a convenient put-in.
0.8–1.1	Gold Ledge Campground (left bank).
1.3–1.5	Difficult boulder gardens.
2	Springhill Primitive Camping Area (left bank).
2.8	Corral Creek Picnic Grounds (left bank) is not a campground.
3.2	Corral Creek enters on the left.
3.5	**SQUASHED PADDLER (V).** Big holes block the river.
3.8	**SOCK-'EM-DOG (V).** Just after the river turns away from the road, it drops into a wall, then turns sharply left. Big holes before and after the turn.
5–5.3	Hospital Flat Campground (left bank).
5.7	**THE FLUME (IV +).** Scout on the left. The river squeezes into a narrow channel and over a big drop.
6	**FENDER BENDER (V).** Scout from the road. A difficult and dangerous maze through rocks and brush.
6.8	**THE CABLE (IV).** Technical, heavily obstructed boulder garden; unrunnable holes at higher flows. Boaters on the Camp 3 run often put in just above this rapid.
6.9–7.2	**TAKE-OUT.** Camp 3 Campground (left bank). Or keep going downstream to the Camp 3 and Powerhouse runs.

5. Camp 3 Run

Camp 3 Campground to the Powerhouse

Difficulty: IV.   **Length:** 2.4 miles.
Season: May–June.   **Gradient:** 50 ft./mi.
Runnable Levels: 1000/1500–5000 cfs at Kernville. Flow is 500 cfs less.

Here the river calms down a bit from the fury upstream, but there is still plenty of white water to hold the boater's attention. This stretch can be combined with the Powerhouse run.

Mile by Mile Guide

0	Camp 3 Campground. Put in at the downstream end. The action starts immediately.
0.1	**THE WALL (IV).** The river cascades into the right bank, then bends sharply left.
0.4	**TOMBSTONE (IV).** A boulder-choked left-hand bend.
0.6–0.8	Headquarters Campground (left bank).
1	**BUZZARD'S PERCH (III +).** At higher flows, trees present a serious hazard toward the end of this left-bending rapid.
1.3	**TEQUILA CHUTE (IV),** the left channel, is the more difficult route. **PEPSI CHALLENGE (III),** the right channel, is the usual choice.
1.5	Bubble Beach (left bank).
1.8	River Kern Beach (left bank).
2	**POWERHOUSE (III +).** Rocks and big holes for over a quarter of a mile.
2.4	*TAKE-OUT.* Take out just below the Powerhouse on the left, or continue downstream to Riverside Park in Kernville.

6. Powerhouse Run

Powerhouse to Riverside Park (Kernville)
or Isabella Reservoir

Difficulty: II–III.   **Length:** 2 miles to Riverside Park.
Season: April–July.   **Gradient:** 30 ft./mi.
Runnable Levels: 300/600–8000 cfs at Kernville.

This is one of California's best runs for novice rafters and kayakers. It is also the site of the Kernville White Water Races every April. Expert open canoeists can run this section at low flows. The U. S. Olympic kayak squad trained here in 1972.

Mile by Mile Guide

0   Just downstream from the Powerhouse, a short paved road leads to the river and the put-in.

0.6   **BIG DADDY (II–III).** The river squeezes against the right bank and drops into a series of runnable holes.

1.7   **EWING'S (II–III).** Beneath Ewing's Restaurant, the river drops between large boulders. A good play rapid for kayakers. At certain flows, nose stands are possible.

2   *TAKE-OUT.* Riverside Park (right bank) is the usual take-out. Slalom competitions are held here during the annual white water races. If the reservoir is low, you can boat up to two more miles, enjoying the good scenery and Class II rapids. There is a lot of brush in this stretch. Take out wherever you find convenient (and legal) vehicle access—for example, just beyond the golf course on the right.

Lower Kern River

Below Main Dam Campground to
Democrat Picnic Area

Difficulty: IVp.   **Gradient:** 28 ft./mi.
Length: 18 miles; 1–2 days. Shorter runs possible.
Elevation at Put-in: 2360'.   **Drainage:** 2258 sq. mi. at take-out.
Season: June–August in average years; May–September in wet years.
Runnable Levels: 500/900–5000 cfs.
Flow Information: (916) 322-3327. Release from Isabella Dam.
Scenery: Good.   **Solitude:** Good.
Rafts: Because of the portage at Royal Flush, it's best not to take too much gear down the river. The Lower Kern is not for novices or intermediates unless guided by veterans who know the run.
Kayaks: Warm water from the shallow reservoir means kayakers often don't have to wear wet suits in summer. (Bring one just in case.) Because Borel Powerhouse (mile 6) releases 570 cfs year round, kayakers can run the lower dozen miles in any season.
Open Canoes: Experts can attempt the first six miles at flows below 1500 cfs, but they should not venture downstream from Hobo Campground (mile 6.9), which is not a river access point at present. Take out at Sandy Flat (mile 6.3).
Special Hazards: (1) Brush and trees in the river bed; (2) Royal Flush, a Class V–VI rapid that is usually portaged.
Permits: Required for private boaters. Contact Greenhorn Ranger District, U.S. Forest Service, 800 Truxton Ave., Room 322, Bakersfield CA 93301 (phone below); or Cannell Ranger District, U.S. Forest Service, PO Box 6, Kernville CA 93238 (phone below).
Commercial Raft Trips: One- and two-day floats. For a list of outfitters, contact the Forest Service in Bakersfield or Kernville.
Water: Warm and not drinkable. Carry your own.
Camping: Because of the portage, it's best not to take overnight gear down the river. If you're on a two-day trip, you can camp with river access for vehicles at Sandy Flat (mile 6.3) or at Miracle Hot Springs private campground (mile 7.3). There is also Main Dam Campground (Forest Service) on Highway 155, just below Isabella Dam.
Maps: Lake Isabella North, Lake Isabella South, Miracle Hot Springs, Democrat Hot Springs (USGS 7.5'); Isabella, Glennville (USGS 15'); Sequoia National Forest; Sequoia, Kern County (AAA); Lower Kern River (Cassady and Calhoun).

Auto Shuttle: 18 miles; 30 minutes.

Emergency Telephone Numbers:
Kern County Sheriff (Lake Isabella): (619) 379-2641.
(Bakersfield): (805) 327-3392.
Forest Service (Kernville): (619) 376-3781.
(Bakersfield): (805) 861-4212.

Logistics: To reach the river area, follow Highway 178 east from Bakersfield into the Kern canyon and past several miles of unrunnable cataracts. About two miles after the road begins to climb higher above the river, a dirt road leads down to the take-out, Democrat Picnic Area.

To reach the put-ins, continue up Highway 178 to the town of Lake Isabella and turn left on Highway 155. About a quarter of a mile before the highway crosses the Kern, just opposite the road leading to Corps of Engineers headquarters, a dirt road on the left leads to one put-in about half a mile downstream on the left bank. There are two more put-ins farther downstream on the right bank. To reach them, cross the Kern on Highway 155 and turn left on Keysville Road (paved) just opposite Main Dam Campground. About three quarters of a mile down the road, turn left onto a dirt road that leads down to the river. Another put-in at mile 2 is reached by continuing south on Keysville Road for another half mile or less and turning left onto a two-mile dirt road. The put-in is under a bridge where Highway 178 crosses the river, but it cannot be reached from the highway.

Below Isabella Reservoir the Kern turns southwest and cuts a deep canyon through the southern end of the Greenhorn Mountains on its way to the valley floor. Boaters enjoy a twenty-mile stretch of river surprisingly well shielded from the highway perched on the wall above. This little bit of wilderness offers excellent advanced white water below Miracle Hot Spring (mile 7.3), which is also used as a put-in for one-day runs. One big rapid, Royal Flush, is almost always portaged, but there are plenty of thrills left. Beyond the take-out the Kern plunges over an old diversion dam, then down a long series of deadly, unrunnable waterfalls.

The wide, shallow reservoir above Isabella Dam (an earth-fill barrier built in 1953 by the Army Corps of Engineers) stores rain and snow runoff eight or nine months a year, releasing only a trickle to the first six miles of the Lower Kern. This allows trees and brush to grow in the river bed—a considerable hazard to boaters. About 570 cfs are diverted at the dam and returned to the river at Borel Powerhouse (mile 6). Boating season coincides with summer irrigation releases to Kern County farms. Summer flows range from 1000 to 3000 cfs and, unlike those on many other dam-controlled rivers, do not drop at night or on weekends.

Mile by Mile Guide

0   Put in on either bank about half a mile downstream from the Highway 155 bridge (see Logistics). The left bank put-in is a couple of hundred yards downstream from the put-in on the right bank.

0–8   ◆ *HAZARD* ◆ For the first eight miles or so, the major danger is brush and trees in the river bed.

0.8   **WALLOW ROCK (III +).** A huge boulder blocks the channel.

1.7   Indian pictographs on the granite wall (right bank) date from about 1500 A.D. and were left by the Tubatulabal Indians (Pine Nut Eaters).

2   *RIVER ACCESS.* Alternate put-in (or emergency take-out) under the Highway 178 bridge. Vehicle access only via Keysville Road, not from the highway (see Logistics).

2.7   **DILLY (III).** Avoid the big hole at the bottom left.

3   **OSCAR'S NIGHTMARE (III +).** Scout this blind left turn from the left bank. Wrap rocks in the center.

3.6   Highway bridge across the river. No vehicle access.

6   Just downstream from another highway bridge, Borel Powerhouse (left bank) adds 570 cfs to the river.

6.3   *RIVER ACCESS.* Sandy Flat (left bank). A designated river access point and primitive campground.

6.9   Hobo Campground (left bank). Not a designated river access point at present. Check with the Forest Service for updated information.

7   **HOBO RAPID (III).** A brushy, bouncy left curve.

7.3   *RIVER ACCESS.* Miracle Hot Springs private campground on the left. The natural hot spring is still there, but the resort hotel where many came for cures in the last century was destroyed by fire in 1975. For information and reservations, call (619) 379-8350 or write Miracle Hot Springs, CA 93288.
         Note: Year-round flows below Borel Powerhouse thin out trees and brush downstream, though they remain a hazard. The rapids become more difficult. Even expert open canoeists should not venture below Miracle Hot Springs.

8.6   Remington Hot Springs (left bank) provides a relaxing wilderness stop.

8.9   **WHITE MAIDEN'S WALKWAY (IV).** The first big rapid on the Lower Kern. A long, foaming ride. At the bottom, the current piles up against a big rock.

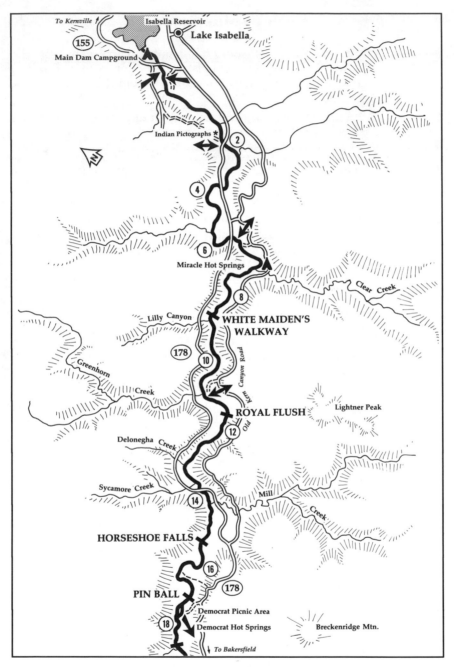

Lower Kern River

9.4   **SUNDOWN FALLS (III +).** A steep but relatively safe drop.

9.5   **SILVER STAIRCASE (III).** A long boulder garden.

10.6   **DEAD MAN'S CURVE (IV).** A horizon line across the river at the end of a pool warns boaters to stop and scout (right bank). Big holes lurk in a right-left kink in the channel.

10.8   *RIVER ACCESS.* River Camp, an unimproved site on the left. Vehicles can reach it via a dirt road leading down from the Old Kern Canyon Road.

11.1   Cable across the river marks the site of the only hard-rock gold mine still operating (sporadically) along the Kern.

11.5   **FALSE FLUSH (III; IV above 2800 cfs).** Two easy Class II rapids follow the cable crossing, then comes False Flush, marked by boulders in the channel. Dangerous at high water because boats and swimmers can be swept into the big one just downstream. Run left of the big hole in the middle, then move quickly right to eddy up above Royal Flush.

11.7   ◆ *PORTAGE* ◆
ROYAL FLUSH (V – VI). A big, heavily obstructed rapid that most boaters should never run. The water drops into a river-wide hole, piles up against a rock ledge blocking the center channel, then surges into the left wall and pours over the final drop. Even experts should not attempt this rapid above 2400 cfs, when the river begins to wash right over the rock ledge in the center, carrying helpless boats into unspeakable dangers. Portage on the right, and choose a put-in site below all the hazards in the rapid.

13.4   Delonegha Hot Springs (right bank). The hotel that once stood here is gone, but the hot spring remains.

13.9   Highway 178 bridge. Not a designated river access point at present. Check with the Forest Service for any changes.

14.7   **SURPRISE (III +).** A big rock hides in the last of a line of standing waves. Surprise!

15.1   **HARI-KARI (IV).** A sharp drop into a right-hand turn is announced by a horizon line across the river at the end of a long pool. Difficult scout on the right.

15.4   **HORSESHOE FALLS (IV).** Next to Royal Flush, this is the most exciting rapid on the Lower Kern. Three drops around a right turn. The second has a big hole that is hard to miss at flows above 2400 cfs.

16.1   **SIDEWINDER (III +).** Also called **Bailmore** and **Patch Corner**. S-turns and some big drops.

16.2–17.3 The river bends around a large peninsula, China Gardens, where immigrant laborers and prospectors from the Far East lived in the last century.

17.6   **PIN BALL (IV).** A difficult boulder garden. Scout left.

18   *TAKE-OUT* ◆ *HAZARD* ◆ Democrat Picnic Area (left bank). The river splits around an island upstream. Take the left channel! If you go to the right, you will miss the take-out. Downstream, the river drops 30 feet over a diversion dam at mile 18.8, then heads into an unrunnable gorge. Do not attempt to take out—except in emergencies—at Democrat Hot Springs (mile 18.3), which is closed and guarded private property.

Oar-paddle combination in big water.   *Brian Fessenden*

Kern River

Rio Bravo Run

Mouth of the Canyon to Lake Ming

Difficulty: III–IVp to mile 2.8 (Rancheria Road); II–III thereafter.

Length: 5 miles. Shorter run possible (from Rancheria Road).

Gradient: 36 ft./mi. (55 ft./mi. to mile 2.8; 15 ft./mi. thereafter.)

Drainage: 2258 sq. mi. at Democrat Hot Springs (15 miles upstream).

Season: All year. From September through May flows are usually only 600–1200 cfs, but they rise to 1200–3000 cfs from June through August due to round-the-clock irrigation releases.

Runnable Levels: 600/900–4000 cfs.

Flow Information: (916) 322-3327. Release from Isabella Dam.

Scenery: Fair.   **Elevation at Put-in:** 700′.

Solitude: Good, except summer weekends when inner-tubers crowd the lower stretch below Rancheria Road.

Rafts: Tricky above 2400 cfs because the current runs through brush and trees.

Kayaks: Excellent kayak run. Site of 1980 national championships.

Open Canoes: The lower stretch below Rancheria Road is a good novice run at low flows (below 1200 cfs) and a good intermediate run up to 1800 cfs. Stay off the river at flows above 1800 cfs. Experts can tackle the upper section below 1800 cfs.

Special Hazards: Above 2400 cfs eddies are scarce the first mile, and the river is beginning to run through the trees on the banks. Brush blocks the river at mile 1.7 and must be portaged. Trees and brush can be a problem all the way down, especially at high flows.

Commercial Raft Trips: One-and-a-half hour trips. Contact Kern River Whitewater Co., Star Route 4, Box 801, Rio Bravo Annex, Bakersfield, CA 93306; phone (805) 872-5792.

Water: Clear and warm but not drinkable.

Camping: Richbar Campground (Sequoia National Forest) is four miles upstream from the put-in. There is a county campground below Lake Ming.

Maps: Rio Bravo Ranch (USGS 7.5′); Sequoia, Kern County (AAA).

Auto Shuttle: 7 miles; 15 minutes.

Emergency Telephone Numbers: See Bakersfield numbers for Lower Kern.

Logistics: To reach the put-in, drive about 13 miles east of Bakersfield on Highway 178 to a turnout on the left side of the road just before you reach the mouth of the canyon. A trail leads to the put-in just upstream from the powerhouse. If you're running the easier lower stretch, turn north off Highway 178 onto Rancheria Road 2.5 miles west of the mouth of the canyon. A bridge crosses the river a mile down the road. To reach the take-out, turn north off Highway 178 four miles west of the canyon mouth onto Alfred Harrell Highway. Follow the signs to Lake Ming and continue past the lake to the Kern River Group Picnic Area's overflow parking lot.

Just upstream, between the mouth of the canyon and Democrat Hot Springs, the Kern is violent and unrunnable, dropping at more than 100 feet per mile over one deadly waterfall after another. As the river flows out into the valley, its gradient slackens and its difficulty eases, first to Class IV, then to III, then to II. Downstream from the take-out for the Rio Bravo Run—named for nearby Rio Bravo Ranch—are ten more miles of even easier Class I–II water.

The river here is a peaceful oasis on the burning valley floor, though it has its hazards—principally trees and brush. At flows below 1800 cfs, most brush is still along the edge of the river, and there are enough eddies to permit recovery from a mistake. At higher flows, strong currents run through the willows, cottonwoods, and sycamores, and the eddies shrink and disappear. Summer irrigation releases from Isabella Dam can range up to 3000 cfs and more. Let boaters beware.

This run, long the site of annual white water kayak meets, is threatened by plans for a hydroelectric project. A local water district and the owners of the private Rio Bravo Ranch have applied for federal permission to construct a diversion dam near the put-in that would dry up the river. These same landowners attempted to deny the public access to this stretch of the Kern in the early seventies. In subsequent years, decisions in a series of court cases tended to uphold public access rights but sometimes concentrated on narrow technicalities. Public access is now permitted but remains a subject of local controversy.

Mile by Mile Guide

0	Put in on the left bank just upstream from the Powerhouse.
0–0.9	A continuous Class III–IV rock garden that becomes much more difficult at higher flows, when holes appear, eddies disappear, and the current grows swift.
1.1	**SCOUT CAMP RAPID (IV).** Big hole at the bottom.
1.5	**UNNAMED RAPID (III–IV).** Rocks become holes at higher flows.

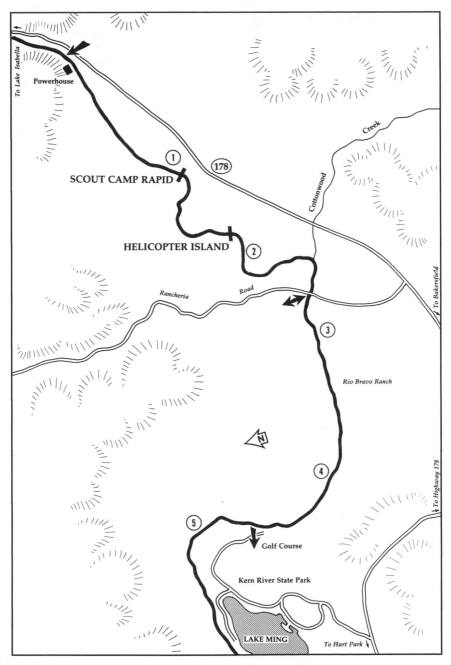

Kern River: Rio Bravo Run

1.7   ◆ *PORTAGE* ◆

HELICOPTER ISLAND (U). The river splits into three impassible channels, each blocked by brush. Easy portage on the left. So named because many stranded inner-tubers have been rescued by the Kern County Sheriff's whirlybird.

2–2.8   Class II–III white water, with no major difficulties.

2.6   Cottonwood Creek enters on the left.

2.8   *RIVER ACCESS.* Rancheria Road bridge. Only one Class III rapid downstream; Class II otherwise. Many inner-tubers launch here.

3.1   **UNNAMED RAPID (III).** This is the hardest rapid on the lower stretch, but it requires only a few easy maneuvers at low flows and washes out into a series of large waves at higher flows.

4.8   *TAKE-OUT.* Kern River Group Picnic Area overflow parking lot (left bank). Downstream are ten miles of Class I–II water and, on summer weekends, wall-to-wall inner-tubers.

Kaweah River

East Fork Confluence to
Terminus Reservoir (Lake Kaweah)

Difficulty: Vp first 6 miles; III₄ last 4 miles.

Difficulty: Vp first 6 miles; III_4 last 4 miles.

Length: 10 miles. Shorter runs possible.

Gradient: 50 ft./mi. overall; 85 ft./mi. first 3 miles.

Elevation at Put-in: 1220'.   **Drainage:** 418 sq. mi. at Three Rivers.

Season: April–late June.

Runnable Levels: 600/1000–4000 cfs (inflow into Terminus Reservoir)

Flow Information: (916) 322-3327. Inflow into Terminus Reservoir. Actual flow at the put-in is about two thirds of this figure. Expect peak water in late May.

Scenery: Good.   **Solitude:** Fair.

Rafts: The upper section is for experts only. Others should put in at the North Fork Road bridge (mile 6.2). Small rafts only below 1500 cfs.

Kayaks: Experts only above mile 6.2.

Open Canoes: Experts can run the river below mile 6.2 at flows below 1000 cfs with one portage around the Class IV rapid at mile 9.

Commercial Raft Trips: None so far.

Maps: Kaweah (USGS 15'); Sequoia National Forest; Sequoia (AAA).

Water: Clear and probably drinkable. Purify to be sure.

Camping: Most land along the river is privately owned and unavailable for camping. There are campgrounds in Sequoia National Park, a few miles up the highway, and private campgrounds in the Three Rivers area.

Auto Shuttle: 12 miles; 20 minutes.

Emergency Telephone Numbers:
Tulare County Sheriff (Visalia): (209) 733-6211.

Logistics: Follow Highway 198 about 30 miles east of Visalia to the upper end of Terminus Reservoir (Lake Kaweah). A boat launching area on the reservoir provides an easy take-out, but if the reservoir is full, river runners must cross nearly a mile of flat water to get there. If you're running only the lower four miles, put in at the bridge where the North Fork meets the Main Kaweah. The put-in for the upper stretch is at the bridge just downstream from the mouth of the East Fork.

The Kaweah is one of America's steepest rivers, dropping from 12,000' headwaters to the 1200' level at the East Fork confluence in only twenty miles. The river drains Sequoia National Park and the western slope of the Great Western Divide (also known as the Kern-Kaweah Divide). The old silver mining town of Mineral King is far up its East Fork. Along with the Tule and Kings Rivers, the Kaweah—named for a Yokut Indian tribe that once lived along its north bank—once emptied into Tulare Lake. Since 1962, when the Army Corps of Engineers completed Terminus Dam, an earth-and-rock structure which generates no electricity, much of the river's water has been collected in the reservoir and used for irrigation. Farther upstream, a small amount of water—too little to affect the Kaweah's flow significantly—is diverted and then returned to the river at two powerhouses below the East Fork confluence.

One of the smaller and lesser-known Sierra rivers, the Kaweah deserves more attention from advanced and expert boaters. The Kaweah runs swift, clear, and free through some of the most exciting rapids in the state. The scenery is good. Highway 198 runs alongside and provides easy access, but it is rarely obtrusive. Most of the private homes that dot the banks are well above river level.

The six-mile expert stretch from the mouth of the East Fork to the mouth of the North Fork drops at an average rate of 70 feet per mile through nearly continuous Class IV and V rapids—including some that may require portaging. The toughest passages cannot be seen from the road, so boaters should stop and scout at every opportunity. Below North Fork Drive bridge the Kaweah's gradient slackens to 30 feet per mile, and most of the rapids are Class III, with one Class IV drop at mile 9.

Mile by Mile Guide

0	East Fork Kaweah enters from the left. Put in beneath the bridge on the left bank, across the river from the Gateway Restaurant and just downstream from the confluence. The bank is steep and the put-in area is small.
0–3	The river drops at 85 feet per mile. Class IV and V rapids are nearly continuous. Scout at every opportunity. Be prepared to portage some rapids at unfavorable flows.
2.2	Hammond Powerhouse (left bank) adds 100 cfs to the river.
2.1–2.4	◆ *POSSIBLE PORTAGE* ◆ A series of Class V rapids. Boulders and large, boat-swallowing holes block the river.
3.1	*RIVER ACCESS.* Dineley Drive bridge. Difficult river access on the right bank.

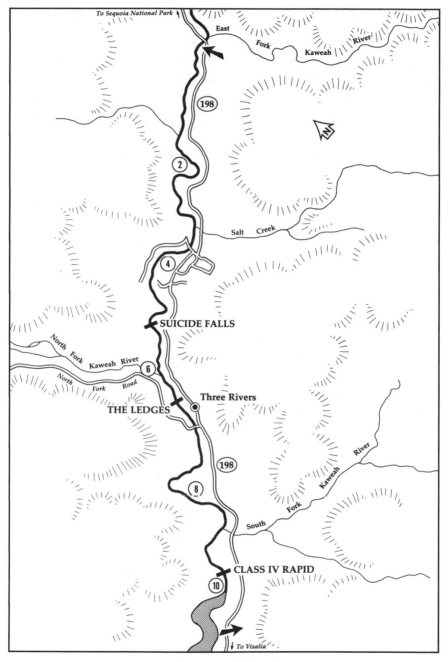

Kaweah River

3.8   Powerhouse No. 2 (right bank) adds 100 cfs to the river.

4.6   ◆ *POSSIBLE PORTAGE* ◆
SUICIDE FALLS (V–VI). A river-wide ledge. Sneak routes on right and left. Scout, and portage if necessary, on the right.

5.3   North Fork Kaweah enters on the right.

5.6   Vacant lot on the left bank (next to the Chevron station) has often been used as a take-out to avoid the very difficult rapid just downstream. Uncertain legal status. Respect property rights.

5.7   ◆ *POSSIBLE PORTAGE* ◆
THE LEDGES (V–VI). A tough passage right behind the Chevron station. The two biggest drops are about a hundred yards apart. The reversal below the second drop has held a kayak for five minutes. Scout and/or portage on the left.

6.2   *RIVER ACCESS.* North Fork Drive bridge. Put in here to run the easier section downstream.

8.1   South Fork Kaweah enters on the left.

9   UNNAMED RAPID (IV). This is the only Class IV rapid on the lower stretch. The river turns right, then drops down a slot into big holes. Scout on the left.

10   *TAKE-OUT.* Take out at the boat launching area on Terminus Reservoir or at any convenient spot upstream.

Kings River

In the highest reaches of California's mountains, where the rugged summits of the Great Western Divide meet the still taller pinnacles of the Sierra crest, Junction Peak (elevation 13,888') towers over the watersheds of three rivers: the Kern, whose headwaters are marked by Mount Whitney (14,495') to the south; the Owens, only ten miles to the east but 10,000 feet below; and the Kings, which drains the western slopes of a long spine of summits stretching northward from Junction Peak to Palisades Glacier, biggest in the Sierra Nevada. The river was named "Rio de los Santos Reyes"—River of the Holy Kings—because it was first seen by Spanish explorers in 1805 on the feast day of the biblical wise men.

Before the white man arrived with plow and shovel, the Kings emptied into the vast marsh known as Tulare Lake, which covered some 700 square miles of the valley floor. A Mississippi-style steamboat provided ferry service across the lake in the nineteenth century. By 1878, a scant three decades after the Gold Rush began, farming was so well established here that more than a thousand miles of irrigation canals had been dug in the Kings River Delta and in the valley near Fresno. Around 1880, this area was the setting for the violent conflicts between wheat ranchers and monopolistic railroad interests depicted in Frank Norris's famous muckraking novel, *The Octopus* (1901). In this century, when large-scale agriculture demanded more land, much of Tulare Lake was drained and brought under cultivation.

The high elevation of its vast drainage gives the Kings the longest boating season of any undammed river in the state. Most of its watershed is protected as Kings Canyon National Park, the John Muir Wilderness, and the High Sierra Primitive Area. The Kings, one of the state's largest rivers, runs free above Pine Flat Dam, a concrete gravity barrier built by the Army Corps of Engineers in 1954 to provide irrigation water for valley farmers. Only recently, three decades after its construction, was the dam retrofitted to generate electrical power.

The runs described in this book are on the boundary between Sequoia and Sierra National Forests, upstream from Pine Flat Reservoir. Kirch Flat Campground is a traditional meeting place for river runners from northern and southern California. Kayak races are often held on the Kings in the spring, and commercial outfitters run daily raft trips throughout most of the summer. There is also a Class I–II canoe run on the Lower Kings below the reservoir.

Upper Kings

Confluence of Middle and South Forks
to Garnet Dike Campground

Difficulty: V + p. **Length:** 10 miles; 1–3 days.
Gradient: 100 ft./mi. **Elevation at Put-in:** 2240′.
Drainage: 950 sq. mi. at Rodgers Crossing (downstream).
Season: About a month, sometime in the summer. Usually too high or too low for boating, so the season is short.
Runnable Levels: 400/700–2000 cfs.
Flow Information: (916) 322-3327. Flow at Rodgers Crossing will be a bit higher than flow at put-in for Upper Kings.
Scenery: Excellent. **Solitude:** Excellent.
Rafts and Kayaks: This section of the Kings is too difficult for all but fearless, seasoned experts who don't mind carrying their gear down a two-mile trail and portaging several rapids.
Open Canoes: No way. **Commercial Raft Trips:** None.
Special Hazards: Remote, inaccessible wilderness canyon. The river is the only way out; rescue would be difficult or impossible. Injury or loss of boats could be disastrous.
Water: Clear, cold, usually drinkable. Purify to be sure.
Camping: Scarce because the canyon is so rugged. There is a good one about mile 4.7, between Rough Creek and Garlic Falls.
Maps: Tehipite Dome, Patterson Mountain (USGS 15′); Sequoia National Forest; Sierra National Forest; Sequoia (AAA).
Auto Shuttle: 50–80 miles; 2.5 hours.
Emergency Telephone Numbers: See next Kings run.
Logistics: To reach the take-out at Garnet Dike Campground, follow directions to the put-in for the next Kings run. To reach the put-in, follow Highway 180 east from Fresno and Centerville toward Kings Canyon National Park. (If you're driving from the take-out, you can save some miles and a little time by turning south at Piedra onto Elwood Road, which leads southeast to Highway 180). Stop at Yucca Point, 16 miles northeast of Grant Grove Village. A two-mile trail leads from Yucca Point down to the put-in. True, Highway 180 crosses the South Fork Kings three and a half miles upstream, but don't even think about putting in there. The South Fork drops more than 200 feet per mile and includes unrunnable sections that can't be scouted or portaged.

Only a few daring kayakers and rafters have seen this rugged stretch of river. Even hikers and fishermen can't reach it. The Upper Kings and the gorge of the Middle Fork Feather are the most difficult rivers in this guide book. A few others—like the Upper Tuolumne and Burnt Ranch Gorge of the Trinity—are nearly as difficult, but the Feather and Kings canyons are much more remote and inaccessible. That means little chance of help if you run into trouble.

Still, the fantastic white water and the spectacular virgin wilderness lure boaters from time to time. Roger Paris, Maynard Munger, and Bryce Whitmore made the first kayak run—with frequent portages—in the early sixties. In 1973 another hardy group of kayakers—Dick Sunderland, Chuck Koteen, and Chuck and Bill Stanley—repeated the feat, portaging eight or nine rapids along the way. Since then, a few others have floated the river in kayaks. Jim Cassady led the first raft run of the Upper Kings in early July 1981.

Our group was made up of seven river guides—all tired from working commercial trips the previous day—in two small rafts. We got around to shopping so late for our planned two-day float that we had to buy our provisions from a liquor store. At least we knew to pack light.

On the morning of the first day, we hiked our gear down the trail and put in around noon. The going was slow, with one big drop following another and everyone peering around the corners in expectation of even worse rapids. We camped around mile 3. The next day was even slower, as we made our way down the Rough Creek–Garlic Meadow Creek section that drops at 160 feet per mile. The current was so swift at 1800 cfs that we had to take emergency measures so our boats could stop between rapids. We ran one raft at a time, and members of our team were stationed downstream to throw lines from shore and pull them into the tiny eddies. Even without serious problems, we covered only two miles.

We were so far behind schedule that we had to ration our food. But we camped just upstream from one of the most gorgeous spots in the Sierra, Garlic Meadow Creek's thousand-foot waterfall. The sight of the moon rising over the canyon wall and the knowledge that few humans had ever been there were worth all the trouble. We made it out the next day. If I ever float the Upper Kings again, I'll make sure I use a self-bailing raft.　　　　　　　　　　　—Jim Cassady

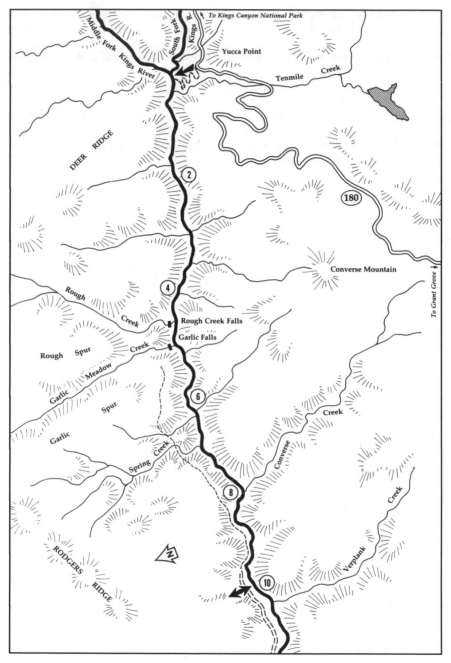

Upper Kings River

Mile by Mile Guide

0	Confluence of Middle and South Forks of the Kings. A two-mile trail leads down to the put-in from Yucca Point on Highway 180. There is a nice spot to rest part way down, beside the falls on Ten Mile Creek.
0–3	Class IV rapids for the first three miles, except for a Class V passage near mile 2.
3–5	Survival boating for the next two miles as the river drops at a rate of 160 ft./mi. Three or four possible portages in this stretch.
4.5	A possible portage (left bank) around a big rapid. Rough Creek enters on the right via a spectacular waterfall.
4.7	Good campsite—rare in this canyon—on the right. Another rapid that may require portaging.
4.9	Garlic Falls (Garlic Meadow Creek).
5–10	In the last half of the run the gradient "eases" to 90 feet per mile, but the river is still laced with Class V rapids that must be scouted. One or two of them may need to be portaged.
10	*TAKE-OUT.* Garnet Dike Campground (right bank). Take out at an open spot about 100 yards downstream, or continue downstream to an easier take-out.

It's always a special thrill to be one of the first boaters to run a wild river. Maybe that's why I let myself get talked into kayaking the upper Middle Fork of the San Joaquin in 1980. I went with a couple of experts, Royal Robbins and Doug Tompkins, who were better known for their climbing feats. Royal was the first to climb Half Dome and to solo El Capitan, among other achievements, and Doug has scaled peaks all over the world, including Mount Fitzroy in Patagonia. We had just kayaked the Bio-Bio in Chile, and right away we started talking about comparable adventures here in California. The next thing I knew, we were in Doug's plane over the Sierra Nevada, scouting the South Fork Merced and the Middle San Joaquin by air.

We thought we could do the South Fork Merced in two days. It took us four days and cost Royal a dislocated shoulder. (He was ready to go again the following week.) So we approached the upper Middle Fork of the San Joaquin much more cautiously. And why not? In the 25 miles from the put-in above Devil's Postpile to the top of Mammoth Pool Reservoir, the river drops 4700 feet. Some stretches have gradients above 400 feet per mile as the river plunges over huge granite aprons.

We took climbing gear, sleeping bags, five pounds of food (dried fruit, nuts, chocolate bars, and tea), and almost nothing else. The trip totaled six days, a couple more than we had planned, so each of us ate only about four ounces of food per day. At one point I found a nice camera not far from one of the rare trails, but I left it behind because I didn't want to make my kayak three pounds heavier.

When we started, we had no idea whether we could really finish the run. Time after time we had to portage by lowering our boats on ropes and carefully climbing down after them. I would have been glad to take out at the Cassidy foot bridge, where a trail crosses the river, but Royal and Doug wanted to press on through Balloon Dome Gorge. We agreed that if necessary, we would abandon the boats and climb out of the canyon—assuming we could find a way up the 3000' walls. I felt we were flirting with forbidden dangers, doing something we shouldn't be doing, but Royal and Doug simply refused to believe we couldn't find a way down. Every move, whether in the boat or on the rock face, was made with more concentration than I had ever mustered. All the little details, from the grain of the granite to the color of the water, stood out more sharply than usual.

When we emerged from the gorge, we knew we were going to make it. But the trip was tough all the way to the end. Difficult rapids continued to the reservoir, then we had to paddle six miles against a 30 mile-an-hour wind. After that we hiked two miles, hitched a ride to the nearest phone, and waited several hours to be picked up. At last we sat down to a fine midnight dinner at Royal's home in Modesto. An hour later, just when I was about to relax, Royal reached into a drawer and pulled out a stack of maps. "Can you keep a secret?" he asked. He was already planning our next first descent: the headwaters of the Kern. — Reg Lake

Kings River

Garnet Dike Campground to Kirch Flat Campground

Difficulty: III; IV above 8000 cfs.   **Length:** 9.5 miles.

Gradient: 35 ft./mi.   **Drainage:** 950 sq. mi. at mile 6.5.

Season: April–late July.   **Elevation at Put-in:** 1280'.

Runnable Levels: 700/1000–15,000 cfs.

Flow Information: (916) 322-3327. Flow at Rodgers Crossing (mile 6.5) or inflow into Pine Flat Reservoir.

Scenery: Very good.   **Solitude:** Good. A dirt road follows the river.

Rafts and Kayaks: An excellent run for intermediate and advanced boaters who want to get used to big water.

Open Canoes: Experts only, and only at flows below 1500 cfs.

Commercial Raft Trips: One- and two-day floats. For a list of outfitters, contact Kings River Ranger District, Sierra National Forest, Trimmer Route, Sanger, CA 93657; phone below.

Water: Clear and cold. Purify to be sure.

Camping: Several Forest Service campgrounds along the river.

Maps: Patterson Mountain (USGS 15'); Sequoia National Forest; Sierra National Forest; Sequoia (AAA).

Auto Shuttle: 9.5 miles; 30–45 minutes.

Emergency Telephone Numbers:
   Forest Service (Kings River Ranger Station): (209) 855-8321.
   Fresno County Sheriff (Fresno): (209) 445-3111 or 488-3111.

Logistics: From Centerville, 18 miles east of Fresno on Highway 180, follow Trimmer Springs Road past Piedra and around the north side of Pine Flat Reservoir. Thirty winding miles later, you'll reach the river. Just upstream is the take-out, Kirch Flat Campground. Continue up the road, crossing one bridge to the left bank and another back to the right (north) bank of the Kings. At this point the pavement ends, and the dirt road becomes more difficult as you proceed upstream. It is nearly impassable by the time you reach the put-in just below Garnet Dike Campground (called Upper Kings Campground on Forest Service maps).

The Kings means big water. In May and June, when a heavy snow pack combines with warm weather to swell the river above 10,000 cfs, the Kings provides California boaters with a chance to test their skills against hydraulics (waves, holes, and currents) on the scale of the Grand Canyon. The river bed is wide and not heavily obstructed, so even at high flows the Kings isn't exceptionally hazardous. Of course, big water always calls for extra precautions. Most of the rapids can be seen and scouted from the road. In general this run is roughly comparable in difficulty to the South Fork American between Chili Bar and Salmon Falls. If you have time, hike five miles up the trail from the put-in and peer over the rim of the canyon where Garlic Falls plummets a thousand feet into the Kings.

Mile by Mile Guide

0	Garnet Dike Campground (right bank). Put in at an open spot 100 yards downstream. There are plenty of alternate put-in sites all along the run; you can find them from the road.
0.3	**BANZAI (III).** At lower flows, watch for a boat-eating hole in the middle of the river. This hole is washed out at higher levels, but bigger holes appear elsewhere in the rapid.
2.8	**MULE ROCK (III).** The current piles into a midstream rock (hole above 3000 cfs).
3.7	**FANG TOOTH (III).** Nearly a quarter mile of boulder dodging.
4.5	Mill Flat Creek enters on the left. Good campsite. A short hike up the creek leads to a refreshing swimming hole.
7.4	North Fork of the Kings enters on the right, just downstream from the bridge across the main river.
7.8	**SIDEWINDER (III).** A large rock on the left becomes a big hole at high flows.
8.2	**RANCH RAPID (III).** Also known as **Rooster Tail.** The river splits; most of the water turns left into a sharp drop. At higher flows the right channel provides a "chicken route"—not a bad idea.
8.5	Bridge across the river.
9.5	*TAKE-OUT.* Kirch Flat Campground (right bank).

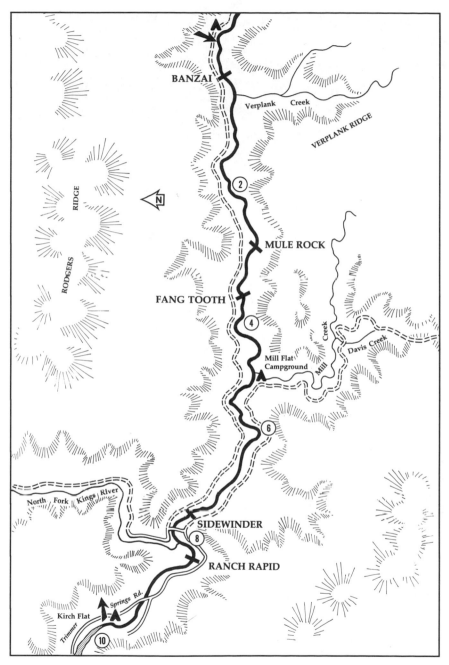

Kings River

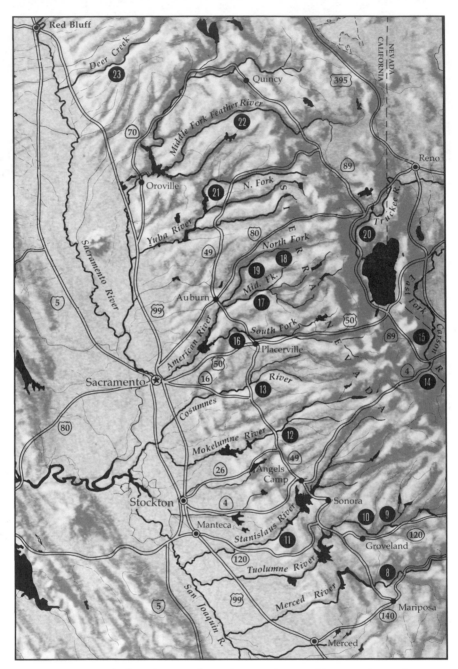

Rivers of the Central and Northern Sierra Nevada

Rivers of the Central and Northern Sierra Nevada

8. Merced

9. Upper Tuolumne

10. Tuolumne

11. Lower Stanislaus

12. Mokelumne

13. Cosumnes

14. Upper East Fork Carson

15. East Fork Carson: Wilderness Run

16. South Fork American

17. Middle Fork American

18. North Fork American: Giant Gap Run

19. North Fork American: Chamberlain Falls and Big Bend Runs

20. Truckee

21. North Fork Yuba

22. Middle Fork Feather

23. Deer Creek

Merced River

Red Bud Picnic Area to Bagby

Difficulty: IVp; II between miles 9 and 16.

Length: 29 miles; 2 days. Shorter runs possible.

Gradient: 34 ft./mi.   **Elevation at Put-in:** 1700'.

Season: March–June.   **Drainage:** 691 sq. mi. at Briceburg.

Flow Information: (916) 322-3327. Inflow into McClure Reservoir.

Runnable Levels: 300/600–10,000 cfs above mile 20; upper limit 5000 cfs above mile 2.8 and below mile 20 (see Special Hazards).

Scenery: Very good.   **Solitude:** Good, especially below Briceburg.

Rafts: Advanced boating except for a seven-mile Class II stretch which novices can handle. Experts sometimes put in above Red Bud.

Kayaks: Same skill levels as for rafts (above). Kayaks can often run the river well into July.

Open Canoes: Experienced intermediates can run the section from the foot bridge to Briceburg below 1200 cfs. Other stretches are too rough for open canoes.

Special Hazards: Portage North Fork Falls (mile 22.8), a strenuous undertaking in spite of the boat ramps. Pack light. At higher flows it is dangerous to run Quarter Mile Rapid (mile 22.3) because boats could be swept over North Fork Falls. Even experts should take out at the end of the road (Railroad Flat Campground, mile 20.5) when the flow is 4000–5000 cfs or higher.

Commercial Raft Trips: One- and two-day trips. For a list of outfitters, contact Bureau of Land Management, 63 Natoma Street, Folsom CA 95630; phone below.

Water: Cold and clear, but since the river runs through Yosemite Valley and along the highway, water should be purified before you drink it.

Camping: Both private and public campgrounds along the highway are crowded on spring weekends and all week during the summer. Below Briceburg, boaters can find numerous campsites. Those on the left bank are more secluded. Gold dredgers often occupy right-bank campsites.

Maps: El Portal, Coulterville (USGS 15'); El Portal, Kinsley, Feliciana Mtn., Bear Valley (USGS 7.5'); Yosemite (AAA).

Auto Shuttle: 47 miles; 1 hour 15 minutes.

Emergency Telephone Numbers:
BLM (Folsom): (916) 985-4474.
Mariposa County Sheriff (Mariposa): 911.

Logistics: The put-in for private boaters is at Red Bud Picnic Area, 29 miles east of Mariposa on Highway 140 and just a few miles west of the El Portal entrance to Yosemite Park. Commercial outfitters launch from the right bank. The take-out is near the recreational settlement of Bagby, near the eastern end of McClure Reservoir. To reach Bagby, drive 18 miles north of Mariposa on Highway 49 and turn right on a dirt road leading up the left bank of the reservoir. There are a number of alternate river access points between the put-in and mile 20. Shuttles are quick and easy down to Briceburg.

Fifteen miles west of its headwaters along the glacier-studded slopes of Mount Lyell (13,114'), the Merced drops down the spectacular cataracts of Nevada and Vernal Falls into Yosemite Valley, where for a time it becomes a peaceful, meandering stream. Yosemite Valley, which became a national park in 1890, was inhabited by the Awani Indians before whites routed them in the early years of the Gold Rush. (The new arrivals thought "Yosemite" was the Indians' tribal name, but it apparently meant "grizzly bear" in their language.) Thanks to the popularity of Yosemite, the Merced — "mercy" in Spanish — is one of the few Sierra rivers left undammed in its upper reaches.

Just west of the park the river surges forward again, tumbling down several miles of breathtakingly steep chutes until it begins to slacken above El Portal. Its cold, clear, free-flowing waters rise to a peak in May and, except in years of heavy snowfall, drop quickly after mid-June. By July in average years, the river offers only a cooling trickle to inner-tubers and fishermen escaping the summer heat. The Merced is at its best in the spring, when redbuds and poppies splash the rugged hillsides with bright colors and Yosemite Park is not yet spilling over with tourists.

The Merced's boating season may be short, but it is intense. At El Portal, where some experts start their runs, the river's gradient is over 120 feet per mile; a mile downstream at the Highway 140 bridge, another alternate put-in, the stream is dropping at 100 feet per mile; and at Red Bud Picnic Area, the most popular put-in, the gradient is still 75. Below the South Fork (mile 6) the pace slackens a bit, but several major rapids still lie in wait. Toughest among them is Quarter Mile Rapid (mile 22.3), one of the best in the state — a long, rough boulder slalom that should not be run at high water because of the danger of being swept over North Fork Falls just downstream.

But the river also has its calm stretches, especially between the foot bridge (mile 9) and Briceburg (mile 15), population nine and a half, where honorary mayor Jack Bass presides over a flock of hummingbirds and several gold-dredging operations downstream. Here Highway 140 leaves the river, but a dirt road follows the right bank of the Merced for five more miles. Even after the road ends, the abandoned road bed of the old Yosemite Railroad—defunct since 1945—follows the right bank all the way to McClure Reservoir, providing a good way to hike out in case of emergency.

Mile by Mile Guide

0   Red Bud Picnic Area. Experts sometimes put in upstream at the Highway 140 bridge to run an extra mile of continuous Class IV rapids (not visible from the highway). Really salty boaters occasionally launch near the cafe and gas station at El Portal about two miles upstream from Red Bud (continuous Class IV).

0–1.1   Continuous Class III–IV white water. Few eddies except at lower flows.

1.2   **NIGHTMARE ISLAND (IV). Recognition:** The river jogs right, then splits around an island as it turns sharply left. Scout both this rapid and Chipped Tooth at the same time, from either or both banks. **The rapid:** Above 3000 cfs most boaters run the left side, but at lower flows this channel ends in a nasty boulder sieve and boaters usually run the right side's sharp, narrow drops.

1.4   **CHIPPED TOOTH (IV).** A short staircase rapid with a sizable rock (hole at higher flows) in the middle. At higher flows this rapid merges with the one above.

1.5–6   Unnamed Class II–III rapids, frequent at first, less so downstream as the river's gradient slackens. Occasionally, brushy islands split the stream bed.

2.8   *RIVER ACCESS.* Cranberry Gulch. An alternate put-in; recommended at high flows to avoid the rapids upstream.

5.6   South Fork of the Merced enters on the left. Expert kayakers sometimes run this river.

7.5   **NED'S GULCH (IV). Recognition:** The river bends sharply left. Ned's Gulch, a creek entering from the right, is marked by a house and other signs of human habitation. Scout from either side. **The rapid:** A staircase rapid; the third and last drop is the biggest. At high water the holes become huge but runnable cresting waves.

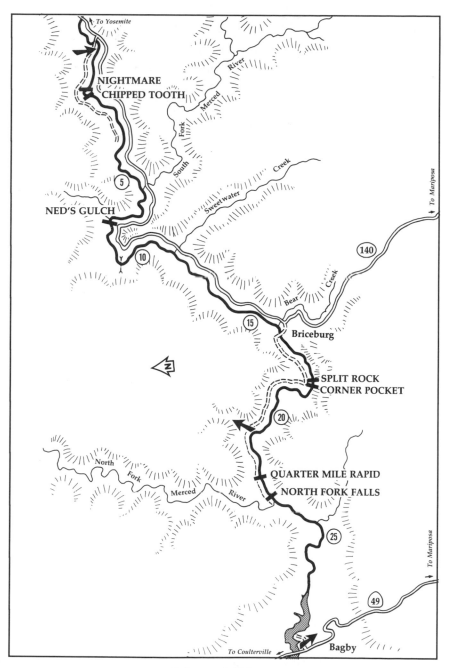

To Yosemite

NIGHTMARE
CHIPPED TOOTH

Merced

River

South

Fork

5

Creek

Sweetwater

NED'S GULCH

Y

10

To Mariposa

140

Bear

Creek

15

Briceburg

N

SPLIT ROCK
CORNER POCKET

20

North

Fork

Merced

River

QUARTER MILE RAPID

NORTH FORK FALLS

25

To Mariposa

49

To Coulterville

Bagby

Merced River

9   **RIVER ACCESS.** Foot bridge across the river. Easy Class II water and a 20-foot-per-mile gradient for the next seven miles. River access via the steep left bank.

15   Briceburg—a private residence, not a town. Bear Creek enters from the left. River access only by advance permission; call Jack Bass at (209) 379-2439. Contribute something if you use the site. Highway 140 leaves the river here, but a bridge crosses to the right bank and a dirt road continues downstream, providing frequent river access for the next five miles.

17.2   **SPLIT ROCK (IV).** A huge rock (hole at higher flows) blocks the middle of the river. Scout both this rapid and the next at the same time, from the right bank.

17.4   **CORNER POCKET (IV).** The river turns sharply right, and most of the current pours into a boat-eating hole.

20.2   Railroad Flat Campground (right bank). End of the road. A trail continues downstream along the old rail bed. Take out here at higher flows (4000–5000 cfs and up) to avoid the risk of running Quarter Mile Rapid unsuccessfully and being swept into North Fork Falls.

21.8   ♦ *HAZARD* ♦ An old four-foot weir (diversion dam) crossed the river here until the BLM dynamited it a few years ago. It's still a good idea to stop upstream and scout it for dangerous debris, especially at low flows.

22   **QUARTER MILE RAPID (IV +).** Longer than its name indicates. A complex boulder slalom at lower flows; big, powerful waves and holes at higher flows. Scout carefully from the right bank, memorizing your entire route. Station rescue parties with throw bags downstream. Check the short pool separating the end of the rapid from North Fork Falls. If you're not sure you can stop in time, don't run this rapid.

22.6   ♦ *PORTAGE* ♦
          NORTH FORK FALLS (U). A 25-foot vertical drop decorated with huge boulders. Sure, a few crazies have run the far left side, but that's no reason for you to try it. Use the boat ramps on the right bank to portage. North Fork of the Merced enters on the right just downstream. Class II rapids from here on.

26.8   High-water mark of McClure Reservoir (capacity 1 million acre-feet). New Exchequer Dam, a rock fill structure completed in 1966, furnishes water and power for the Merced Irrigation District.

28.3   *TAKE-OUT.* End of the dirt road that runs up the left bank from Bagby. A small fee is required to use the road. Take out at any convenient spot.

29   Highway 49 bridge crosses the reservoir at Bagby.

Tuolumne River

The Tuolumne, California's premier white water river, courses through one of the most spectacular canyons in the Sierra. The river's watershed makes up a larger portion of Yosemite Park than that of the Merced, which flows through Yosemite Valley just to the south. The Tuolumne* drains the western slopes of the Sierra Crest, from an area southwest of Mono Lake northward to the Emigrant Wilderness. Its headwaters, the Lyell and Dana Forks, rise on Mount Lyell (13,114') and Mount Dana (13,053'), named for eminent geologists of the last century. Northwest of Tuolumne Meadows, the great granite walls of the Grand Canyon of the Tuolumne open onto Hetch Hetchy Valley, described by John Muir as "another Yosemite Valley."

That valley has long been buried under the waters of Hetch Hetchy Reservoir, a San Francisco city project approved by Congress in 1913 over the objections of Muir's young Sierra Club. Hetch Hetchy is the only sizable commercial reservoir in the country permitted in a national park. O'Shaughnessy Dam, completed in 1923 and named for its builder, is relatively small. The concrete gravity barrier's height was raised in 1938, but the reservoir's capacity is still only 360,000 acre-feet. The City of San Francisco not only drinks the Tuolumne but realizes about $30 million a year from selling Hetch Hetchy power. Such is, apparently, the price of another Yosemite Valley.**

Between Hetch Hetchy (elevation 3796') and the backwaters of New Don Pedro Reservoir some 36 miles downstream, the Tuolumne flows like a wild river in winter and spring and at the behest of dam operators from about mid-summer on. San Francisco also operates reservoirs and powerhouses on two major tributaries of the Tuolumne, Cherry Creek and Eleanor Creek, and another powerhouse downstream on Moccasin Creek. Below Ward's Ferry the Tuolumne has been harnessed again by New Don Pedro Dam, owned by the Modesto and Turlock irrigation districts.

What remains of the Tuolumne has long been a candidate for the National Wild and Scenic Rivers System, but so far the Modesto and Turlock irrigation districts and their political allies have prevented the river's friends from passing a bill to extend this protection. Even though the Tuolumne already supplies their customers with cheap and plentiful water and electricity, the Modesto and Turlock districts are studying a

Tuolumne River downstream from Lumsden Bridge.   *Brian Fessenden*

new series of dams and powerhouses that would dry up much of the remaining river canyon. Their projects would wipe out one of the best fishing streams in the Sierra, both white water runs, and the city of Berkeley's summer camp at Hardin Flat on the South Fork. They would adversely affect summer camps on the Middle Fork belonging to the San Francisco Jewish Community Center and the city of San Jose. San Francisco, to its credit, has recently opposed further dams on the river. As this book goes to press, the river's fate is still in doubt.***

For river runners the loss of the Tuolumne, with two of the country's finest stretches of white water, would be a disaster. Most of California's best rafters and kayakers cut their teeth on the exciting, boulder-strewn rapids downstream from Meral's Pool. Until even more difficult runs were opened in recent years, this section of the "T" was considered the state's prime test of technical boating, and it remains one of the best river experiences anywhere. But upstream the Tuolumne is truly fierce. Clavey Falls, the biggest drop between Meral's Pool and Ward's Ferry, would be just an average rapid on the Cherry Creek run of the Upper Tuolumne. This may be the toughest regularly-boated white water in the country. Yet commercial raft trips have been offered since 1981, and the Cherry Creek run grows in popularity every season.

*"Tuolumne" is an attempt at "talmalamne," or "people of the stone dwellings," and was the name of Miwok who lived, perhaps in caves, near this river and the nearby Stanislaus. For more on the natural and human history of the Tuolumne, see John Cassidy, *A Guide to Three Rivers* (Friends of the River Books).

**Power from the Hetch Hetchy system is generated at Cherry, Early Intake, and Moccasin powerhouses, sold by San Francisco, and distributed by PG&E from transmission lines at Newark. Recently, San Francisco's net profit from electricity produced on the Tuolumne has ranged from $6 million in dry years to $70 million or more in the very wet year of 1983.

***More information is available from the Tuolumne River Preservation Trust, one of the organizations leading the fight to save the river, at Fort Mason Center, Building C, San Francisco, CA 94123; (415) 441-8778.

Upper Tuolumne

Cherry Creek Run

Cherry (Holm) Powerhouse to Meral's Pool

Difficulty: Vp. **Length:** 9 miles.

Gradient: 105 ft./mi. **Drainage:** 723 sq. mi. at Cherry Creek.

Season: March to mid-May and July through October. This extremely difficult stretch of white water should be attempted only at low flows, either in the spring before snow melt, or from mid-summer on, after heavy snow melt is over and the Tuolumne's flow is largely controlled by upstream hydroelectric facilities—primarily Cherry (Holm) Powerhouse.

Runnable Levels: 300/600–2000 cfs. **Elevation at Put-in:** 2225'.

Flow Information: (916) 322-3327. Flow at Meral's Pool. Dam-controlled summer flows usually range from 900 to 1300 cfs weekdays, 600 to 800 Saturdays, and 500 or below Sundays. Water comes up slowly in the morning and drops early in the evening. Most of the water is released from Cherry (Holm) Powerhouse down Cherry Creek, while Early Intake (Kirkwood) Powerhouse upstream on the Tuolumne usually adds only 200 to 300 cfs to the total flow at Meral's Pool, and the South Fork (at the end of the run) even less.

Scenery: Excellent. **Solitude:** Excellent.

Rafts: An extremely difficult run for experts only, preferably in self-bailing boats.

Kayaks: Only experts with foolproof rolls should try this river. It's no place to take a swim.

Open Canoes: Totally inappropriate.

Special Hazards: Lumsden Falls and Flat Rock Falls.

Permits: Required for private boaters. See next run.

Commercial Raft Trips: This may be the toughest white water in the country with regularly-scheduled raft trips. Guests must be in good physical shape and have previous white water experience. For outfitter information, contact the Forest Service in Groveland (see next run).

Water: Always cold, so wear wet suit even in the heat of summer. Usually drinkable, but giardia has been reported. Purify to be sure.

Camping: Don't try to carry camping gear down the river. Camp at Lumsden Bridge Campground (right bank, just downstream from the bridge) or at other sites near the road. Get an early start. If darkness catches you on the river, tie up the boats, climb up the right bank to the road, and finish the run in the morning.

Maps: Lake Eleanor NW, Duckwall Mtn., Jawbone Ridge (USGS 7.5'); Lake Eleanor, Tuolumne City (USGS 15'); Stanislaus National Forest; Yosemite (AAA).

Auto Shuttle: 12 miles; up to 1 hour via back roads. Longer route partially via Highway 120 if you need gas or supplies.

Emergency Telephone Numbers: See next run.

Logistics: To reach the take-out, follow directions to the put-in for the next Tuolumne run and continue upstream to Lumsden Bridge. To reach the put-in from the take-out, keep driving upstream on Lumsden Road, ford Jawbone Creek, and turn right about two miles farther onto a paved road. Almost immediately, turn right again onto Cherry Lake Road. Cross Cherry Creek and turn right on a paved road that leads to the put-in just downstream from the powerhouse. (If you find yourself on a bridge crossing the Tuolumne, you've gone too far.)

If you're driving to the put-in first, take Highway 120 toward Yosemite. Turn north onto Cherry Lake Road at the San Jose Camp 14 miles east of Groveland. Seven miles farther the road crosses the Tuolumne at Early Intake Powerhouse. A mile and a half beyond this bridge, turn left on a paved road that leads to the put-in on Cherry Creek.

Floating the Cherry Creek run puts boaters on the leading edge of the sport. Here in Jawbone Canyon, the Tuolumne plummets at an average rate of more than 100 feet per mile over granite boulders torn from the eroded bedrock of the Sierra. In one mile-long section the river falls 200 feet. This is one of the most difficult stretches of river in this book, and its few competitors (such as the Middle Fork Feather Gorge, Deer Creek, and the Upper Kings) are rarely boated.

Kayakers Dick Sunderland and Gerald Meral were the first to run the Upper Tuolumne in 1968. Marty McDonnell and Walt Harvest made the first raft trip in 1973, and McDonnell's company, Sierra Mac River Trips (Sonora), pioneered commercial rafting here in 1981. The run is emphatically for experts only, and only at low summer flows. Even guests on commercial raft trips are required to have white water experience and to pass a physical test before embarking. Self-bailing rafts are advisable on the Upper "T." The rapids are separated by very short pools, and a swamped boat can get into trouble in a hurry. Kayakers must have a strong, dependable roll.

The guide below lists only the very toughest rapids. Aside from Lumsden Falls, the three most feared by boaters are Mushroom, Lewis's Leap, and Flat Rock Falls. But there are plenty of others difficult enough to cause trouble. Stop and scout whenever possible, even though this probably means contact with poison oak—another good reason to wear a wet suit even in the heat of summer. Don't get overconfident when you make it to the halfway point: the pools grow shorter and the rapids even more difficult the rest of the way. Be sure you recognize Flat Rock Falls (mile 6.8); most boaters wisely portage this dangerous drop. Lumsden Falls is even worse and should be considered unrunnable.

Mile by Mile Guide

0   Put in on the right (south) bank of Cherry Creek just below the bridge, or at a primitive campsite on the opposite bank. Most of the Tuolumne's flow after mid-summer is released down Cherry Creek from the powerhouse, so boaters put in on the creek and float a mile of continuous Class IV rapids down to the river.

1   Confluence of Cherry Creek and the Tuolumne, which enters from the left.

2   **CORKSCREW (V).** A horizon line across the river marks the top of the rapid. Avoid an undercut rock at the left bottom. Scout on the left.

2.4   **JAWBONE (V).** Jawbone Creek enters on the right. Boulders block the river channel. Scout on the right.

3.2–3.4 **MUSHROOM (V+).** The rapid begins just beyond a sharp right turn. Scout left. In the first 50 yards the river falls 30 vertical feet as it tumbles over ledges, into holes, and against a huge flake of rock that has split away from the right wall. The flake divides a sharp vertical drop onto a great foaming boulder. Just downstream, a final Class V vertical (also called **Toadstool**) splits around another big rock that catches a lot of the current. An eddy on the left just above this final drop is hard to escape. Downstream, half a mile of Class IV boulder gardens that can be seen from the road continue to the next big rapid.

3.9   **CATAPULT (V).** Also called **Unknown Soldier**. As a cable crosses the river and the road comes into view high on the right bank, the Tuolumne surges through a rocky slalom leading to a sharp drop down a right-hand chute. Scout this final drop, either from the right bank before you start down the rapid, or from one of the small eddies on either side just above the drop.

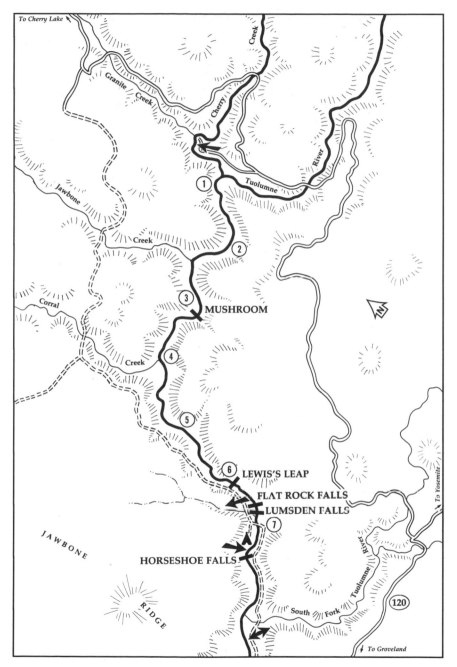

Upper Tuolomne River

4-5   **MIRACLE MILE (V).** Continuous action as the river drops 200 feet in a mile. A big gulch on the right (mile 4.3) announces **Just a Slalom** (also called **Gar's Lunch**), a brutal quarter-mile boulder garden laced with steep drops. The worst ones—like "Chuck's Wave"—are near the top, so a mistake could lead to a nasty swim. Scout right, then enter left and think fast. Around mile 4.7 comes **Blind Alley**, a steep, rough chute leading to a tiny pool. Then the current piles into **Coffin Rock**. Some boaters avoid it by running a drop on the far right behind a large boulder. Scout on either side.

5–6   Another mile of continuous Class V white water: first a boulder slalom; then a wide, shallow rock garden; next a series of wrap rocks. Near the end of the stretch, the river turns right, and boaters should stop to scout **Christmas Hole**, an eight-foot vertical just downstream. White water continues to the lip of the falls, so don't wait too long to eddy up.

6.1   **AIRPLANE TURN (V).** After flowing through a large pool, the river turns left and drops into a hole that has held boats for a minute or more. Scout on the right.

6.4   **LEWIS'S LEAP (V+).** Also called **Number Two**. Boaters must negotiate some sharp drops and maneuver around boulders to have the privilege of making the leap into a huge, river-wide hole. Amazingly, most boats emerge upright. No guarantees. Scout on the right.

6.7   *ALTERNATE TAKE-OUT.* Boaters often take out above Flat Rock Falls, but it's a very difficult task. Choose between scrambling up a steep embankment to the road on the right, or carrying gear out via a long trail on the left that isn't very steep but is laced with poison oak.

6.8   ◆ *POSSIBLE PORTAGE* ◆
        FLAT ROCK FALLS (V–VI). A technical boulder garden leads to a ten-foot falls onto a severely undercut rock. Boaters trapped in the reversal could drown. This drop should be portaged at most flows. Some boaters flirt with disaster to reach a slightly less intimidating vertical chute on the right. Scout either side. Portage (a tough one) on the left.

7   ◆ *PORTAGE* ◆ *ALTERNATE TAKE-OUT.*
        LUMSDEN FALLS (U). Look at this one from the bridge. You may think you see a way down this long, turbulent rapid's shelves and ledges, but don't even think about testing your theory. For the record, though, we have heard of three successful runs of Lumsden Falls—two by a paddle raft crew from Texas, and one by kayaker Gordon Patchin in 1983.

7.1   *RIVER ACCESS.* Lumsden Bridge. A Forest Service campground just downstream sometimes serves as a put-in.

7.5   **AGAINST THE WALL (IV).** A blind right turn leads to a big hole in the middle of the river.

7.7   **HORSESHOE FALLS (IV+).** A staircase rapid similar to Clavey Falls. The second drop is the biggest. Scout from the island of the right.

8.3   South Fork Tuolumne enters on the right.

8.4   Lumsden Campground (left bank). Kayakers sometimes take out or put in here.

8.5   **MERAL'S POOL TABLE (IV).** A rock garden. At lower flows, watch for an undercut ledge on the left.

8.6   *TAKE-OUT.* Meral's Pool. This is the put-in for the run to Ward's Ferry.

I've seen a lot of changes in white water boating in California. Back in the early sixties, when I first started floating rivers, the South Fork American and the Stanislaus were the hot runs, and it was rare to see a kayaker wearing a helmet or a rafter wearing a life jacket. By the late sixties, when boaters started running the main Tuolumne below Lumsden Campground, techniques, equipment, and safety procedures had improved considerably. Then, running the main "T" was putting yourself out on the leading edge of the sport, and Clavey Falls was the ultimate rapid.

When I heard about the first kayak run of the Upper Tuolumne in 1968, I was intrigued. The Tuolumne, then as now, was a candidate for Wild and Scenic status on the one hand and for more dams on the other. Jerry Meral and Dick Sunderland wanted to show that there was another boatable section of the river. They took a couple of days to float the seven miles down to Lumsden Falls, and they portaged a lot of rapids, but they made their point. For the next few years I fantasized about rafting that stretch, but I figured it was too tough. Eventually, though, we learned enough on the main Tuolumne to think we had a chance. We had developed boats appropriate for the run: modified Huck Finns, which we called "spider boats" or "catarafts" because they had only two tubes, one on each side, held together by rowing frames and rigging. They were light, quick, and impossible to swamp, though they would flip.

In April 1973 Walt Harvest, one of the strongest and shrewdest kayakers and rafters I've ever known, joined me for a first raft run of the Cherry Creek stretch. We each rowed a spider boat with one experienced river runner as a passenger—Mark DuBois with me, Fred Dennis with Walt. (Being a passenger on a spider boat is a very active job, because these light rafts need fast high-siding and counterbalancing to prevent flips. Now we use stabler boats for this run, full Huck Finns or a newer type of self-bailing raft.) We wore helmets—unusual for rafters in those days—and took climbing gear in case we needed to line our boats through rapids or belay them down the sheer walls of the canyon if we portaged.

We found our way to the put-in at night and lowered the boats over a sheer 60-foot cliff down to the river. If the put-in was this tough, we thought, how bad would the river be? We couldn't help feeling apprehensive. By dawn we were on the water, picking our way down the boulder gardens, with first one raft leading the way, then the other. Our plan was to spend a couple of days on the river, since we were scouting every rapid. But we made much better time than we had expected. We were nearly two miles downstream, scouting a rapid we later named Corkscrew, when the sun finally appeared above the canyon wall.

It was like a dream come true. To our amazement, we found that we were able to run one after another of these fearsome chutes and drops. The rapids that later became Mushroom, Lewis's Leap, and Flat Rock Falls caused us the most hesitation. (At the time, we referred to them as Numbers One, Two, and Three.) But we made it every time, and at the bottom of the rapid we'd just look at each other and laugh. We could hardly believe we were really doing it. Our euphoria almost ran away with us, and we started talking about running Lumsden Falls as well. But when we finally got there and looked at this dangerous pitch, we sobered up soon enough. Lumsden Falls has no feasible entrance, a very tough boulder field in the middle, and a bad exit that takes boats toward an undercut ledge. So we quit while we were ahead and hauled the rafts up the steep bank to the road.

We ran the Upper Tuolumne twice more that spring, and by the time summer came around, our concept of rafting had been transformed. After that, though we continued to respect it, the main Tuolumne run looked almost flat.

—Marty McDonnell

Tuolumne River

Meral's Pool to Ward's Ferry

Difficulty: IV +; V above 4000 cfs.   **Length:** 18 miles; 1–3 days.

Gradient: 40 ft./mi.   **Drainage:** 1350 sq. mi. at take-out.

Season: March–October. Often too high from late May to early July during peak snow melt.

Runnable Levels: 300/600–8000 cfs.   **Elevation at Put-in:** 1430'.

Flow Information: (916) 322-3327. Flow at Lumsden (Meral's Pool). After snow melt is over, dam-controlled summer flows usually range from 900 to 1300 cfs weekdays, 600 to 800 Saturdays, and 500 or less Sundays. Water comes up slowly in the morning and drops early in the evening.

Scenery: Excellent.   **Solitude:** Excellent.

Rafts: At low summer flows—especially on Sundays—all but the smallest rafts have a tough time getting down the steep, rocky rapids in the first couple of miles. Put in on weekdays if possible (Friday for weekend floats).

Kayaks: Advanced and expert kayakers can run the river in one day, but a tight schedule cuts down on time for play in the rapids.

Open Canoes: Not recommended. A few experts have run the river at very low flows.

Special Hazards: For years a huge log jam blocked the top of New Don Pedro Reservoir, upstream from the Ward's Ferry take-out, after mid-summer. Kayaks could make it through, but for rafts the going was tough and often impossible. The Modesto and Turlock irrigation districts, legally responsible for maintaining the reservoir, chose to deal with the problem by charging private and commercial rafters to be towed through the log jam. In the winter of 1983-1984 work was finally begun on the project of clearing the debris. Check with the Forest Service in Groveland or with the irrigation districts themselves for updated information.

Permits: Required for private boaters. Contact Groveland Ranger District, Stanislaus National Forest, PO Box 709, Groveland, CA 95321; phone below.

Commercial Raft Trips: Two- to three-day floats are popular and heavily booked in summer. For a list of outfitters, contact the Forest Service in Groveland.

Water: Clear and cold. Usually drinkable in the past, but recently there have been reports of giardia. Avoid taking water from side streams, including the Clavey River. Purify to be sure.

Camping: Large campsites are fairly scarce above mile 15. Forest Service insists on reservations for major sites.

Maps: Jawbone Ridge, Groveland, Tuolumne, Standard, Moccasin (USGS 7.5'); Tuolumne, Sonora (USGS 15'); Yosemite (AAA); Tuolumne River (Cassady and Calhoun).

Auto Shuttle: 25 miles; 1.5 hours.

Emergency Telephone Numbers:

Tuolumne County Sheriff (Sonora): 911 (within 209 area code), or (209) 533-5911.

Forest Service (Groveland): (209) 962-7825.

Logistics: To reach the take-out, turn north off Highway 120 at Big Oak Flat (two miles west of Groveland) onto Ward's Ferry Road (paved) and follow it seven miles to the bridge across the upper end of New Don Pedro Reservoir. To reach the put-in, continue east on Highway 120. About 7.5 miles east of Groveland, turn left onto Ferretti Road (paved). After about a mile, immediately after crossing the second cattle guard, turn right onto Lumsden Road, a steep, rough dirt road that reaches the river five miles later. The put-in at Meral's Pool is a couple of hundred yards downstream from Lumsden Campground, complete with toilets, tables, fire pits, and plenty of poison oak. Another campground may be found about two miles upstream, just below Lumsden Bridge.*

*When you drive shuttle, you can save a few minutes by taking Deer Flat Road, which connects Ward's Ferry Road with the highway just west of Groveland. If you descend from the foothills via Highway 120, be sure not to take steep, dangerous Old Priest Grade, which is too much for the brakes of many vehicles, especially if they're loaded with gear and people. The New Priest Grade (the main stem of the highway) is much safer.

When kayakers and rafters began to tackle this run in the sixties, they usually portaged its biggest rapid, Clavey Falls. The first kayaker to run all the rapids in this stretch was solo kayaker Noel DeBord in 1965, but the early descents by Dick Sunderland, Gerald Meral, and Jim Morehouse had more to do with turning boaters' attention to the Tuolumne. In 1968 Bryce Whitmore and Martin McDonnell made the first raft run without portages. Whitmore also organized the first commercial raft trips here in 1969.

Things are different now. The Tuolumne's popularity soared as white water sport took off during the last decade. Even though the river is often too high to run from late May to early July, some 6000 people float the Tuolumne every year, and that number would be considerably higher without the Forest Service's fairly tight restrictions on both private and commercial boaters.

This is a challenging run for advanced boaters at any level and for experts only above 4000 cfs. It is no river for novices or intermediates unless they are guided by seasoned veterans at low flows. More than a dozen rapids rated Class IV or higher dot the run, and there are many good Class III and III+ rapids which remain nameless.

Mile by Mile Guide

0   Meral's Pool. There are two good put-in sites on the left bank. A flow gauge is located at the river's edge, and a conversion chart is on the bank above it. Kayakers who want to run an extra rapid sometimes put in upstream at Lumsden Campground, but this alternate put-in is a little difficult for rafts. Another put-in is farther upstream, just below Lumsden Bridge (see Cherry Creek run).

0.1   **ROCK GARDEN (IV).** This boulder slalom is toughest at low water, when rafts usually have to cross from right to left part way down to find a runnable channel. At very high flows there is a dangerous reversal at the bottom.

0.4   **NEMESIS (IV).** Another low-water nightmare just after a sharp left-hand bend. The Nemesis is a big boulder cluster about half way down. At low flows there are no clear routes, but it's safest to run left of the obstacle.

0.8   **SUNDERLAND'S CHUTE (IV+).** At the end of a short pool, the river turns sharply right and tumbles down a rough chute. The current pushes boats toward a big rock (hole at higher flows) guarding the right side. Scouting from the right involves a difficult clamber over huge boulders and around poison oak. Wear your life jacket—securely fastened—when you scout.

1   **HACKAMACK HOLE (IV).** A sharp drop divided by two big rocks. At high flows they form a river-wide reversal that is hard to miss.

1.5   **RAM'S HEAD (IV; V above 3500 cfs).** The river bends left and drops down a rocky pitch whose exit is plugged by a boulder. At medium and high flows the boulder creates a powerful, spouting hole. Fortunately, there is a good recovery pool below. Stop well upstream to scout (either bank). Walk all the way down to look at the bottom of the rapid.

1.9–2.1   **INDIA and LOWER INDIA (IV).** Two shorter chutes separated by a small pool. Both finish with sharp drops plugged by big rocks—at high water, river-wide holes. Scout both rapids at the same time (left bank).

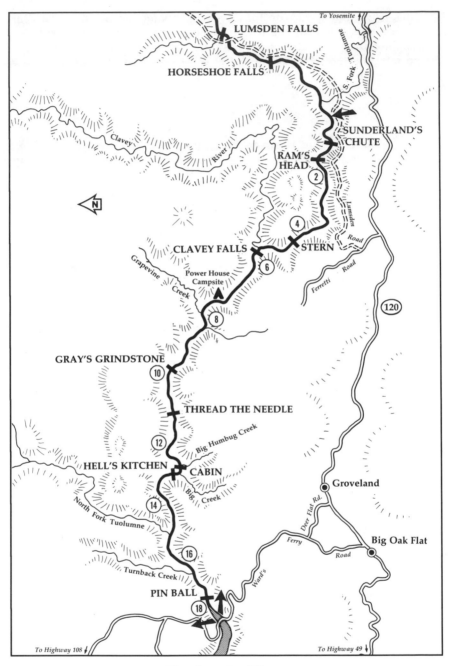

Tuolumne River

3.3 Tin Can Cabin Camp (left bank) is sometimes used by fishermen who hike down a steep trail from Lumsden Road.

4.4 **STERN (IV).** At low flows, big boulders blocking the river create a problem for rafts, which must run a narrow chute between the left wall and a van-sized rock. Don't get turned sideways!

4.7 **EVANGELIST (IV).** The river bends right into a series of short drops with a big rock/hole right center.

5.4 At the end of a long pool, the Clavey River enters from the right, and the Tuolumne turns sharply left into Clavey Falls, the biggest rapid on this run. Small campsites on both banks of the Tuolumne. A trail leads from the left bank downstream and then out of the canyon. Good hiking (with poison oak) and fishing up the Clavey, but both activities are dangerous at high water. When the Clavey is running high, it can be difficult to get rafts across its mouth in order to eddy up on the right bank of the Tuolumne above the falls.

5.4 ♦ *POSSIBLE PORTAGE* ♦
   CLAVEY FALLS (V). The first two drops in this dramatic staircase rapid are the biggest. The first, an eight-foot vertical called "The Falls," takes boats into a foaming current that pushes them toward the left wall. The second drop is guarded by a boat-eating hole across the left half of the river. Rafts have a hard time avoiding it at flows above 2000 cfs. Kayaks can choose alternate routes that avoid most of the problems. When boats run the Falls, station rescue parties downstream. Portage on the right if you don't like the looks of this rapid.

5.9 The trail that begins above Clavey Falls climbs out of the canyon to Ferretti Road from above the left bank.

The Tuolumne River on a perfect June morning: green and white thunder against a gray cliff, yellow sun in a shimmering sky of blue. While we ate breakfast, two members of another boating party dangled fishing lines in the pool at the mouth of the Clavey River. We broke camp and stowed our gear in the rafts with particular care—"rigging for a flip." As we studied Clavey Falls, other boats began to arrive from upstream, and a crowd soon formed on the banks. Some were passengers on commercial trips, wielding cameras and already showing the first signs of sunburn. Others wore the professional river guide's simple summer garb: worn-out sneakers, nylon shorts, belt festooned with knife and other river tools.

  Our small private party could not have chanced on the canyon at a better moment. We had expected low water, but upstream reservoirs were full, and releases had mounted to 3700 cfs by the time of our put-in around noon on the previous day. We had an exhilarating run at this medium-high flow. The river sparkled and danced all the way. The heat of the sun in a cloudless sky quickly overcame the water's chill, and the rugged canyon ridges, studded with green groves of oak and pine, wore the golden color of summer in the Sierra foothills. We made five miles and camped just above the Falls. Night came on so mild that it was late before we reached for sweaters, and the cascading melody of a canyon wren awakened me just before the morning sun topped the ridge behind the camp.

We didn't stare too long at Clavey Falls; it just looks worse and worse. My passengers, two robust journalists, had never seen a Class V rapid. In fact, it was the first raft trip for one of them. But they eagerly followed my instructions, poised in the bow of the fourteen-foot Falcon I was rowing, ready to throw their weight forward to help the raft through the big stopper wave.

A good thing, too. The hole stood the little raft almost on end. But we came down right side up and washed over the big wave, only to be caught briefly in the left-hand whirlpool eddy where I had found myself floating in my life jacket after a less successful run of Clavey years earlier. This time, though, we were all in the boat—swamped, awash to the gunnels, but safe and sound. Whoops from the crowd echoed against the cliff as our heavy craft blundered down the rest of the rapid. My passengers bailed furiously, exultant grins on their faces. Made it again, I thought. Thanks be to the river gods. —Fryar Calhoun

7.5	Powerhouse Campsite, a big sandy beach, on the right. The powerhouse provided electricity for mines early in the century and was destroyed by flood in 1937. A trail on the left bank leads downstream to Indian Creek and then out of the canyon.
7.9	Grapevine Creek enters from the right. Grapevine Campsite is downstream on the left.
8.2	Abandoned hard rock mine shaft on the left.
8.3	Indian Creek enters from the left. An old road climbs out of the canyon from a point just downstream. Large campsite on river right.
9.5	**GRAY'S GRINDSTONE (IV).** At the end of a long pool, boulders block the left side of the river and announce the beginning of this thousand-yard maze. At high flows a big hole hides in a row of standing waves just below the top of the rapid.
11	**THREAD THE NEEDLE (IV).** Rocks block most of the river. Even at low flows, boaters are advised to take the "Chicken Shot" on the left rather than attempt to "thread the needle" between the rocks in the center. Two campsites on the left in the next half mile.
12.2	Quartz mine shafts on both banks were abandoned around 1909. A huge old steam engine (right bank) is worth a look. A trail leads out of the canyon from the left bank.

12.6   **CABIN (IV).** Big Humbug Creek enters from the left. The river bends right and drops down a curving chute with a big rock/hole just below the entrance.

12.8   Big Creek enters from the left. A short hike up the creek leads to a nice waterfall. Indian mortar holes near the creek's mouth. Large campsite.

12.9   **HELL'S KITCHEN (IV).** A wide chute is almost blocked by a boulder jumble extending out from the right bank. There is a runnable slalom course down the left side, made even tighter in recent years by a snag caught on a rock.

14.4   Tattered suspension bridge marks the site of the abandoned Mohican and Mary Ellen quartz mines. Old mining equipment, including a stamp mill, on the left. The Mohican Trail leads out of the canyon from the left bank.

15.1   North Fork of the Tuolumne enters on the right. Good campsites from here on. A mile up the tributary is the site of an old bridge, Devil's Gate, which once linked Tuolumne City with the Mohican Trail via the old suspension bridge upriver.

15.8   High-water mark of New Don Pedro Reservoir. When the reservoir is low, more white water action lies ahead.

16.5   Turnback Creek enters on the right. Its name commemorates a discreet strategic decision made by two miners who stumbled upon an Indian camp. This creek was the site of an intense gold rush in 1856.

17.5   **PIN BALL (IV +).** One of the best rapids on this run, almost in sight of the take-out, is usually covered by the reservoir. When Pin Ball emerges, boaters must find routes over a river-wide ledge guarded by a jumbled boulder fence.

18   *TAKE-OUT.* Ward's Ferry Bridge. Take out on either bank.

Stanislaus River

In May 1982 one of the loveliest rivers in the country, the Stanislaus* below Camp Nine, disappeared under the rising waters of New Melones Reservoir. Those of us lucky enough to have known the Stanislaus remember it as a nearly perfect river. Lush riverside vegetation was displayed against the canyon's sculpted limestone walls—rare in the Sierra. At low summer flows its forgiving Class II–III rapids delighted thousands of commercial rafting passengers and provided an excellent run for novice and intermediate kayakers and rafters. During high water, especially in the glorious Mays and Junes of peak snow melt, the river became a surging torrent of green and white, attracting advanced and expert boaters from all around the state.

In the end sixteen miles of living river canyon and all that made it special—the limestone grotto of Crystal Cave, Miwok mortar holes on the banks, abandoned artifacts of gold mining days at the mouth of the South Fork, the giant fig tree at Duck Bar—were drowned by a reservoir of questionable necessity. California farmers are so well supplied with irrigation water that the U.S. Bureau of Reclamation, which now operates New Melones, has yet to find buyers for all the cheap, federally-subsidized water stored behind the dam. Electrical power generated at the dam is sold at a fraction of its true cost to municipal utilities and agricultural irrigation districts. The GAO, a federal watchdog agency, recently reported that New Melones will not pay for itself before the year 2062, if ever.

The struggle to save the "Stan" went on for more than a decade—years laced with emotion, fruitless appeals to reason, confrontations, heroics, and villainy. In 1974 a statewide referendum to stop the dam was narrowly defeated due to a confusing ballot and a costly and misleading advertising campaign. A later poll indicated that a majority of voters had intended to save the river, but too many were uncertain about what "yes" and "no" votes meant. Meanwhile, in 1978, the Army Corps of Engineers completed New Melones Dam, a colossal rock pile that is one of the largest structures of its type in the world, and the waters of the reservoir began to rise.

In May 1979 seven miles of the canyon had already been flooded when Friends of the River Director Mark Dubois chained himself to a rock in a hidden location not far downstream from Parrott's Ferry and sent word that he would remain there to drown. After official search parties were unable to find him, the Army Corps opened the flood gates and halted the rising waters, leaving the upper nine miles of the river largely untouched. Dubois's dramatic gamble saved the river for two more years, while its defenders—including the administration of Governor Jerry Brown—argued in court and in Washington for a reprieve. Those years also saw protesters arrested for blocking roads into the canyon, as well as some nasty incidents initiated by pro-dam factions.**

As geological time goes, of course, the dam's victory will be short-lived. In the course of coming centuries, New Melones will fail or silt up and be abandoned. Eventually, the river will break through the great heap of rocks and tumble them slowly downstream. As the stagnant reservoir waters fall, the canyon will gradually come back to life. Ferns, alders, and willows will re-establish themselves along the banks, and pines and oaks will creep downhill to join them. Life will again flourish along the river. It is only for our lifetimes—and those of our children, and their children, and their children's children—that the river is buried and lost.

*The Spaniards called the river Rio Guadalupe, but in 1844 it was baptized the Stanislaus by the romantic explorer John C. Fremont in honor of "Estanislao." This was the name given a young California Indian caught up in the net of Catholic conversion. In the 1820's Estanislao fled to the Sierra foothills, where for years he led a band of rebel Indians in guerrilla warfare against the Mexican authorities. Doubtless Fremont, who would himself lead a Californian uprising against Mexico only a few years later, liked the subversive ring of the name.

**For a full account, see Tim Palmer, *Stanislaus: The Struggle for a River* (Univ. of California Press, 1982). For more on the human and natural history of the Stanislaus, see John Cassidy, *A Guide to Three Rivers* (Friends of the River Books, 1981).

Stanislaus River

Goodwin Dam to Knight's Ferry

Difficulty: V; III–IV with several portages.   **Length:** 4 miles.

Gradient: 30 ft./mi.   **Drainage:** 986 sq. mi.

Season: Year round in theory, but dependent on dam releases. See comments below.

Runnable Levels: 400/600–5000 cfs.   **Elevation at Put-in:** 300'.

Flow Information: (916) 322-3327. Flow at Orange Blossom Bridge.

Scenery: Good.   **Solitude:** Very good.

Rafts: An expert run unless you plan to do some portaging. Small rafts only below 1000 cfs. Paddle boats recommended for ease of portaging. Pack light.

Kayaks: This river is for experts, but advanced boaters and even gutsy intermediates can run it (with several portages) if accompanied by experts.

Open Canoes: Experts could make this run below 900 cfs with several portages.

Special Hazards: Several tough rapids may require portaging. At higher flows trees and brush become major dangers.

Commercial Raft Trips: For information, contact Army Corps of Engineers, 12748 Rodden Road, Oakdale CA 95361; phone (209) 847-0225.

Water: Cold, because it comes from the bottom of the reservoir. Probably not drinkable. Purify to be sure.

Camping: No public campgrounds. Private campground at Knight's Ferry Resort, PO Box 863, 17525 Sonora Road, Knight's Ferry CA 95361; phone (209) 881-3349.

Maps: Knight's Ferry (USGS 7.5'); Copperopolis (USGS 15'); Yosemite (AAA).

Auto Shuttle: 6 miles; 15 minutes.

Emergency Telephone Numbers:
Tuolumne and Stanislaus County Sheriffs: 911.
Army Corps of Engineers: (209) 847-0225.

Logistics: To reach the put-in, turn north off Highway 108/120 about 15 miles east of Oakdale onto Tulloch Road toward Goodwin Dam. Put in on the Army Corps of Engineers property (left bank) near a metal gate about half a mile downstream from the dam. Gear must be carried about 50 yards. To reach the take-out, turn north off the highway 12 miles east of Oakdale. Take out either at the Knight's Ferry bridge or at the parking lot on the left bank half a mile downstream.

Between the headwaters of its North, Middle, and South Forks, which drain 9000' and 10,000' peaks along the Sierra Crest between Ebbetts Pass and Sonora Pass, and its confluence with the San Joaquin near Tracy and Modesto, the Stanislaus is interrupted by fourteen major dams. New Melones is only the latest and biggest. Yet there is still boatable white water on the river—both higher up on the North Fork* and far downstream, below Goodwin Dam, where the Stanislaus empties onto the floor of the San Joaquin Valley.

The short, difficult Goodwin Dam run will never take the place of the river that was lost upstream, but since the take-out at Knight's Ferry is less than a hundred miles from the Bay Area and only a short drive from Tuolumne River country, and since the lower Stanislaus is theoretically runnable year round, this run should attract its share of advanced and expert boaters in the years to come—that is, if the government continues to release water into the river bed.

During the campaign for New Melones, the Army Corps of Engineers proposed to "mitigate" the loss of the Stanislaus upstream by improving access and building a chain of parks along the river below Goodwin Dam, and by releasing enough water, even during summer irrigation season, to provide a minimum flow of 600 to 900 cfs for boating. Sad to say, these promises have not been kept. The agency in charge of Goodwin and Tulloch dams is the U.S. Bureau of Reclamation, which guarantees a minimum of 650 cfs only one month of the year— from April 10 to May 10—for spawning season. The rest of the year, except in periods of heavy runoff when upstream reservoirs are full, the Bureau promises a mere 200 cfs or less. Boaters can only hope that actual flows will be higher, as they were in 1983 (a very wet year).

The canyon of the lower Stanislaus is much smaller and less imposing than the one farther upstream, but the scenery in this mini-wilderness is very good. The river flows through striking granite formations capped here and there by the remnants of old lava flows. The overall gradient is moderate, with long pools between the drops, but the tight, rocky rapids are occasionally very steep. Because upstream dams rarely allow the lower Stanislaus to flood and scour out the vegetation, trees and brush clog the river channel and add to the hazards of this stretch. At certain flows one or more portages may be required, even for experts.

*A four-mile stretch of the North Fork between Board's Crossing and Calaveras Big Trees State Park (Class IV–V), presently runnable only in spring and early summer, may have year-round flows sufficient for low-water boating if upstream reservoirs are enlarged as planned. The dam builders give and the dam builders take away. See our chapter *More California Rivers*.

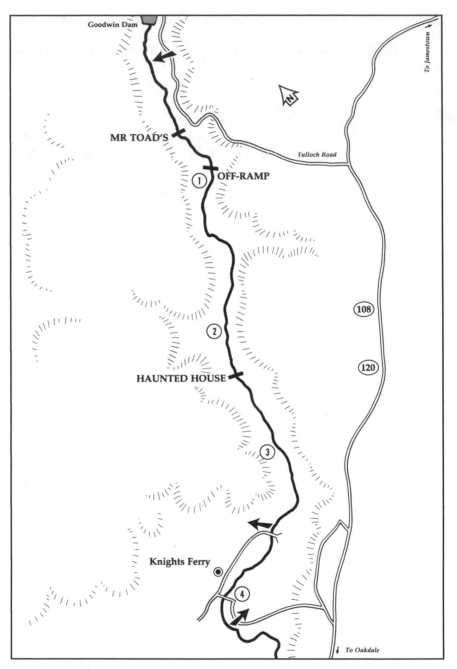

Lower Stanislaus River

Mile by Mile Guide

0	Put in on the left bank half a mile downstream from the dam (see **Logistics**).
0.6	◆ *POSSIBLE PORTAGE* ◆ **MR. TOAD'S (V).** A long, dangerous chute punctuated by big holes. Toward the bottom most of the current runs beneath an undercut wall on the right. Especially difficult at higher flows. A long, hard portage on the right is sometimes necessary. Scout on the right.
0.9	◆ *POSSIBLE PORTAGE* ◆ **OFF-RAMP (IV–V).** A river-wide ledge with rocks just below the surface. Scout and portage on either side.
2.3	◆ *POSSIBLE PORTAGE* ◆ **HAUNTED HOUSE (IV–VI).** A five-foot drop onto a partially submerged boulder creates a powerful reversal. Boats are sometimes stopped there or, at higher flows, in the strong eddy on the left. The difficulty of this rapid varies considerably at different flows. Scout either side. Easy portage on the right if necessary.
3.2	**UNNAMED RAPID (IV).** A clean drop over a river-wide ledge.
3.8	*TAKE-OUT.* Knight's Ferry. The covered bridge is the first take-out. There is an easier take-out downstream.
4.3	*ALTERNATE TAKE-OUT.* Parking area (left bank). Open canoeists and inner-tubers enjoy 14 miles of Class I–II river between this point and the town of Oakdale.

Mokelumne River

Electra Run

Electra Picnic Area to Highway 49

Difficulty: II (III above 3000 cfs).   **Length:** 3 miles.

Gradient: 23 ft./mi.   **Drainage:** 544 sq.mi. at put-in.

Season: Year-round. During the summer, Electra Powerhouse releases about 800 cfs to the river.

Runnable Levels: 300/500–6000 cfs.   **Elevation at Put-in:** 670'.

Flow Information: (916) 322-3327. Inflow into Pardee Reservoir.

Scenery: Very good.

Solitude: Good except for crowded summer weekends.

Rafts and Kayaks: An ideal run for beginners and novices.

Open Canoes: Advanced canoeists can try it at low flows.

Commercial Raft Trips: Not available.

Water: Cold and probably drinkable, but purify to be sure.

Camping: Primitive campsites along the river and Electra Road.

Maps: Mokelumne Hill (USGS 7.5'); Lake Tahoe (AAA).

Auto Shuttle: 3 miles; 10 minutes.

Emergency Telephone Numbers:
   Amador County Sheriff (Jackson): 911.

Logistics: The take-out is at the Highway 49 bridge across the Mokelumne, five miles south of Jackson. To reach the put-in, drive three miles east on Electra Road, which intersects the highway just north of the take-out.

For years beginning kayakers have developed their skills on the Mokelumne*—among them Jim Cassady, co-author of this book, back in 1974-1975. The run is short, but the shuttle is so easy that boaters can float it two or three times in a single day. Even inner-tubing is feasible—though tubers should always wear life jackets. No wonder the Mokelumne is popular. The old Gold Rush towns of Jackson and Mokelumne Hill are close by, the river is convenient to the Bay Area and the towns of the Central Valley, and the scenic canyon gives boaters the feeling of floating a wild river.

The Mokelumne's headwaters drain 9000' and 10,000' peaks south of Lake Tahoe and Carson Pass. The river is dammed at higher elevations by PG&E and at lower elevations by the East Bay Municipal Utility District, whose reservoirs supply drinking water for Oakland, Berkeley, and other East Bay communities.

The short run described in this book could be nearly doubled in length if EBMUD permitted boating below Highway 49 down to Middle Bar Road, but river runners are not allowed to float more than a quarter mile downstream from the Highway 49 bridge. The official reason for this prohibition is fear of contamination of East Bay water supplies, but in fact EBMUD probably wants to keep this stretch of river from becoming popular because of a pending dam project. Though it is not normally in the business of generating electrical power, EBMUD has been unable to resist the prospect of a "cash register" dam on the lower Mokelumne just above Pardee Reservoir. The smaller version of the proposed Middle Bar project would flood five miles of the river canyon up to Electra Powerhouse. The larger version would inundate more than eight miles of the canyon, all the way to Ponderosa Way (and would destroy the existing Electra Powerhouse).

In addition to the run described below, boaters can find more white water upstream. There is a sparkling twelve-mile Class IV–V run (with one portage) beginning at the mouth of a major tributary, the Bear River, and ending at Tiger Creek. But this experts-only section of the Mokelumne is runnable only when Salt Springs Reservoir is full and water is allowed to spill into the river bed (usually in late spring); otherwise, the river's entire flow is diverted to Tiger Creek Powerhouse.

*Name of local Indians. "Umne" meant "people"; what "Mok" or "Mokel" meant is unknown.

Mile by Mile Guide

0   Put in at the pool beside the Electra Picnic Area, or choose another convenient location downstream. The road follows the river all the way to the take-out.

1.3   **THE SLOT (II).** An unobstructed chute with good waves where beginners can learn to handle river hydraulics.

2   **S-TURN (II).** A pint-sized version of Troublemaker Rapid on the South Fork American. The river bends right, then left. An excellent spot for beginning kayakers to play.

2.3   **BRIDGE RAPID (II).** Just below the ruins of an old bridge, the river drops down an open chute.

3   *TAKE-OUT.* You can take out on the right just above the Highway 49 bridge, or you can continue downstream to run one more rapid.

3.1   *TAKE-OUT.*
         DEVIL'S TOILET (II +). About 100 yards below the bridge. Take out immediately below the rapid on the left bank. A trail leads up the hill to a turnout beside Highway 49. If you plan to use this take-out, scout it from the road before you put in. EBMUD prohibits boating below this point.

Clavey Falls, Tuolumne River.   *Brian Fessenden*

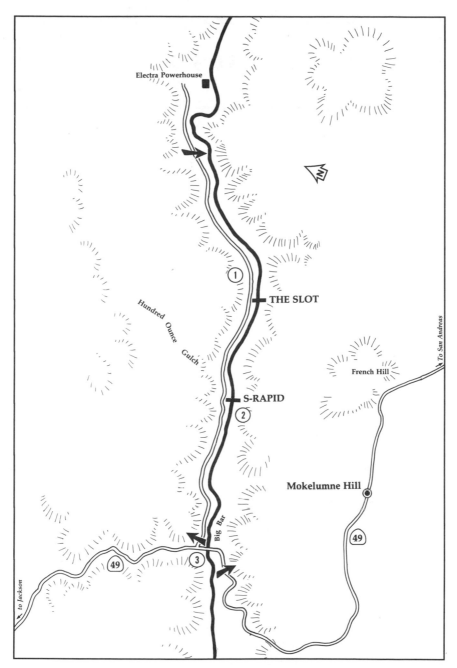

Mokelumne River

Cosumnes River

Highway 49 Bridge to Highway 16 Bridge

Difficulty: II–Vp above Latrobe Road (mile 10.2); III–IVp downstream.

Length: 20 miles; 2 days. Usually run as two one-day trips.

Gradient: 40 ft./mi. above Latrobe Road (100 ft./mi. first 2 miles); 25 ft./mi. downstream.

Drainage: 538 sq. mi. at Michigan Bar.   **Elevation at Put-in:** 770'.

Season: March–early May.   **Runnable Levels:** 300/600–3000 cfs.

Flow Information: (916) 322-3327. Flow at Michigan Bar.

Solitude: Excellent.

Scenery: Excellent first three and last ten miles; good elsewhere.

Rafts: Because of the portages, use small rafts and travel light.

Kayaks: A fine advanced and expert run above Latrobe Road. Experienced intermediates can handle the lower section at moderate and low flows.

Open Canoes: Not recommended. Experts could run the lower stretch at low water with several portages.

Special Hazards: Mandatory portages at miles 1.6, 10.8, and 18.2. Fallen trees and brush can be a major hazard in this small river. Heavy rains turn the Cosumnes into a raging torrent; don't try it at high water.

Commercial Raft Trips: Not available at present. Difficult portages are a limiting factor.

Water: Possibly drinkable. Purify to be sure.

Camping: Fine beaches along the river are rarely used by boaters, who prefer not to carry camping gear because of the portages. Respect private property rights along the river.

Maps: Fiddletown, Latrobe, Folsom SE (USGS 7.5'); Lake Tahoe (AAA).

Auto Shuttle: 20 miles; 30 minutes.

Emergency Telephone Numbers:
Amador County Sheriff (Jackson): 911.
El Dorado County Sheriff (Placerville): 911.
Sacramento County Sheriff (Sacramento): (916) 440-5111.

Logistics: The take-out is at the Highway 16 bridge across the Cosumnes at Rancho Murieta, about 16 miles east of downtown Sacramento. To reach the put-in, continue another 15 miles east on Highway 16, then turn north on Highway 49 for about five miles to the bridge across the river. Avoid trespassing on private property; use only the public right-of-way beside the bridge for the put-in.

To reach the halfway point, turn north on Latrobe Road from Highway 16 a few miles west of its junction with Highway 49 and drive about seven miles north to the Latrobe Road bridge across the Cosumnes. Because of heavy use by swimmers in the summer, no-parking signs are posted for a considerable distance on each side of the bridge; the nearest legal parking is about a quarter of a mile south.

The Cosumnes* is one of the smallest runnable rivers in the Sierra foothills. Because its upper watershed is cut off by the larger canyons of the South Fork American and the Mokelumne, the river's headwaters rise ten miles west of the Sierra crest at only 7000'. Consequently, the boating season for this undammed stream is short. But the Cosumnes is close to Sacramento and the Bay Area, and experienced river runners who catch it at the right time, know how to travel light, and don't mind carrying their boats around unrunnable rapids will be richly rewarded by a spring trip on this tiny jewel of a river.

Because of the portages, boaters usually run the Cosumnes in two one-day floats, with the Latrobe Road bridge (mile 10.2) serving as a halfway point. Either section is an adventure. The upper stretch begins with a very tough couple of miles (Class IV–V) and includes the most spectacular portage in this guide book, a carry around a three-tiered, 50-foot waterfall. Then it becomes an easy Class II float. The lower section takes boaters through a delightful five-mile gorge (Class III–IV), then eases to Class II. There is another portage just below Latrobe Road, and a third at mile 18.2. In addition, the Cosumnes has some of the worst vehicle access problems in California—not because of the lack of roads, but because of local restrictions both formal and informal. An enormous no-parking zone around the bridge makes the Latrobe Road access point inconvenient, and though a county road crosses the river at Michigan Bar (mile 16.6), public access is privately denied by the landowners.

---

*The river's name—"salmon people" in Miwok—is derived from an Indian tribe that once lived along its banks.

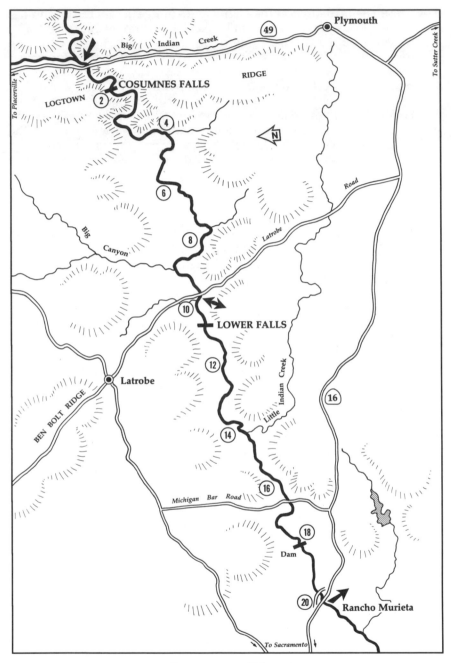

Cosumnes River

Mile by Mile Guide

0   Confluence of North and South Forks of the Cosumnes. Put in downstream from the Highway 49 bridge. Class IV–V action begins immediately. If you want to warm up on easier Class II water, put in several miles upstream on the North Fork at the old Sand Ridge Road bridge just east of Highway 49.

0–2   Continuous Class IV–V rapids for the first two miles or more. The river drops quickly as it cuts through the old fault line parallel to Highway 49. If you can't see the end of a rapid from upstream, stop to scout it. One of them ends in a deadly waterfall at mile 1.6.

1.6   ◆ *PORTAGE* ◆
        COSUMNES FALLS (U). An easy rapid turns into a spectacular 50-foot waterfall. Use a trail on the right to portage.

1.8–2.2 Below the falls there are a few more Class IV rapids, then the canyon opens up into scenic pastoral country. Between mile 2.2 and the Latrobe Road bridge, rapids are only Class II.

10.2   *RIVER ACCESS.* Latrobe Road bridge. River access on the right bank just upstream from the bridge.

10.8   ◆ *PORTAGE* ◆
        LOWER FALLS (VI). A series of big drops choked with boulders. It has been run at favorable water levels, but it's wiser to portage on either side.

11–16   Enjoyable five-mile stretch of Class III–IV rapids through a narrow gorge. Some of the drops are quite sharp. The canyon opens up half a mile above the bridge.

16.6   Michigan Bar Road bridge. The public probably has the right to take out here, but hostile landowners have been known to make the experience less than pleasant. And since there's no place to park shuttle vehicles, most boaters prefer to continue on to the Highway 16 bridge. The float is a pleasant one through a valley marked by old mine tailings, but there is one more portage.

18.2   ◆ *PORTAGE* ◆ At the end of half a mile or so of flat water backed up by a diversion dam, the river divides around an island. Take the right channel. Stop upstream from the dam and portage on the left.

18.3   Easy Class II rapids from here to the take-out.

20   *TAKE-OUT.* Take out at any convenient location near the new Highway 16 bridge, which is downstream from the ruins of the old bridge. In the old days this was Bridge House, where a lonely country road crossed the river. Now it is the site of Rancho Murieta, a planned community of houses, condominiums, and a golf course.

East Fork Carson River

Rivers that drain the steep eastern side of the Sierra Nevada—like the Carson*, the Walker, and the Truckee—contrast sharply with the bigger, more numerous rivers flowing down the wetter and more gradual western slopes. Since their watersheds lie in the partial rain shadow of the Sierra crest, eastern-slope streams carry smaller volumes of water and have shorter seasons. They fall quickly and steadily down the steep back side of the great range, and their nearly continuous rapids are less severe than those of typical pool-and-drop rivers on the west side. The East Fork Carson above Hangman's Bridge drops at a rate of 65 feet per mile, yet its most difficult rapids are only Class III. On the western slope, rivers with gradients over 50 feet per mile are typically Class IV and V.

The East Carson rises at the base of 11,000' Sonora Peak, north of Yosemite, and its tributaries drain mountains just across the Sierra crest from the headwaters of the Stanislaus and the Mokelumne. The river flows north between two parallel fault zones and is undammed until well after it crosses the border into Nevada. There it irrigates the fertile Carson Valley and then meanders north and east across the desert toward the Carson Sink, the dry bed of a large glacial-era lake (Lahontan, 10,000 to 20,000 years ago).

Two different runs await boaters on the East Carson. The upper section features seven miles of continuous Class III rapids in a mile-high pine forest. Highway 89 is close by. The lower run takes boaters through twenty miles of spectacular wilderness. Snow-capped Sierra peaks tower over the river as it plunges into high desert country. In spite of the respectable gradient of 27 feet per mile, the rapids are only Class II. Added attractions include nearby Grover Hot Springs; the colorful old town of Markleeville, seat of California's least-populated county (Alpine County has slightly more than a thousand residents); and another hot spring along the river in the wilderness section. Bring wet suits and warm clothing. Days are usually warm in late May and June, but nights are cold at these high elevations, and late-season storms have been known to drop snow as late as Memorial Day.

*Named by John C. Fremont for Kit Carson, who guided him across the Sierra Nevada in 1844. For more on the region, see Shane Murphy, *The Lore and Legend of the East Fork* (Carson River Conservation Fund, P.O. Box 1221, Zephyr Cove, NV 89448).

Upper East Fork Carson

Cave Rock to Hangman's Bridge

Difficulty: III.   **Gradient:** 65 ft./mi.

Length: 7.3 miles. Shorter runs possible.

Drainage: 276 sq. mi. two miles below put-in.

Season: May–late June.   **Elevation at Put-in:** 6000'.

Runnable Levels: 400/600–3000 cfs.

Flow Information: (916) 322-3327. Flow near Gardnerville.

Scenery: Excellent.   **Solitude:** Good. Road along river.

Rafts: Continuous gradient means few eddies at high water. At low flows only small rafts can negotiate the rocky channels.

Kayaks: Don't try this run at higher flows unless you have a good roll; lack of eddies makes river rescue difficult.

Open Canoes: Experts only, and only at low water.

Special Hazards: Watch for recently fallen trees. A kayaker died here in 1980 because of a new "strainer" in the river.

Commercial Raft Trips: This section is rarely run commercially except in combination with the wilderness run downstream. For a list of outfitters contact Carson Ranger District, U.S. Forest Service, 1536 S. Carson, Carson City NV 89701; phone below.

Water: Clear, cold, and probably drinkable. Purify to be sure.

Camping: There is a Forest Service campground beside Markleeville Creek, one mile north of Hangman's Bridge, and a primitive campground at the put-in.

Maps: Topaz Lake, Markleeville (USGS 15'); Toiyabe National Forest; Lake Tahoe (AAA).

Auto Shuttle: 7 miles; 15 minutes.

Emergency Telephone Numbers:
Alpine County Sheriff (Markleeville): 911.
Forest Service (Carson City, Nevada): (702) 882-2766.

Logistics: To reach the take-out, drive two miles southeast from Markleeville on combined Highways 89 and 4 to the bridge across the East Carson. To reach the put-in, continue upstream, following Highway 4 when it splits from 89. About three miles south of this junction, turn left on Wolf Creek Road (which follows the river while the highway turns up Silver Creek). Put in about a mile and a half up Wolf Creek Road, just before the road leaves the river bank. An alternate put-in is on Silver Creek just below the Wolf Creek Road bridge.

Mile by Mile Guide

0   Put in at any convenient spot downstream from Cave Rock. Don't venture upstream; the rapids are treacherous. This run consists of continuous Class III rapids all the way to the take-out. Most scouting can be done from the road. No individual rapids are listed here.

1.2   *ALTERNATE PUT-IN* just below the Wolf Creek Road bridge on Silver Creek, which enters from the left. Don't try to run any rapids higher up on the creek.

1.6   *RIVER ACCESS.* Centreville Bridge (Highway 4).

3.7   Monitor Creek enters from the right. Junction of Highways 4 and 89.

7.3   *TAKE-OUT.* Hangman's Bridge. Take out on the right, unless you are continuing downstream on the wilderness run.

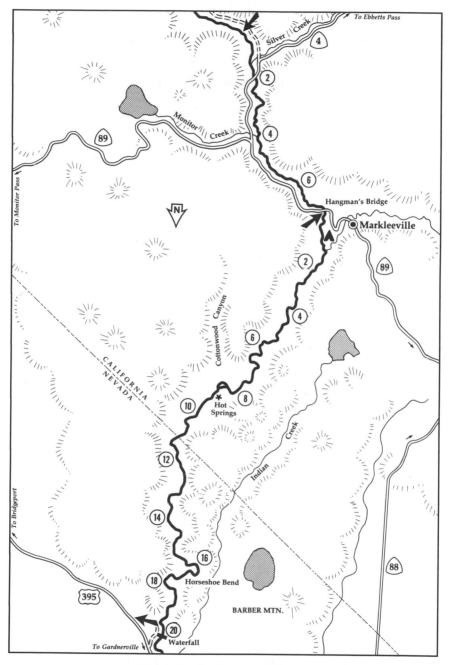

East Fork Carson River

East Fork Carson River

Wilderness Run

Hangman's Bridge to Diversion Dam

Difficulty: II. **Length:** 20 miles; 2 days.

Gradient: 27 ft./mi. **Drainage:** 341 sq. mi. near take-out.

Season: May–June. **Elevation at Put-in:** 5500'.

Runnable Levels: 250/400–5000 cfs.

Flow Information: (916) 322-3327. Flow near Gardnerville.

Scenery: Excellent. **Solitude:** Excellent.

Rafts and Kayaks: A good river for beginners and novices (in the company of more experienced boaters).

Open Canoes: A favorite run for intermediate canoeists, but only at flows below 1500 cfs.

Special Hazards: There is a deadly waterfall over a 30-foot dam a few hundred yards downstream from the take-out.

Commercial Raft Trips: Two-day floats. See Upper East Carson.

Water: Clear and cold, but after Markleeville Creek enters at mile 1.6, the quality of the river water declines. Purify to be sure.

Camping: The favorite rendezvous for Carson trips is off the river, at Markleeville National Forest Campground between Hangman's Bridge and the town of Markleeville. Downriver there are many wilderness campsites, enough for all even though the Forest Service marks and reserves ten of them for commercial outfitters. Favorites include those near the hot spring at mile 9.

Maps: Markleeville, Mt. Siegel (USGS 15'); Toiyabe National Forest; Lake Tahoe (AAA).

Auto Shuttle: 30 miles; 1 hour.

Emergency Telephone Numbers:
Douglas (Nevada) County Sheriff: (702) 782-8111.
See also emergency numbers for Upper East Carson.

Logistics: Put in at Hangman's Bridge, two miles southeast of Markleeville, where combined Highways 89 and 4 cross the East Carson. To reach the take-out, drive seven miles north from Markleeville on 89, turn right on Highway 88, follow it for 14 miles, and turn right (south) on Highway 395. About five miles south of Gardnerville, turn right off the highway onto a dirt road leading to a developed take-out and parking area on the river bank just upstream from Ruhenstroth Dam.

Mile by Mile Guide

0   Put in at Hangman's Bridge. Local vigilantes claimed they lynched a confessed murdered here in 1874 to save the bankrupt county court costs. Continuous Class I and II rapids throughout the run.

1.6   Markleeville Creek enters on the left. Spectacular view of the Sierra crest. Don't drink from the creek; the water is polluted by humans and cattle upstream.

8.6   **SIDEWINDER (II).** Perhaps the toughest rapid on the run. Open canoeists and novice rafters and kayakers might want to scout it.

9.0   Hot spring on left bank is the favorite stopping place on the river. Water is about 104°.

15.5   The canyon narrows here. The Army Corps of Engineers proposed a 300-foot dam for this beautiful gorge. The project, which would wipe out this run, was recently shelved.

16.5   The river has carved a lovely canyon around Horseshoe Bend.

20   *TAKE-OUT* ◆ *HAZARD* ◆ BLM boat ramp on the right. Don't miss it—there's a 30-foot waterfall downstream.

Brian Fessenden

American River

The American is the classic Gold Country river. Its three forks rise in the Desolation Wilderness west of Lake Tahoe, flow through the rich foothills of the Mother Lode between Auburn and Placerville, and eventually empty into Folsom Reservoir. Downstream from Folsom Dam, the American joins the Sacramento River not far from the State Capitol.

In January 1848 James Marshall discovered gold at John Sutter's mill on the banks of the South Fork and touched off the great invasion that made California irretrievably American. Yet the river's name stems from a case of mistaken identity. Western explorer Jedediah Smith called it the "Wild River" in 1828, but later it was dubbed "Rio de los Americanos" by Spanish-speaking Indians because Canadian trappers forded the river a few miles upstream from Sutter's fort at Sacramento. In 1841 Sutter translated the Spanish name for a map, and it stuck.

The American River is also one of the birthplaces of modern white water boating in California. In the fifties and sixties the state's earliest kayakers practiced their techniques on the easy rapids of the Coloma-to-Lotus run on the South Fork American before moving up to the Chili Bar and Gorge runs, the Stanislaus, and other rivers. Now the South Fork American between Chili Bar and Salmon Falls (Class III) is the second most popular white water river in the country—to Pennsylvania's Youghiogheny. But that is not all the American River offers. The Middle Fork and the North Fork are considerably more challenging (Class IV–V) and have attracted increasing numbers of boaters in recent years. The South Fork itself has more runnable white water upstream between Kyburz and Riverton. (See our chapter *More California Rivers*.)

Like most rivers, the American lives in the shadow of proposed dams—in spite of the numerous installations already in place on the river and its tributaries. The largest of these, Folsom Dam, a 1956 federal project that backs up water into both the main stem and the South Fork, generates electrical power and releases irrigation water to San Joaquin Valley farmers via the Delta-Mendota Canal.

But the U.S. Bureau of Reclamation has even more ambitious designs on what is left of the American. Two decades ago plans were announced for a 700-foot-high concrete arch dam one mile southeast of Auburn, just downstream from the confluence of the North and Middle Forks. In 1975

96

work on its foundations was under way when a sizable earthquake (5.7 on the Richter scale) shook nearby Oroville and proved that the numerous faults in the Sierra foothills, including some at the Auburn Dam site, should be considered potentially active. Critics warned that if Auburn Dam failed, Sacramento would be flooded in less than an hour and that losses would total billions of dollars. Work was abandoned.

Recently, though, the Auburn Dam project has been revived with a new design as a massive concrete gravity barrier 685 feet high, 465 feet thick at the base, and 4150 feet wide from canyon wall to canyon wall. It would be the sixth highest dam in the world, and its $2.2 billion price tag would make Auburn the most expensive dam ever built in the United States and one of the biggest boondoggles in our history. It is highly unlikely that the dam would ever pay for itself. Its federally-subsidized electrical power would be sold at half its true cost, and water would go even cheaper ($20 to $30 per acre-foot for water that would cost $100 to $350 per acre-foot to develop). Federal taxpayers would make up the difference. Auburn Dam would have to devote two decades of electrical production to generate as much energy as its construction would expend — the equivalent of 12 million barrels of oil.

If it is built, Auburn Reservoir will wipe out twenty miles of the North Fork American and the entire twenty-five mile stretch of the Middle Fork now enjoyed by boaters. Their living canyons will become narrow fingers of stagnant water. The reservoir's level will fluctuate a hundred feet or more each year, exposing large bathtub rings of dirt, rock, dead vegetation, and debris. Experience has shown that the recreational value of such artificial lakes is vastly overrated by the proponents of more dams. In contrast, a local coalition* is not only coordinating opposition to the dam but also proposing an alternative: the creation of a national recreation area encompassing the canyons of the North and Middle Forks of the American River.

*PARC (Protect American River Canyons), PO Box 1395, Auburn, CA 95603; phone (916) 823-9891. The American River Recreation Association is also involved. See South Fork American.

South Fork American River

Chili Bar and Gorge Runs

Chili Bar to Salmon Falls Bridge

Difficulty: III.
Gradient: 25 ft./mi.
Length: 20 miles; 1–2 days. Shorter runs possible.
Drainage: 673 sq. mi. at Lotus.
Elevation at Put-in: 930′.
Season: Year round.
Runnable Levels: 400/800–10,000 cfs.
Flow Information: (916) 322-3327. Flow at Chili Bar.
Scenery: Very good.
Solitude: Good above Coloma and below Lotus except summer weekends.
Rafts and Kayaks: A challenging intermediate run. Novices should stick to the Coloma–Lotus section. Beware of high water. On summer weekends the river is so crowded with rafts that kayakers have little chance to play.
Open Canoes: This river is too difficult for beginners and novices. Intermediates can handle the Coloma–Lotus stretch at low flows. Expert open canoeists have run the entire river at low flows.
Permits: Private boaters are required to register at the put-in.
Commercial Raft Trips: One- and two-day floats. For a list of outfitters, contact American River Recreation Association, PO Box 221, Coloma CA 95613, phone (916) 626-7113; or El Dorado County Department of Planning, 360 Fair Lane, Placerville CA 95667; phone (916) 626-2438.
Water: Since it comes from the bottom of upstream reservoirs, the river water remains cold all summer. Wear wet suit at least until peak runoff (May–June) is over. Don't drink river water without purifying it. Better yet, bring your own.
Camping: Convenient private campgrounds with vehicle access along the river: Chili Bar (put-in), Camp Coloma (mile 5), Coloma Resort (mile 5.5), Point Pleasant (mile 6), and Camp Lotus (mile 9). Reserve well in advance.

Commercial rafters often camp on public lands in the lower half of the river. The Bureau of Land Management says all its lands are open to private boaters as well. A campsite at mile 9.8 has been set aside for privates only. For details contact the BLM, 63 Natoma St., Folsom CA 95630; phone below.

Maps: Garden Valley, Coloma, Pilot Hill (USGS 7.5′); Georgetown, Auburn (USGS 15′); Lake Tahoe (AAA); South Fork American River (Cassady and Calhoun).

Auto Shuttle: 25 miles (paved roads); 1 hour or more.

Emergency Telephone Numbers:
El Dorado County Sheriff River Patrol (Placerville): (916) 626-4911.
Bureau of Land Management (Folsom): (916) 985-4474.
Fire (California Department of Forestry, Placerville): 911,
   or (916) 644-2344.

Logistics: To reach the put-in, follow Highway 49 to the north side of Placerville and take the right fork of a "Y" intersection. Highway 193 leads down into the river canyon and crosses the South Fork at Chili Bar. To reach the take-out, return to Placerville on Highway 193, turn sharply right at the "Y" onto Highway 49, and follow it north through Coloma. About eight miles after the highway crosses the river, turn left at the hamlet of Pilot Hill onto Salmon Falls Road and follow it to the take-out at Salmon Falls Bridge. See mile by mile guide for other access points.

The South Fork American, California's most popular white water river, provides 100,000 people a year with a thrilling ride through the heart of Gold Rush Country. Those who put in at Chili Bar find themselves on a lively stream dropping quickly through a remote, steep-walled canyon cut into metamorphic volcanic rocks. Five miles farther, where the canyon opens up into the gentle Coloma Valley, Troublemaker Rapid provides the climax of the Chili Bar stretch. Civilization is close at hand for the next four easy miles between Coloma and Lotus. Then the river heads into back country again, winds through the foothills, and finally plunges into the exhilarating, nearly continuous chutes and drops of the South Fork Gorge before it merges with the still waters of Folsom Reservoir.

Dam-controlled flows make the river runnable year round, though water levels are low on summer weekends, when the river is always very crowded. But weekday boaters can still enjoy the scenery and the bouncy but forgiving rapids in relative solitude. The Chili Bar and Gorge runs become considerably more difficult at flows above 3000 cfs, but they are tough enough even at low and moderate levels to get the inexperienced into trouble. Beginners and novices should stick to the Class II stretch between Coloma and Lotus. Below Folsom Reservoir open canoeists and inner-tubers enjoy summer floats down eleven miles of easy Class I–II river between Sunrise Avenue and Watt Avenue in eastern Sacramento.

More dams have been proposed on the South Fork, including one at the site of Troublemaker Rapid. After complex negotiations involving river runners, landowners, and El Dorado County, in 1982 the California Legislature passed a bill that will delay new dam proposals for at least ten years (provided that a series of dam and diversion projects is approved for the upper South Fork, above Kyburz).*

Another problem is the extensive private property along much of the river below Chili Bar—an important factor in El Dorado County's abortive attempt to prohibit white water sport on the South Fork a few years ago. After the courts ruled that the public had the right to run the river, El Dorado County took over the task of regulating boating. The county patrols the river, requires private river runners to register at the put-in, and asks all boaters to observe a "quiet zone" between miles 4.4 and 11.5. Use fees from commercial rafting outfitters have provided the county with a tidy sum over the past few seasons.

*For updated information, stay tuned to the American River Recreation Association, PO Box 221, Coloma, CA 95613; phone (916) 626-7113.

Mile by Mile Guide

0   Put in at Chili Bar, on the right bank just downstream from the Highway 193 bridge. Small fee. Chili Bar also has overnight camping; phone (916) 622-6104. Though misspelled, Chili Bar was named for Chilean miners who lived and worked here during the Gold Rush.

0.6   **MEATGRINDER (III+).** A long, rough rock garden with big waves and a hidden boulder at the bottom. Scout on the right.

1.3   **RACEHORSE BEND (II+).** A sharp left forces boats toward the right wall.

1.5   **MAYA (II–III).** No problem at low water, but at high flows big, dangerous holes block the channel. Sneak far right.

3   Site of old miner's cabin (right bank).

3.1   **TRIPLE THREAT (III).** Three separate drops. Exposed rocks at low water, strong hydraulics at high flows. The third drop is at a sharp left-hand bend.

4.4   Indian Creek enters from the left. California's first gold quartz mine was located just upstream. Private homes and campgrounds begin to appear. El Dorado County asks boaters to observe a "quiet zone" from here to mile 11.5.

5.1   **TROUBLEMAKER (III+).** The biggest rapid on the Chili Bar stretch, a river-wide ledge strewn with boulders, is almost always run on the far left. Scout on the left, but stay close to the river and avoid walking through the private campsites.

5.2–10.6   Town of Coloma (left bank). Easy Class I and II rapids for more than five miles.

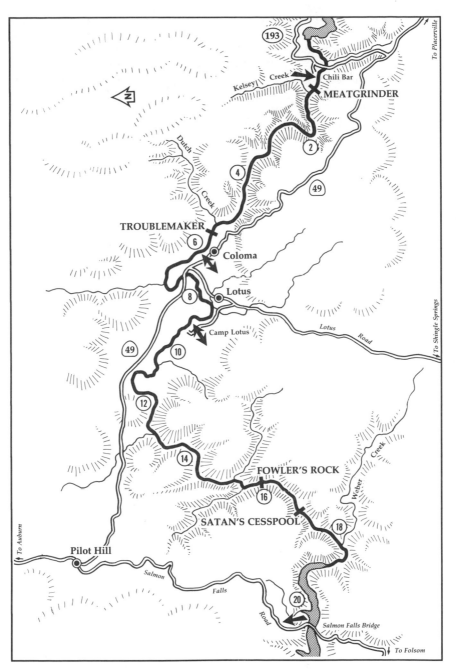

South Fork American River

5.7   *RIVER ACCESS.* Marshall Gold Discovery State Park (left bank). A stone monument marks the site of Sutter's Mill, where the Gold Rush started. A full-scale replica of the mill is nearby, and a good mining museum is just across the highway. There are picnic tables and public toilets near the river. Boaters may put in or take out at the northern (downstream) end of the park for a fee.

7.1   **OLD SCARY (II).** Once this was the most difficult rapid on the Coloma–Lotus stretch. Old Scary was rearranged by high water in winter 1982 and is now little more than a riffle.

7.4   *RIVER ACCESS.* Highway 49 bridge. Small parties can launch on the left. No parking.

9   *RIVER ACCESS.* Camp Lotus (left bank) has long been the favorite meeting place for river runners on the South Fork and a popular overnight spot for two-day trips. Store, hot showers, toilets. Reserve in advance. (916) 622-8672.

9.8   BLM land on the right has been set aside as campsites for non-commercial boaters. Most of the land, even in the gorge, is privately owned.

10.6   **CURRENT DIVIDER (II+).** A rocky chute with a wrap rock in the center.

11.1   **HIGHWAY RAPID (II+).** A long, curving rock garden. No vehicle access across private land, even though Highway 49 is nearby.

11.5   Greenwood Creek enters on the right. End of El Dorado County "quiet zone."

12.1   BLM land (public) on both banks between miles 12.1–12.3 and miles 12.7–13.5. Portable toilets on the right.

15.8   **FOWLER'S ROCK (III).** First of the big rapids in the gorge. The river bends left into a short pool, then back to the right where a boulder cluster marks the entrance to the rapid. You may want to scout on the left. Fowler's is the wrap rock in the center just below the entrance. There is a second sharp drop just downstream. This rapid deserves special respect at high water.

16.9   **SATAN'S CESSPOOL (III+).** The biggest rapid in the gorge. At the end of a long pool, the river pours over a sharp drop (sometimes called **Lost Hat**), then bends left and right into a bigger drop against the left wall. The rapid can be scouted on the left, but most boats end up running the big drop and its back-curling wave anyway. There is a small eddy on the left just downstream. A rock above the final drop provides a good vantage point for photographers and spectators. If you miss the eddy, watch out for **Dead Man's Drop** (II+) just below. Stay right.

C-1 white water canoe in Satan's Cesspool.   *R. Valentine Atkinson*

17.4   **SCISSORS (III).** The river turns left down a narrow, rocky chute with big, irregular waves.

17.6   **LOWER HAYSTACK CANYON (II+).** Big standing waves and short drops in a narrow section of the gorge.

17.7–18.1 BLM land on both banks provides good stopping places. There is a nice half-mile hike up Weber Creek, which enters from the left at mile 18.1, before you reach private property.

18.2   **BOUNCING ROCK (II+).** Big but runnable hole on the far right.

18.6   **HOSPITAL BAR (III).** Named for a medical tent set up here in the Gold Rush. The last big ride in the gorge, a rocky chute that bends left, then right. Big side curlers at the bottom.

18.8   **RECOVERY ROOM (II+).** Clean drops and big waves.

19   High water mark of Folsom Reservoir. In dry years or at other times when the reservoir is low, Class II+ rapids continue to the take-out.

20.5   *TAKE-OUT.* Salmon Falls Bridge. Take out on the right, upstream from the bridge. Parking facilities are limited for the big summer crowds. Park only your shuttle vehicle in the paved lot; other vehicles should be parked on the other side of the bridge (left bank).

Middle Fork American River

Oxbow Bend to Highway 49 Bridge

Difficulty: IV–Vp; II from Greenwood bridge site to Mammoth Bar (miles 16-23).

Length: 25 miles. Shorter runs possible.

Gradient: 23 ft./mi.   **Drainage:** 524 sq. mi. at mile 2.5.

Season: May–September.   **Elevation at Put-in:** 1100'.

Runnable Levels: 400/700–3000 cfs.

Flow Information: (916) 322-3327. Flow below Oxbow Dam. Summer irrigation releases from Ralston Afterbay rarely exceed 1000 cfs once the snow melt is over.

Scenery: Very good.   **Solitude:** Very good.

Rafts and Kayaks: Intermediates can run the section above mile 16 at flows below 1800 cfs—provided they are accompanied by advanced boaters who know the run, and provided they portage the big drops. Novices can handle the Class II stretch below mile 16 if they take out above Murderer's Bar Rapid.

Open Canoes: At low flows, experts can tackle the upper section but should be prepared to portage several rapids. Intermediates can run the lower section with one long portage around Murderer's Bar or with an early take-out at Mammoth Bar (mile 23).

Special Hazards: Tunnel Chute (mile 2.5), Ruck-a-Chucky (mile 14.5), and difficulties with miners and private landowners.

Commercial Raft Trips: One- to three-day floats. For a list of outfitters, contact California Department of Parks and Recreation, 7806 Folsom-Auburn Road, Folsom, CA 95630; phone (916) 988-0205.

Water: Undrinkable. Purify or carry your own.

Camping: Because of one or two portages in the first 15 miles, few boaters carry overnight gear down the river. Instead, they drive it in via Ruck-a-Chucky Road to the old Greenwood Bridge site (mile 16).

Maps: Michigan Bluff, Foresthill, Georgetown, Auburn, Greenwood (USGS 7.5'); Duncan Peak, Colfax, Georgetown (USGS 15'); Lake Tahoe (AAA).

Auto Shuttle: 25 miles; 1.5 hours.

Emergency Telephone Numbers:
El Dorado County Sheriff (Placerville): 911.
Placer County Sheriff (Auburn): 911.
BLM (Folsom): (916) 985-4474.
El Dorado National Forest (Placerville): (916) 622-5061.

Logistics: The take-out for the Middle Fork run is three miles southeast of Auburn, upstream from the Highway 49 bridge across the North Fork American and just below the confluence with the Middle Fork. To reach the put-in, follow the Auburn-Foresthill Road east about 17 miles from Auburn. Just before you reach the town of Foresthill, turn right and follow the curves of Mosquito Ridge Road down to and across the North Fork of the Middle Fork American. About two miles beyond this tributary, turn right and drive down to the Middle Fork put-in, just downstream from Ralston Powerhouse.

There is also river access at the old Greenwood Bridge site (mile 16). Turn south on McKeon Road off the Auburn-Foresthill Road five miles west of Foresthill. McKeon Road soon becomes a decent dirt road and winds its way down to the river. Another road suitable only for four-wheel drive vehicles leads upriver from the bridge site to Ruck-a-Chucky Rapid. Greenwood Bridge was washed out by the wall of water that scoured the river canyon when Hell Hole Dam, then under construction, gave way in 1964.

The Middle Fork American rises in the mountains just west of Squaw Valley. The Rubicon River, its principal tributary, drains peaks west of Alpine Meadows as well as the northern part of the Desolation Wilderness. Both streams are dammed high up. In December 1964, when the Placer County Water Agency was building Hell Hole Dam on the Rubicon, flood waters swept it away and knocked out downstream bridges all the way to Folsom Reservoir. The agency promptly rebuilt Hell Hole, a rockfill barrier. Another Placer County project in the mid-sixties was Anderson Dam, an earthfill structure which created French Meadows Reservoir on the upper Middle Fork.

The Middle Fork is a legendary Gold Rush river. In the nineteenth century, mining towns sprang up along its banks, and miners diverted the river at Horseshoe Bend to glean riches from its dry stream bed. It is said that more gold has been found in the Middle Fork canyon than in any other. Successful mining and dredging operations continue to this day.

Though it is only 140 miles from the Bay Area and offers runnable flows throughout most summers, the Middle Fork does not receive much attention from boaters. The shuttle is long and slow, and then there are the portages: mandatory at Ruck-a-Chucky; optional but recommended at Tunnel Chute, Murderer's Bar, and—at high water—Cartwheel. But river runners willing to deal with these difficulties will enjoy a much more challenging and secluded summer run than the nearby South Fork American.

On occasion, boaters on the Middle Fork have run afoul of private landowners and miners along the river. A few years ago a caretaker brandished a shotgun to emphasize his point. One landowner, a Bay Area businessman, has for years discouraged river running by contending that the Tunnel Chute is too dangerous to run and that portaging entails trespass on his property. His attitude may stem in part from his reported intention to have a hydroelectric facility built at that spot. Nevertheless, the law upholds the public's right to boat on navigable rivers. If you have to portage, be quick and polite about it. Stay close to the river itself. And never argue with a shotgun.

Mile by Mile Guide

0   Oxbow Bend. Put in at the eddy just below the penstock that releases water from Ralston Powerhouse.

1   The North Fork of the Middle Fork enters on the right.

2.5   ◆ *POSSIBLE PORTAGE* ◆
TUNNEL CHUTE (V–VI). The tunnel blasted by miners through a narrow ridge is flat and easy. But the dynamited chute leading down to it has sharp sides that can rip rafts and fiberglass kayaks, and it ends in a big drop with a powerful reversal. Portaging the chute on the left is easy, but at flows over 2000 cfs it can be difficult to get the boats back into the river above the tunnel. A private four-wheel drive road—for emergencies only—leads out of the canyon from this point, but the landowner is not friendly to river runners (see above).

2.7–4.7   Numerous Class III rapids.

5   ◆ *POSSIBLE PORTAGE* ◆
CARTWHEEL (IV; V above 1500 cfs). At the end of a large pool, the river tumbles off to the right. Several big reversals obstruct the channel, and at the bottom the current sweeps boats toward a rock wall on the right. Easy scout and portage on the left.

5.2–14.2 A pleasant nine-mile stretch of Class I and II rapids affords boaters the opportunity to enjoy the fine scenery.

6   *RIVER ACCESS.* Cash Rock. A poor four-wheel-drive road used primarily by miners leads from the left bank to Volcanoville.

14.2   *RIVER ACCESS.* A poorly-maintained dirt road leads downstream to the Greenwood Bridge site and a better road out of the canyon. If your vehicle can navigate it, you can avoid the upcoming portage by taking out here.

14.3   **UPPER RUCK-A-CHUCKY RAPID (IV).** This is the beginning of Ruck-a-Chucky, named by miners in the last century. You can shorten the portage by running this drop, but don't try it if the flow is too high. The next drop is just downstream, and it is definitely out of the question. Station rescuers downstream. Scout on the right.

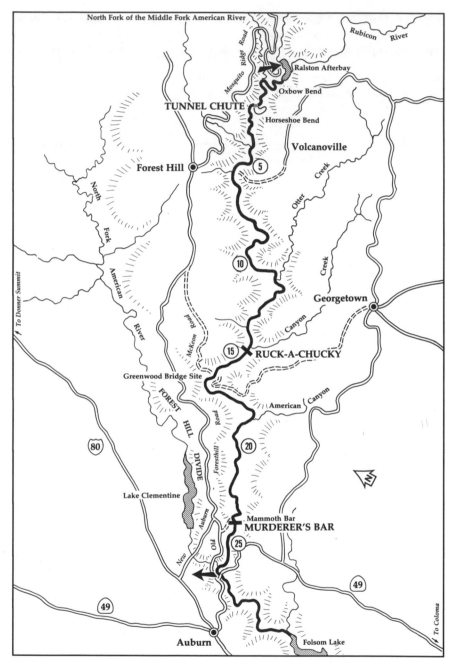

Middle Fork American River

14.5 **♦ PORTAGE ♦**

  RUCK-A-CHUCKY (U). Even crazed daredevils don't run this one. The river drops 20 feet through a sieve of huge boulders. Portage on the right—a tough task, but necessary. Many of the rocks are severely undercut. Extend your portage far enough downstream to bypass all the dangers.

14.7 **LOWER RUCK-A-CHUCKY (IV).** This rapid begins just below the six-foot drop that terminates Ruck-a-Chucky proper. Scout from the left bank. Boaters usually start down a narrow, runnable chute in the center, then cut to the left.

14.8–16 Enjoyable Class III rapids.

16 *RIVER ACCESS.* Greenwood Bridge site. Primitive campsite on the right. A road leads out of the canyon.

16–23 A lovely stretch of wilderness and Class II rapids.

19 American Canyon on the left. Beautiful waterfall and fine swimming holes up the canyon.

23.1 *RIVER ACCESS.* Mammoth Bar (right bank). A dirt road leads from this point to the old Auburn-Foresthill Road. Take out here to avoid Murderer's Bar Rapid just downstream.

23.2 **♦ POSSIBLE PORTAGE ♦**

  MURDERER'S BAR RAPID (V–VI). The rapid is upstream from Murderer's Bar, so stop at Mammoth Bar and walk down to scout it. If you choose not to run it, take out at Mammoth Bar; the portage around the big rapid is very difficult. Murderer's Bar was so named because five Oregonians were killed here in 1849 by Indians as an act of vengeance.

23.3–25.3 Class II rapids.

25.3 *TAKE-OUT.* Confluence of Middle Fork and North Fork American. Choose a convenient take-out on the right bank upstream from the bridge. A good one is just above the confluence.

25.4 *TAKE-OUT.* Highway 49 bridge. Don't float too far below it, or you'll end up having to navigate 10 miles of Folsom Reservoir to reach the next take-out. Worse, only three miles below the Highway 49 bridge, water is diverted around the site of controversial Auburn Dam through a tunnel that would be very dangerous for boaters, especially at high flows.

North Fork American

From the bottom of the North Fork American's steep-walled canyon, it looks like a long way back to civilization. Yet busy Interstate 80 climbs toward Tahoe along the back of a ridge only a few miles distant, and Sacramento is less than an hour away. Here and there country roads cross the river, providing boaters with access to its banks and dividing the North Fork into runs of varying difficulty.

In the past few years, as white water sport has exploded, the North Fork has evolved from a little-known kayaking run to one of the state's most popular rivers in spring and early summer. Higher up, where the river slices through Giant Gap Ridge in a continuous series of thundering drops, is one of the toughest runs in this guide book. Below the Colfax-Iowa Hill Road bridge, where the Chamberlain Falls run begins, the North Fork's clear, green waters flow through several miles of exhilarating Class IV and IV+ rapids. Just downstream from Shirttail Canyon, the river gradually eases into a peaceful Class II float. Boaters can choose the section that fits their skills.

The headwaters of the North Fork rise at only 8500', so its boating season is shorter than that of most other Sierra rivers. In dry years the season may begin and end in May, and even in wet years the river drops too low for rafts by the end of June—though kayakers can scrape down for a few more weeks. Flows usually peak in May when warm weather or rain storms melt the snow pack.

North Fork American River

Giant Gap Run

Eucre Bar to Colfax-Iowa Hill Road

Difficulty: V. **Length:** 14 miles.

Gradient: 55 ft./mi. **Drainage:** About 200 sq. mi. at put-in.

Season: April–early June. **Elevation at Put-in:** 1890'.

Runnable Levels: 200/500–2000 cfs.

Flow Information: (916) 322-3327. Best guess is three quarters of the North Fork's flow at Lake Clementine.

Scenery: Excellent. **Solitude:** Excellent.

Rafts: Outstanding run for seasoned experts only. Paddle boats recommended because of the long carry to the put-in.

Kayaks: Experts only.

Open Canoes: Absolutely not recommended, though expert Joe Willie Jones ran Giant Gap in 1981 without a portage—a remarkable feat.

Special Hazards: Rugged, isolated canyon with little chance of help in case of trouble.

Commercial Raft Trips: None offered in 1984. For information on possible future trips, stay in touch with Tahoe National Forest, Highway 49 and Coyote Road, Nevada City, CA 95959; phone below.

Water: Clear, cold, and probably drinkable. Purify to be sure.

Camping: Excellent beaches except in Giant Gap itself (miles 2.5–5.4). Primitive campsite at the take-out.

Maps: Dutch Flat, Foresthill, Colfax (USGS 7.5'), Colfax (USGS 15'); Tahoe National Forest; Lake Tahoe (AAA).

Auto Shuttle: 18 miles; 1 hour. There's also a two-mile trail to the put-in.

Emergency Telephone Numbers:
    Placer County Sheriff (Auburn): 911.
    Tahoe National Forest (Nevada City): (916) 265-4531.

Logistics: To reach the put-in, drive about 30 miles north of Auburn on Interstate 80 and exit at Alta. Turn south on Casa Loma Road and drive about three miles to a sign marking the trail head. From this point a wide two-mile trail leads down to the put-in at Eucre Bar, just downstream from a foot bridge across the river. To reach the take-out, drive south on I-80, exit at Colfax, cross to the south side of the freeway, turn right on Canyon Way for a short distance, and then turn left on Colfax-Iowa Hill Road. Take out on either bank where the road crosses the river. This is the put-in for the Chamberlain Falls run.

Including the Giant Gap run in this guide book is evidence of how far white water boating has come in the last decade or so. Giant Gap is one of the most spectacular river canyons in California. Narrow rock walls tower more than 2000 feet above the clear, green stream as it splashes down steep rapids choked by huge boulders. In June 1971 a team of expert kayakers abandoned their pioneering run through Giant Gap because they felt the flow (1800 cfs) was too high. John Ramirez came back three weeks later when the flow had dropped by half, recovered the kayak he had left on the bank, and finished the run—with numerous portages—just before nightfall. John Googins and Charles Martin waited until Labor Day to rescue their kayaks and float through the gorge at 100 cfs. All these adventures are recounted in Martin's early guide book, *Sierra Whitewater* (1974), which declared Giant Gap "unsuitable for river running, in the usual sense, at any water level."

Since then, things have changed. In the 1980's most expert kayakers and rafters (usually in paddle boats) run Giant Gap without portaging at all. Amazingly, Giant Gap has even been run in an open canoe, though such a stunt is off limits to all but daredevil experts.

The run is long and difficult, so boaters should get an early start if they plan a one-day trip. The three-mile gorge itself, where the river cuts through Giant Gap Ridge, is inaccessible except by boat, but hikers and river runners whose skills aren't up to the level demanded by this run can get a taste of the upper North Fork American by hiking down the trails to Eucre Bar, Green Valley, Pickering Bar, and Tommy Cain Ravine. The latter two trails are not marked on USGS topo maps.

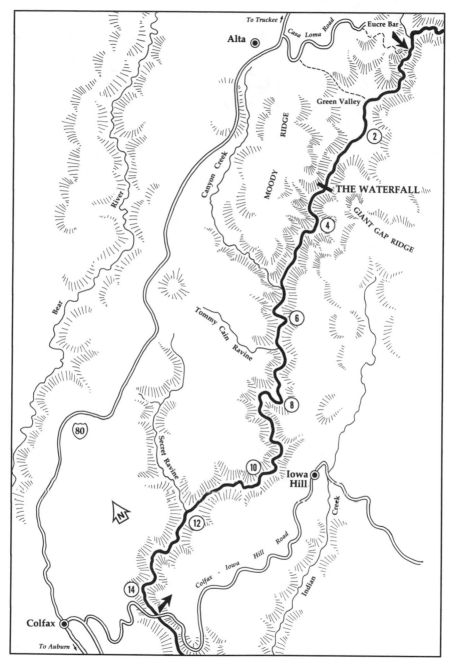

North Fork American: Giant Gap Run

Mile by Mile Guide

0	Eucre Bar. Put in just downstream from the foot bridge. At low water a lovely swimming hole awaits tired hikers.
0–1	Class IV rapids in a scenic gorge.
1–2.5	Green Valley. The canyon opens up and the rapids ease. Several trails lead out of the canyon from the right bank.
2.5–5.4	Giant Gap. Here the river has cut a narrow chasm between spectacular 2000-foot walls. There are several Class V rapids in this stretch. Even experts should make their first trips at flows below 1000 cfs; above that level, the pools between drops are so swift that rescue is very difficult. Scout at every opportunity. The third drop is the biggest (see immediately below).
3.5	◆ *POSSIBLE PORTAGE* ◆ **THE WATERFALL (V–V+).** A sharp six-foot vertical drop into a big reversal. Scout, and portage if necessary, on the right.
5.4	Canyon Creek enters on the right. There are several waterfalls a short hike up the creek. Excellent lunch spot.
5.4–6.6	Class V rapids continue to Tommy Cain Ravine.
6	Pickering Bar (left bank). A trail leads out of the canyon from the right bank.
6.6	Tommy Cain Ravine. A trail leads out from the right bank.
6.6–13.9	Fine scenery and Class III–IV rapids.
13.9	**UNNAMED RAPID (IV+).** A tough technical test at a left-hand bend. Around the corner the bridge comes into view.
14.2	*TAKE-OUT.* Colfax-Iowa Hill Road bridge. Take out on the left above the bridge or on the right just below it. This is the put-in for the Chamberlain Falls run.

North Fork American

Chamberlain Falls and Big Bend Runs

Colfax-Iowa Hill Road to Ponderosa Way

Difficulty: IV+ above Shirttail Canyon (mile 5); II below it.

Length: 5 or 9 miles.   **Season:** March–mid-June.

Gradient: 34 ft./mi. overall; 50 ft./mi. first 5 miles; 15 ft/mi. last 4 miles.

Drainage: 342 sq. mi. downstream at Clementine Reservoir.

Runnable Levels: 300/500–5000 cfs.   **Elevation at Put-in:** 1100'.

Flow Information: (916) 322-3327. Inflow into Clementine Reservoir.

Scenery: Excellent.

Solitude: Very good; excellent weekdays and early in the season.

Rafts: A challenging run for advanced boaters. Small rafts below 900 cfs.

Kayaks: Advanced boaters above Shirttail Canyon (mile 5); below it is a good novice run.

Open Canoes: Advanced canoeists can put in at mile 5, though they might want to portage one of the early rapids in the lower stretch.

Special Hazards: Narrow stream bed means hydraulics become severe at what might appear to be moderate flows. Experts only above 3000 cfs.

Commercial Raft Trips: One- and two-day floats. For a list of outfitters, contact California Department of Parks and Recreation, Folsom Lake Area Headquarters, 7806 Folsom-Auburn Road, Folsom CA 95630; phone below.

Water: Cold, clear, probably drinkable. Purify to be sure.

Camping: Primitive camping at the put-in (left bank). Closest developed campsite is Bear River Campground a few miles southwest of Colfax.

Maps: Colfax (USGS 7.5'); Colfax (USGS 15'); Lake Tahoe (AAA).

Auto Shuttle: 15 miles; 45 minutes.

Emergency Telephone Numbers:
Placer County Sheriff (Auburn): 911.
California Dept. of Parks & Recreation (Folsom): (916) 885-4527.

Logistics: To reach the put-in, drive 16 miles north of Auburn on Interstate 80 and exit at Colfax. Turn south on Canyon Way for a short distance, then left onto Colfax-Iowa Hill Road, which descends into the canyon. Put in at the bridge on either bank. To reach the first take-out and alternate put-in at Shirttail Canyon (mile 5), drive south from Colfax on Canyon Way, turn left on Colfax-Foresthill Road, and follow it across the river. River access is on the left bank upstream from the bridge. To reach the second take-out, continue south on Canyon Way, turn left onto Ponderosa Way, and take out on the right bank below the bridge.

Just downstream from the put-in, the North Fork plunges into a narrow gorge. Big rapids follow in quick succession for most of the next five miles. At moderate and high flows eddies become scarce and hard to catch, and boats must negotiate some big holes—especially at Chamberlain Falls and Staircase. Below Staircase (mile 3.3) the river eases a bit, but a couple of unnamed Class III rapids can surprise the unwary boater. At Shirttail Canyon (mile 5) the river changes into a Class II float, the Big Bend run. Novice and intermediate boaters often put in here.

If it weren't for North Fork Dam, river runners could continue to enjoy the scenery and solitude all the way to Auburn, ten miles below the Ponderosa Way take-out. Unfortunately, this old debris dam—built by the WPA in 1939 to catch rocks and sludge from upstream mining, but rendered unnecessary when Folsom Dam was finished in 1956—is still in place. It has recently been retrofitted to generate a small amount of electrical power. As a result, the waters of tiny Clementine Reservoir cover five miles of the North Fork canyon, turning half of the run below Ponderosa Way into a flat-water paddle. But North Fork Dam is a minor problem compared to the behemoth planned by the U.S. Bureau of Reclamation for a site farther downstream. Auburn Dam would wipe out the Chamberlain Falls and Big Bend runs, the Middle Fork run, and North Fork Dam's new hydroelectric facility, not to mention archaeological sites along the rivers.

Mile by Mile Guide

0   Colfax-Iowa Hill Road bridge. Put in on either bank.

0.4   **SLAUGHTER'S SLUICE (III–IV).** There is a blind entry to this boulder slalom because of a huge rock in midstream. Scout on the left. Enter right, then work quickly left behind the rock. The series of drops continues down to Chamberlain Falls.

0.8   **CHAMBERLAIN FALLS (IV +).** A narrow slot with an eight-foot vertical drop funnels boats into a big reversal. If you try to run too far left, you may be caught by a violent eddy between the reversal and the left bank. At certain flows the only way to rescue boats trapped in this eddy is to drag them out with a line. Scout on the left, but remember that the small eddy above the rapid is hard to catch at high water. The rapid was named for early kayaker Mike Chamberlain, whose less than successful run here was immortalized on film.

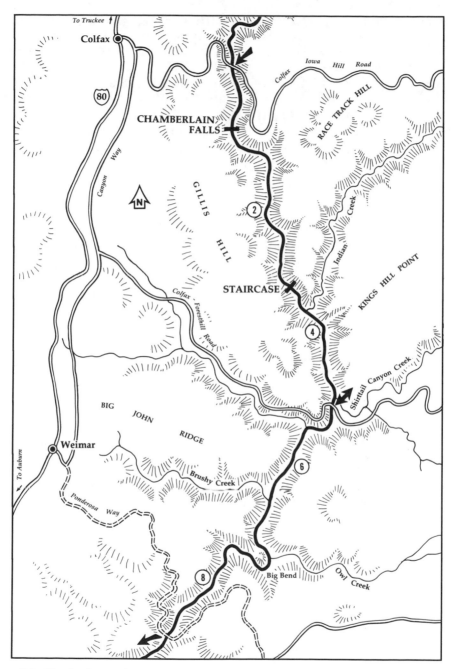

N. Fork American: Chamberlain Falls & Big Bend Runs

1.1   **TONGUE AND GROOVE (III–IV). Recognition:** A horizon line across the river. **The rapid:** The tongue on the left provides the easiest route; the groove (left center) requires maneuvering.

1.6   **ZIG-ZAG (IV).** Tricky boulder dodging. Start center, move right, then quickly back to the left.

2.4   **ACHILLES' HEEL (III–IV).** Another boulder slalom. Toughest at low water, when the right side becomes very rocky.

2.7   **BOGUS THUNDER (IV).** A ledge creates a river-wide reversal. Scout from either bank.

3   **GRAND SLALOM (IV).** Huge boulders form a long, technical maze. Scout the entry from the right bank. It's difficult to scout the entire rapid. At lower flows, catch an eddy behind a midstream rock to look for a route through the last half.

3.3   **STAIRCASE (IV–V).** Three river-wide ledges, with a vicious keeper hole waiting below the second. Scout right. Class III rapids from here to Shirttail Canyon.

3.8   Indian Creek enters on the left. There is a nice waterfall about a quarter of a mile up the creek.

5   *RIVER ACCESS.* Shirttail Canyon Creek enters on the left, just above the Colfax-Foresthill Road bridge. Put in or take out on the left bank upstream from the bridge.

6.5   Brushy Creek enters on the right.

7.5   Big Bend. The river makes a long right-hand horseshoe bend.

9   *TAKE-OUT.* Ponderosa Way bridge. Take out just downstream on the right. Novice kayakers and intermediate open canoeists might be interested in the Class I-II float downstream from this point: four miles of easy rapids, then five miles of flat water on Clementine Reservoir to the take-out at North Fork Dam (reached via New Foresthill Road from an I-80 exit just north of Auburn).

Truckee River

River Ranch to Floriston

Difficulty: II–III.   **Length:** 27 miles; 2–3 days.

Gradient: 32 ft./mi.

Drainage: 506 sq. mi. near put-in; 932 sq. mi. at take-out.

Season: April–October. High elevation (6200' at put-in) means chance of cold weather in spring and fall.

Runnable Levels: 150/300–1500 cfs. Low bridges across the stream make it impossible to run the Truckee at higher flows.

Flow Information: (916) 322-3327. Flow at Tahoe City (Fanny Bridge).

Scenery: Good. Fine Alpine forest the first half; drier country downstream.

Solitude: Fair. Either Highway 89 or Interstate 80 is close by most of the time.

Rafts: Small rafts only below 600 cfs.

Kayaks: Novices and intermediates will find this a good run for learning how to handle rocky, technical rivers.

Open Canoes: Suitable for advanced canoeists below 600 cfs.

Special Hazards: (1)Low bridges across the river. (2) Dangerous diversion dam downstream from take-out.

Commercial Raft Trips: Several companies rent small rafts for self-guided trips on the three-mile Class I stretch between Tahoe City and River Ranch. No commercial floats are currently allowed downstream from River Ranch on the run described here. For updated information, contact Truckee Ranger District, Tahoe National Forest, PO Box 399, Truckee CA 95734; phone below.

Water: Clear, cold, and beautiful above Truckee. Quality deteriorates downstream. Since there is plenty of human habitation along the way, avoid drinking the river. Side streams may be OK. Purify to be sure.

Camping: Developed Forest Service campgrounds at Silver Creek (mile 2.8), Goose Meadow (5.5), Granite Flat (9), and Polaris (14.3).

Maps: Tahoe City, Truckee, Martis Peak, Boca (USGS 7.5'); Tahoe, Truckee (USGS 15'); Tahoe National Forest; Lake Tahoe (AAA).

Auto Shuttle: 26 miles; 40 minutes.

Emergency Telephone Numbers:
Tahoe National Forest (Truckee): (916) 587-3558.
Placer County Sheriff (Tahoe City): 911.
Nevada County Sheriff (Truckee): 911.
Logistics: To reach the put-in, turn south off Interstate 80 just west of Truckee onto Highway 89. Put in 11 miles upstream, at the picnic area just downstream from Alpine Meadows Road. River Ranch, just upstream, is often crowded and has limited parking. To reach the take-out, return to I-80 and follow it east about 15 miles. Exit at Floriston and take out just upstream from the I-80 bridge.

The Truckee gave birth to Lake Tahoe 1.5 million years ago, when volcanic eruptions plugged the north end of a down-faulted valley on the eastern edge of the young Sierra Nevada. The river's headwaters rise just north of Carson Pass, among peaks towering well above 9000', and feed one of the world's largest natural fresh water lakes. With its 122 million acre-feet, Tahoe dwarfs California's biggest man-made lake, Shasta Reservoir (capacity 4.5 million). The Truckee becomes a river again where the lake overflows its northwest corner at Tahoe City. A small dam regulates the flow. From this outlet on, volcanic formations abound on both banks.

Like other rivers on the eastern slope of the Sierra, the Truckee falls continuously instead of in the pools and drops characteristic of western-slope and Coast Range streams. The river flows north through wooded country past the well-known ski areas, Alpine Meadows and Squaw Valley, until it reaches the historic railroad town of Truckee (mile 10) just east of Donner Pass. There it turns northeast toward the Nevada desert. Downstream, Derby Dam provides power and water for Reno residents and Nevada farmers and releases only a trickle to the lower end of the Truckee. As a consequence, the river is almost dry by the time it reaches its final destination, Pyramid Lake.*

The run begins three miles downstream from Tahoe City. In the summer, the short Class I stretch upstream, from Tahoe City to River Ranch, is crowded with inner tubes and rubber duckies (small, cheap plastic dime-store rafts guaranteed to rip). Below River Ranch the Class II and easy Class III rapids are continuous in many stretches. Vehicle access to the river is easy throughout the run because of the highway alongside. The take-out at Floriston is potentially dangerous because of a diversion dam just downstream. There is also a very tough series of steep Class III boulder gardens above Floriston; less experienced boaters might want to portage or to take out upstream.

*Pyramid Lake, successfully defended by the Paiutes against the U.S. Army in 1859 and still part of their home land, became a thriving commercial fishery by the end of the last century because of the rich harvest of cutthroat trout to be taken. In the 1920's and 1930's sport fishermen came from all over the world, and the world record cutthroat was caught there. The Paiutes lived largely from the bounties of the lake. Now, because dam releases are so tiny, the fish have trouble reaching their upstream spawning waters. Trout fishing has undergone a deep decline, and another fish—the cui-ui (pronounced KWEE-wee), a sucker unique to Pyramid Lake—is on the endangered species list.

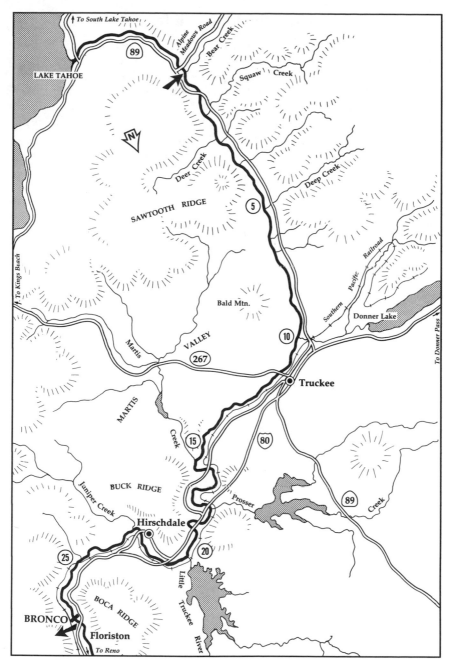

Truckee River

Mile by Mile Guide

0	Put in at the picnic area just downstream from the Alpine Meadows Road bridge. An alternate put-in is a mile upstream at River Ranch, but the Alpine Meadows bridge is lower than the other bridges, and boaters cannot float under it at flows above 1000 cfs.
0–9.5	Highway 89 follows the river for the first 9.5 miles, providing plenty of alternate put-ins and take-outs. Shallow, rocky Class II and III rapids throughout the run. Watch out for low bridges.
1.8	Squaw Creek enters on the left.
9.8	Donner Creek enters on the left, and the river turns east.
10–12	Town of Truckee, founded in 1863-64 as a Central Pacific station, was given its present name in 1868. Both the town and the river were named for a Paiute who guided early explorers, while "Tahoe" was a Washo Indian word meaning "big water." The scenery changes to high desert as the Truckee turns northeast and descends toward Nevada. Continuous Class II–III boulder gardens can cause trouble for novices.
15.2	Martins Creek enters on the right.
18	Interstate 80 bridge across the river. No vehicle access.
18.1	Prosser Creek enters on the left.
18.6	I-80 bridge. No access.
19.4	I-80 bridge. No access.
20.3	Little Truckee River enters from the left. Dam releases from Boca Reservoir on the Little Truckee add considerably to the Truckee's flow during the summer.
21.2	I-80 bridge.
22.4	Bridge across river at town of Hirschdale.
26.5–27	**BRONCO (III).** The gradient suddenly steepens to 100 ft./mi. as the Truckee splashes down several Class III–III+ boulder gardens. Bronco Creek enters on the right.
27.1	*TAKE-OUT* ◆ *HAZARD* ◆ Take out just upstream from the I-80 bridge at Floriston. Don't miss the take-out; a dangerous diversion dam is around the corner. Floriston (originally named Bronco) is an old railroad stop where trains picked up ice to cool their cars in summer. Kayakers sometimes run the eight-mile Class III stretch from Farad Powerhouse, about two miles downstream, to Verdi, but there are some potentially dangerous old diversion dams along the way.

North Fork Yuba

Downieville and Goodyears Bar Runs

Union Flat Campground to Highway 49 Bridge

Difficulty: IV–V above Goodyears Bar (mile 10); III–IV$_5$ thereafter.
Length: 19 miles; 2 days. Shorter runs possible.
Gradient: 59 ft./mi.   **Drainage:** 250 sq. mi. at Goodyears Bar.
Season: April through June.   **Elevation at Put-in:** 3350'.
Runnable Levels: 400/700–3000 above Goodyears Bar; 500/800–8000 below Goodyears Bar.
Flow Information: (916) 322-3327. Above the Downie River (mile 6), about a third of the inflow into New Bullards Bar Reservoir; below the Downie, about half.
Scenery: Excellent.   **Solitude:** Good except summer weekends.
Rafts: The run above Goodyears Bar (mile 10) is for experts only. Especially difficult at high water. Self-bailing rafts recommended.
Kayaks: Difficult, continuous action for the first ten miles—experts only. The stretch below Goodyears Bar is runnable by intermediates if they make a few portages.
Open Canoes: At low flows, experts can tackle the section below Goodyears Bar if they make several portages.
Special Hazards: Maytag Rapid (mile 16.2) is much tougher than any other rapid on the stretch below Goodyears Bar. Depending on the water level, many boaters prefer to portage it.
Commercial Raft Trips: One- and two-day trips. Most put in at Goodyears Bar. For a list of outfitters, contact Downieville Ranger District, U.S. Forest Service, Camptonville, CA 95922; phone below.
Water: Clear, cold, probably drinkable—but there are towns upstream. Purify to be sure.
Camping: Improved Forest Service campgrounds all along the run: Union Flat (put-in), Indian Valley (mile 17), Fiddle Creek (mile 18.3). All are accessible both from the river and from the highway. Another, Ramshorn (mile 12), is not on the river. Campgrounds are usually full on weekends from Memorial Day on.

Maps: Downieville, Goodyears Bar (USGS 7.5'); Downieville (USGS 15'); Tahoe National Forest; Feather River and Yuba River Region (AAA).

Auto Shuttle: 20 miles; 30 minutes.

Emergency Telephone Numbers:
Sierra County Sheriff (Downieville): 911.
Forest Service (Camptonville): (916) 288-3231.

Logistics: Downieville is 45 miles north of Nevada City on Highway 49. The highway follows the right bank of the river, so vehicle access and shuttles are easy. The put-in for the upper stretch, Union Flat Campground, is six miles east of Downieville. Those who want to run only the lower section can put in at Goodyears Bar by taking a side road that crosses to the left bank of the river four miles west of Downieville. Put in on the left bank just downstream from the bridge or a few hundred yards upstream from the cluster of houses that makes up Goodyears Bar.

This high-elevation run through Tahoe National Forest is sure to attract more attention in the future. The North Fork of the Yuba is a medium-sized river draining Yuba Pass and surrounding 8000' peaks. Its flow is almost doubled at the confluence with the Downie River, site of the well-preserved gold mining town of Downieville. The North Fork runs free all the way to New Bullards Bar Reservoir, well downstream from the Downieville run.* (See the end of the mile by mile guide.)

Boaters should not take on the North Yuba lightly. The ten miles from Union Flat to Goodyears Bar is extremely tough, and difficult rapids continue all the way to the Maytag series below mile 16. Good emergency access from Highway 49 along much of the run is a positive factor. However, some of the most difficult rapids cannot be seen from the highway. One that can, Maytag, has caused problems in the past, partly because downstream rapids make recovery difficult. Temperatures are chilly at this high elevation during most of the boating season, so full wet suits are a necessity.

*Experts might be interested in eight additional miles of Class V white water above Downieville, from Haypress Creek to Union Flat Campground, but flows are skimpy, the gradient is 110 feet per mile, and the highway rarely comes close to the river. Beware.

Mile by Mile Guide

0	Put in at Union Flat Campground (right bank).
0–6	Experts only. Avoid at high water. For the first six miles, the gradient is 80 feet per mile, and unnamed Class IV–V rapids are nearly continuous. Stop to scout as often as possible.
2.8	Jim Crow Creek enters on the left. The river passes through Sierra Shangri-La Resort.

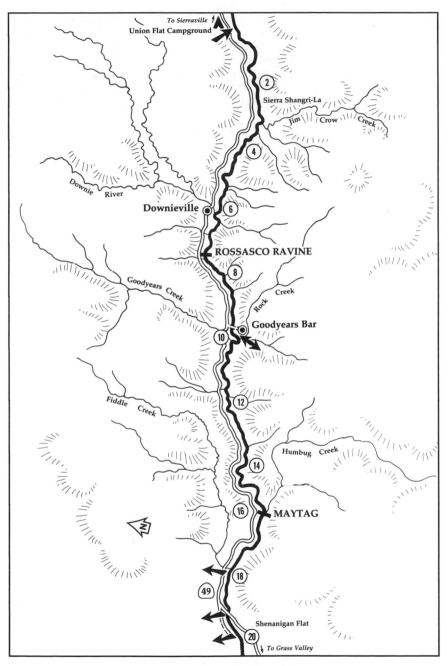

North Fork Yuba River

6   *RIVER ACCESS.* Downieville. The old mining town (population 600), county seat of Sierra County (population 3000), is a quiet, friendly place worth visiting before or after your river trip. The Downie River enters on the right, increasing the North Fork's flow dramatically. River access on the right bank just below the confluence. The big rapids are just ahead.

6.8–8   **ROSSASCO RAVINE (V).** A long series of rapids. The initial chute along the right wall ends in a huge hole. A pool follows, then a string of more technical but less drastic drops that can be seen from turnouts along Highway 49.

8–10   Class II rapids.

10   *RIVER ACCESS.* Goodyears Bar bridge across the river. Easy river access just downstream on the left.

10.2   Rock Creek enters on the right. Most of the rapids the next six miles are Class II–III gravel bars and boulder gardens, with the exceptions noted below.

11.7   **RAMSHORN (IV).** The river divides into three channels. The center channel usually has the most water and the hottest action.

14.9   **TWO PAIR (IV).** Look for a landslide on the right wall. A Class III rapid leads to this double drop.

16.2   ◆ *POSSIBLE PORTAGE* ◆
         MAYTAG (V). Recognition: The river bends right, and Humbug Creek enters from the left. **The rapid:** A pool leads to a big vertical drop. Many boats which manage to negotiate the reversal at its base are then washed against the downstream left wall. More drops and holes follow, and then a Class IV rapid. Consider portaging (either bank), especially at high water.

16.4   **SON OF MAYTAG (IV).** Only a short pool separates the big one upstream from this junior version. At high flows the two rapids merge.

17–20   Class II–III rapids to the take-out.

18.3   *ALTERNATE TAKE-OUT.* Fiddle Creek Campground (right bank).

19   *TAKE–OUT.* Highway 49 bridge across the river. Take out just downstream on the right bank.

20   *TAKE–OUT.* Shenanigan Flat (right bank). A dirt road follows the right bank of the river upstream to the highway bridge. Downstream, the Yuba splashes through six more miles of Class IV rapids before it is swallowed up in New Bullards Bar Reservoir. The problem is that there is no road access to the upper reservoir, so boaters face a 12-mile tow-out to Dark Day Boat Ramp (Dark Canyon Road off Highway 70) and formidable shuttle problems. New Bullards Bar Dam, a thin concrete arch, was built in 1970 to provide irrigation water and electrical power for the Yuba County Water Agency.

arly self-bailing raft on the Upper Tuolumne.

Kayaker playing in a reversal wave.

Wet.

Kayaker in a sharp drop.

Vortex Rapid, Forks of the Kern.

ry Meadow Creek, Forks of the Kern.

A calm stretch in Giant Gap.

Doug Cars

Oar raft on the Upper Kern.

Good times, bad life jacket.

Clavey Falls. Find the passengers.

Daredevil kayaker runs a falls just upstream from the McCloud put-in.

Bill Carlson

Fun.

Brian Fessenden

Salmon River.

Whitewater Voyages

Brian Fessenden

Two views of Chamberlain Falls, North Fork American.

Brian Fessenden

Salmon River.

Big Ike at 15,000 cts. Klamath River.

Upper Burnt Ranch Falls, Trinity River.

Rainy-season rafting.

High brace.

Bloomer Falls (1965-1983), Salmon River.

Smith River in winter.

Feather River

The higher reaches of the Feather give us an idea of what the Sierra rivers were like before the northern part of the great mountain range began to be lifted and tilted toward the west two or three million years ago. The Middle Fork, the biggest branch of the Feather, still originates east of the Sierra crest, as other Sierra rivers like the Yuba, American, and San Joaquin used to. Its headwaters meander through a high, hilly plateau not far from the Nevada border—countryside that resembles in some respects the lower-elevation landscape through which the ancient Sierra rivers once flowed. Below the little town of Sloat, the Middle Fork becomes a "modern" Sierra river as it cuts through the mountains that have risen in its path during the last couple of million years.

The Feather is one of the state's most heavily-developed rivers. Along the North Fork, which drains the Diamond Mountains and the southern slopes of the Lassen area, PG&E has constructed a chain of dams and powerhouses that flood the canyon in some spots and reduce the river to a trickle in others. Until 1969, when its flow was diverted to one of these powerhouses, the North Fork Feather below the little town of Caribou was very popular with fishermen as well as a favorite run for early California kayakers. An irrigation district has dammed the smaller South Fork. Downstream, Oroville Dam—one of the world's biggest earthfill dams and centerpiece of the California Water Project—towers over the old Gold Rush town of Oroville and backs water up into all three forks of the river. As a result of all this engineering, few stretches of the Feather are boatable.

Only the Middle Fork is allowed to run free above the backwaters of Oroville Reservoir, thanks to the resolution of a struggle between wilderness lovers and a dam-minded irrigation district back in 1968. In that year Congress passed the National Wild and Scenic Rivers Act, including the Middle Fork Feather as the sole California stream among the six rivers protected by the original legislation.

White water boaters can choose between two very different sections of the Middle Fork. The English Bar run, an eight-mile stretch of Class III rapids and fine scenery between Sloat and Nelson Point, is suitable for intermediate rafters and kayakers. Its season is somewhat earlier than the run through the Middle Fork Gorge, described below, which is most emphatically for experts only.

127

Middle Fork Feather

Gorge of the Middle Fork

Nelson Point to Milsap Bar

Difficulty: V + p.

Length: 32 miles; 3 days minimum.

Gradient: 75 ft./mi.

Drainage: 1062 sq. mi. at take-out.

Season: Late May–early July.

Elevation at Put-in: 3900'.

Runnable Levels: 200/300–1200 cfs at put-in. Summer flows at the take-out are two or three times higher.

Flow Information: Not available on flow phone. As a very rough guess, use the flow on the North Fork Yuba as a guide (half the inflow to New Bullards Bar Reservoir).

Scenery: Excellent.

Solitude: Excellent.

Rafts: Only for teams of experts in self-bailing rafts.

Kayaks: Experts only; plastic boats preferred.

Open Canoes: Out of the question.   **Commercial Raft Trips:** Not yet.

Special Hazards: Mandatory portage at mile 29; many other likely portages. Remote wilderness area; rescue difficult in case of injury.

Water: Don't drink from the main river. Numerous side creeks should be fine; purify to be sure.

Camping: Plentiful except in a few sheer-walled sections.

Maps: Blue Nose Mountain, Onion Valley, Cascade, Brush Creek (USGS 7.5'); Quincy, Bucks Lake, Mooreville Ridge, Big Bend Mountain (USGS 15'); Plumas National Forest; Feather-Yuba Region (AAA).

Auto Shuttle: 65 miles; 3 hours.

Emergency Telephone Numbers:
Plumas County Sheriff (Quincy): 911.
Butte County Sheriff (Oroville): (916) 534-4321.
Plumas National Forest (Quincy): (916) 283-1131.

Logistics: To reach the put-in, drive three miles east of Quincy on combined Highways 89 and 70 and turn south on La Porte Road (paved for almost the entire seven miles to the river). Put in at a primitive campsite on the right bank just downstream from the bridge. To reach the take-out, return to Oroville on Highway 70 and drive northeast on Highway 162 (Oroville-Quincy Highway) to Brush Creek. Turn south onto Galen Ridge Road, follow it for a few hundred yards, then turn left on Milsap Bar Road which winds down to the bridge across the Middle Fork.

The gorge of the Middle Fork Feather is the most spectacular and most difficult river in this book: 32 miles of Class V—and worse—rapids in a remote, steep-walled canyon. Only a few old logging roads reach the river between Nelson Point and Milsap Bar, and they might prove too much even for four-wheel drive vehicles. The infrequent trails are steep and difficult. Even helicopter rescue might be impossible in some sections of the canyon. None but teams of experts should attempt the Middle Fork Gorge. The minimum time for running the river is three full days; allow more for a safety margin. Those few who successfully negotiate this river will share the wilderness adventure of a lifetime.*

*The first known kayak run down the Middle Fork gorge was made by Bert Welti, Dan Gaut, and Charlie Pike. The first known raft trips were led by Mark Helmus in early July 1983 and by Jim Cassady later that same month.

Mile by Mile Guide

0   Nelson Point. Put in on the right bank beside a primitive campground downstream from the bridge.

0–3   Class III and IV rapids for the first three miles.

1.5   Nelson Creek enters on the left.

3–9   Class V rapids for six miles. One boulder-strewn six-foot drop over a river-wide ledge should probably be portaged.

9–14.5 Four or five miles of "merely" Class IV rapids.

9.5   Grizzly Creek enters on the right. Just downstream on the right bank is Oddie Bar, a large clearing with an emergency trail out of the canyon.

10   Horseshoe Bend, a big curve around a resistant ridge.

12   Cleghorn Bar. An old jeep trail leads out of the canyon from the left bank.

14.5   Onion Valley Creek enters on the left, and the new Pacific Crest Trail crosses the river via a footbridge. The river enters Franklin Canyon. Downstream, turbulent Class V+ rapids alternate with short pools. The river drops 140 feet per mile for the next several miles. Class V rapids continue to the take-out.

14.7   Consider portaging this steep rapid, almost a waterfall.

15   **HOLE-IN-THE-BOX (V+).** The main current plummets down a narrow chute into a big hole. This is only one of many equally tough passages.

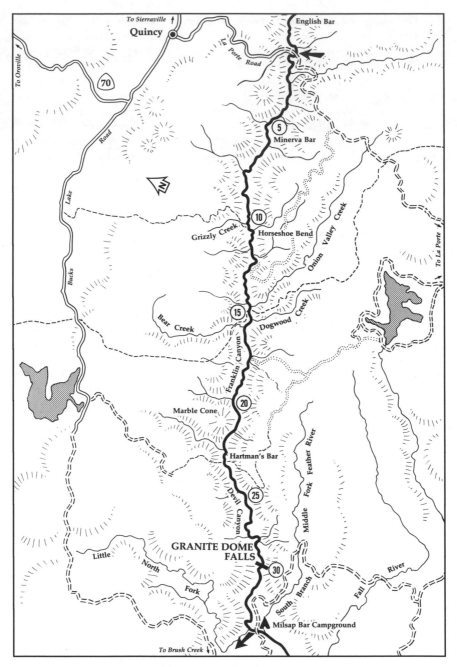

Middle Fork Feather River

15.5   Dogwood Creek drops down a splendid waterfall on the left.

17.5   Stag Point (left bank). A trail leads out of the canyon.

19.5   Little Bear Creek enters on the right. Good campsite.

On our exploratory raft run down the Middle Fork Feather in July 1983, we had just begun our third day on the river when we met veteran inner-tuber Don Turner and some other adventurous souls near Hartman's Bar. Unlike most inner-tubers, who account for the vast majority of drownings on American rivers, Turner and his friends know what they're doing. They wear wet suits and life jackets and carry gear in backpacks strapped to extra tubes. They float through the calm pools and portage or line the big rapids. Turner has been navigating stretches of the Middle Fork in this manner for years—including Bald Rock Canyon, downstream from this run and even more difficult. On this occasion he was on the fifth day of a six-day, six-mile trip from Stag Point to Hartman's Bar. — Jim Cassady.

22   Hartman's Bar. The old Pacific Crest Trail crosses the river via footbridge.

26.5   An old cart trail crosses the river at a wide, shallow spot— probably where the USGS topo map shows Graves Cabin.

28   The river enters Devil Canyon. The gradient remains about 80 feet per mile, but major rapids are formed by huge chunks of granite that have broken off the walls and dropped into the river. By this point side streams have significantly increased the flow, adding to the difficulties.

29   ◆ *PORTAGE* ◆
        GRANITE DOME FALLS (U). Recognition: The river follows a long bend to the right and forms a suspiciously large pool. A granite dome towers over the left bank. **The rapid:** A series of Class V drops climax in a deadly boulder jumble similar to Ruck-a-Chucky on the Middle Fork American. Use a primitive trail on the right for the long, strenuous portage. Rinse off the poison oak in the pool at the bottom.

By the time we got to Granite Dome Falls on our July 1983 float down the Middle Fork gorge, our paddle crew was getting pretty cocky. Thanks in part to our self-bailing raft, we had run 29 miles of outrageous river with no portages and no major problems. But there was a moment when common sense almost turned to putty. After looking over the horrors of the falls, half the crew wanted to run it. For a moment we were tempted. One of the crazies signaled "Let's go!" to our two kayakers, who were scouting from the other bank. They looked at us for a moment across the roaring chute. Then, in unison, each pointed to the frightening drop at the bottom of the rapid with one hand and put the other to his head like a gun. We portaged. —Jim Cassady

30   The canyon begins to open up, but difficult rapids continue to the take-out.

32.5   *TAKE-OUT.* Milsap Bar Road bridge. Little North Fork of the Middle Fork enters on the right just upstream. Take out on the right bank between the Little North Fork and the bridge. Downstream in Bald Rock Canyon the river drops over great slabs of granite at a rate of more than 200 feet per mile. Bald Rock Canyon has been run by some daredevil inner-tubers and by expert kayakers Chuck Stanley, Lars Holbek, and Richard Montgomery. Stanley and Holbek are publishing a book about their many adventures on the state's most outrageous kayak runs.

Deer Creek

Ishi Caves Run

Ponderosa Way to Leininger Road

Difficulty: Vp.   **Length:** 23 miles; 1–3 days.
Gradient: 65 ft./mi. (80 ft./mi. for first 17 miles).
Drainage: 208 sq. mi. near take-out.   **Elevation at Put-in:** 1700′.
Season: April–mid-May. Longer for plastic kayaks. Deer Creek's flows are more consistent from one season to the next and rise less dramatically during rainy weather or snow melt than those of most other California rivers. Volcanic rock in the watershed absorbs water like a sponge and releases it gradually.
Runnable Levels: 200/500–1500 cfs.   **Scenery:** Excellent.
Flow Information: Not on flow phone.   **Solitude:** Excellent.
Rafts: So far as we know, the first raft descent has not yet been made. Narrow stream bed and continuous tricky drops make Deer Creek raftable only by team of experts in small, self-bailing paddle boats.
Kayaks: Fiberglass kayaks would take a beating from the rocks; plastic boats preferred. Lots of eddy-hopping necessary.
Open Canoes: No.   **Commercial Raft Trips:** Not available.
Water: Cold, clear, and almost certainly drinkable. Purify to be sure.
Camping: Few beaches but plenty of beautiful meadows.
Maps: Butte Meadows, Panther Spring (USGS 15′); Lassen National Forest; Northeastern California (AAA).
Auto Shuttle: 45 miles; 2.5 hours.
Emergency Telephone Numbers:
     Tehama County Sheriff (Red Bluff): 911.
     Lassen National Forest (Susanville): (916) 257-5575, 257-5579.
Logistics: To reach the take-out, turn east off Highway 99 some seven miles south of Los Molinos onto Vina Road, then left onto Leininger Road, which soon crosses Deer Creek. To reach the put-in, drive about 11 miles south on 99 from Vina Road and turn east onto Keefer Road, which becomes Cohasset Road (paved). Beyond the hamlet of Cohasset the dirt road is called Ponderosa Way, and the going is rough. In wet weather four-wheel drive might be necessary. Don't turn onto one of the numerous logging roads by mistake. After a long stretch on the ridge, the road finally drops down to the put-in at a bridge across Deer Creek.

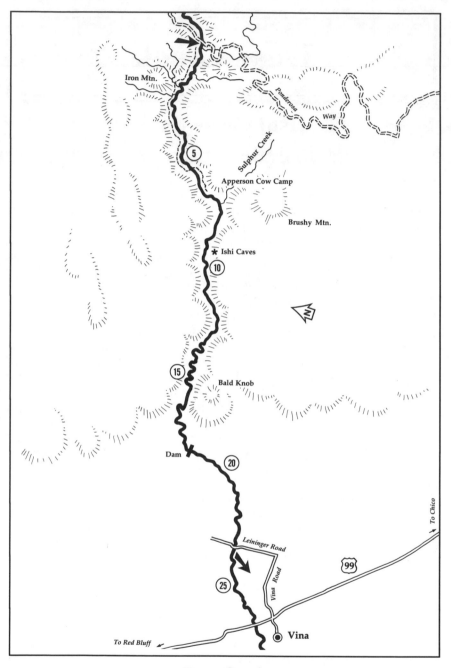

Iron Mtn.

Ponderosa Way

Sulphur Creek

⑤

Apperson Cow Camp

Brushy Mtn.

★ Ishi Caves

⑩

N

⑮

Bald Knob

Dam ⑳

To Chico

Leininger Road

Vina Road

99

㉕

To Red Bluff ←

⊙ Vina

Deer Creek

Deer Creek—actually a small river—rises at the base of Butt Mountain (7866') south of Lassen Volcanic National Park, circles to the north, and then courses southwest toward its eventual confluence with the Sacramento River near the town of Corning. Its spectacular wilderness canyon is cut into relatively young volcanic mud flows (2 to 4 million years ago) that have been tilted gently west toward the valley.

For centuries about two thousand Yahi Indians lived in this area; but by 1872, only a couple of decades after the white man arrived in numbers and began to wage war against them, their population had dwindled to five. This tiny band lived in total seclusion in a remote area along Deer Creek just below its confluence with Sulphur Creek. In 1911 the last surviving Yahi, Ishi, walked out of the wilderness and into the annals of anthropology. His story is told in Theodora Kroeber's classic book, *Ishi in Two Worlds*.

At first glance the reader may wonder why Deer Creek is even listed in this guide book. Kayakers have made this run occasionally since the 1970's. The run is very difficult, studded by big drops through and around volcanic rocks and boulders; the shuttle roads are bad; and the boating season is short. But experts who can handle the non-stop rapids and the possible portages will find themselves in one of the most gorgeous wild river canyons anywhere. The mile by mile guide below gives only the general characteristics of the various sections of the run; no individual rapids are listed.

Mile by Mile Guide

0	Fifty yards downstream from the put-in, Deer Creek begins to drop at a rate of 160 feet per mile. Scout whenever possible.
0.5	Possible portage around a big rapid just after a right turn.
1–8	Gradient in this stretch is 80 feet per mile. But the going is still tough, with lots of scouting and eddy-hopping and possibly a portage or two.
7	Apperson Cow Camp (left bank).
7.5	Sulphur Creek enters on the left. Ishi hid in the caves downstream on the left bank for almost forty years.
8–9.5	Another very steep section (120 ft./mi.); pools between the drops are very short. Another portage or two could be in store.
9.5–18	Class IV rapids. The gradient slackens and the canyon opens up a bit, providing the boater with spectacular vistas of long mesas of columnar basalt, the remnants of lava flows.
18–23	Deer Creek drops into the Sacramento Valley about mile 18; just downstream, a diversion dam shunts water into an irrigation canal on the left bank. The last five miles are easy Class II.
23	*TAKE-OUT.* Leininger Road Bridge.

Rivers of the Coast Ranges

24. Russian
25. Cache Creek
26. Rancheria Creek
27. Stony Creek
28. Eel: Pillsbury Run
29. Eel: Dos Rios to Alderpoint
30. North Fork Eel
31. Middle Fork Eel
32. South Fork Eel
33. Redwood Creek
34. Upper Sacramento

35. Trinity
36. Trinity: Burnt Ranch Gorge
37. Lower Trinity
38. South Fork Trinity
39. Salmon
40. Scott
41. Upper Klamath
42. Klamath
43. North Fork Smith
44. Smith
45. South Fork Smith

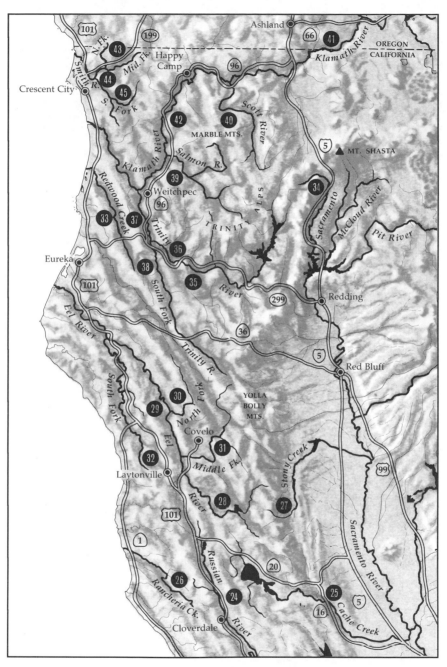

Rivers of the Coast Ranges

Squaw Rock Rapid, Russian River.

Russian River

Squaw Rock Run

Pieta Creek to Cloverdale

Difficulty: II$_3$. **Length:** 8 miles. Shorter runs possible.
Gradient: 17 ft. / mi. **Drainage:** 502 sq. mi. at take-out.
Season: December–May for rafts, year round for kayaks.
Runnable Levels: 200 / 400–10,000 cfs. **Elevation at Put-in:** 440'.
Flow Information: (916) 322-3327.
Scenery: Good. **Solitude:** Fair. Highway 101 is nearby.
Rafts: Best as a rainy-season run, when flows are above 600 cfs. Only tiny rafts can negotiate low summer flows.
Kayaks: Runnable at low summer flows (200–350 cfs). Though rocky, the Russian is a favorite novice run in the summer. Beginners might want to avoid Squaw Rock and Graveyard by putting in just downstream.
Open Canoes: A good run at low flows for advanced canoeists, though they might want to portage here and there. Downstream from Cloverdale, Class I stretches extend for 50 miles and are very popular with beginning canoeists. Bob Trowbridge rents canoes (but not for the Squaw Rock Run) at 20 Healdsburg Avenue, Healdsburg, CA 95448; phone (707) 433-7247.
Commercial Raft Trips: None. **Camping:** None near the river.
Water: Polluted by upstream towns and farms. Don't drink from the river or from side streams.
Maps: Hopland, Cloverdale (USGS 7.5'); Hopland (USGS 15'); Mendocino and Lake Counties, North Bay Counties (AAA).
Auto Shuttle: 8 miles; 15 minutes.
Emergency Telephone Numbers:
  Mendocino County Sheriff (Ukiah): (707) 462-2951.
  Sonoma County Sheriff (Santa Rosa): (707) 527-2121.
Logistics: To reach the put-in, drive eight miles north on Highway 101 from Cloverdale. Put in at a turnout just above Squaw Rock or at a good access point a mile farther north, where Pieta Creek joins the river. The take-out is on the left bank just upstream from the

Highway 101 bridge about two miles north of Cloverdale. A number of alternate river access points are available along the way, but be sure to respect property rights.

The Russian River* rises near the headwaters of the Eel, less than 150 miles north of the Golden Gate. The river probably emptied into a bay covering the Santa Rosa area several million years ago, but uplift and fault movement have altered its path. Now the river flows roughly south beyond Healdsburg, then turns west and empties into the Pacific at Jenner.

Massive Squaw Rock, which dominates the major rapid on this run, is a giant "knocker"—old sea floor bedrock which was smashed against the edge of the continental plate, thrust underground, squeezed, deformed, and carried back to the surface where it has weathered more slowly than the softer Franciscan sedimentary rocks around it. Slides off its face have created the rapid at its base. According to legend, a jilted Indian maiden named Sotuka took revenge on her faithless lover and his new woman by holding a large rock and jumping down on the couple while they were asleep at the base of what became Squaw Rock. In 1956 the rock was registered as a historical landmark.

The Squaw Rock Run, only two hours' drive from San Francisco, has long been a favorite for northern California boaters. The shuttle is easy, and summer flows, though low, are dependable. Every year, beginning in April, water is shunted from Van Arsdale Reservoir on the upper Eel through a tunnel and into the East Fork of the Russian, providing irrigation water for farms and vineyards in the Alexander Valley and all along the Russian River throughout the summer, when the Russian would otherwise be dry. The river is less scenic than most in this guide book because the banks have long been stripped of their forest cover. Solitude is lacking, too: Highway 101 follows the left bank and the tracks of the Northwestern Pacific Railroad are laid along the right bank. But frequent vehicle access to the river adds to the attraction of the Russian as a training run.

In winter and early spring, heavy rains can turn the placid river into a raging torrent, partly because heavy logging throughout its watershed has contributed to the erosion of topsoil which otherwise might absorb some of the runoff. Avoid this—and other—rivers at flood stages. Less experienced open canoeists should stick to the easier Class I stretches below Cloverdale and Healdsburg.

*The river was called the San Ygnacio by the Spanish and the Slaviank ("Slav woman") by Russian colonists in the area, but by the time of the Gold Rush days its present name was generally accepted.

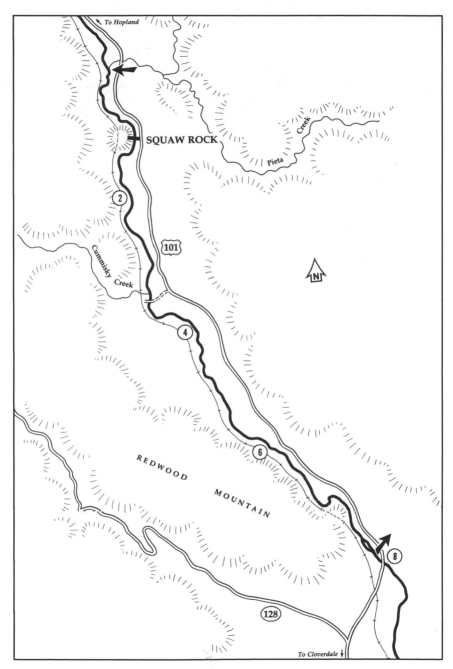

Russian River

Mile by Mile Guide

0   Put in at the mouth of Pieta Creek at the end of a dirt road that may be private property. If it is, use alternate put-in at mile 1.

0–0.7   The river channel is narrow and brushy. Several Class II rapids around and through monolithic rocks in the stream bed.

1   *ALTERNATE PUT-IN*. A turnout beside the highway provides an alternate put-in.

1.1   **SQUAW ROCK RAPID (III).** The river bends left around Squaw Rock and drops through a narrow, rocky slot that becomes a hole at higher flows. Scout from the left bank. The portage on the left is difficult at low water and impossible at higher flows. If you decide not to run the rapid, you should put in downstream.

1.2   **THE GRAVEYARD (II).** A long, technical rock garden with some brush to be avoided as well. Inexperienced boaters might want to skip this one as well and put in downstream.

1.5   **TILDEN FALLS (II).** The river turns left into a short, brushy drop.

3.8   ◆ *HAZARD* ◆ *POSSIBLE PORTAGE* ◆ Cummiskey Creek enters on the right. Low-water bridge across the river is dangerous at high water and must be portaged. At lower flows boats can float under it.

6–7   The river bends away from the highway and flows through a more heavily wooded area.

8   *TAKE-OUT*. Highway 101 bridge across the river just north of Cloverdale. Take out under the bridge on the left bank.

Cache Creek

Rumsey Run

Bear Creek to Rumsey Bridge

Difficulty: II–III.
Length: 8.5 miles. Shorter runs possible.
Gradient: 25 ft./mi.
Drainage: 955 sq. mi. at take-out.
Season: December–August. Summer irrigation releases from Clear Lake range from 400 to 800 cfs. High winter flows attract intermediate and advanced boaters.
Runnable Levels: 250/400–10,000 cfs.
Elevation at Put-in: 630'.
Flow Information: (916) 322-3327. Flow at Rumsey Bridge.
Scenery: Fair.
Solitude: Good in winter, fair in spring, poor on summer weekends.
Rafts: A good training river for novices at moderate flows and for intermediates at higher flows. Small rafts only at flows below 900 cfs.
Kayaks: A favorite beginner's run in the summer for its enjoyable, forgiving rapids and warm water. No wet suit necessary in summer. Good for novices and intermediates at moderate and higher flows, respectively.
Open Canoes: A good run for intermediate and advanced canoeists at lower summer flows.
Special Hazards: A low-water bridge across the river at mile 2.9 creates a dangerous reversal and should be portaged. Always scout it.
Commercial Raft Trips: One- and two-day self-guided trips in small rafts at low summer flows. For a list of outfitters, contact Yolo County Parks Department, 625 Court Street, Woodland, CA 95695; phone below.
Water: Warm and polluted, especially in summer. Undrinkable but pleasant enough for boating.
Camping: Yolo County public campground downstream from the put-in. No camping at other county parks along the river. Private property almost everywhere else. Wilbur Hot Springs is only half an hour's drive north of the put-in; rooms available by reservation— (916) 473-2306.

Maps: Glascock Mountain (USGS 7.5′); Sacramento Valley Region, North Bay Counties (AAA).

Emergency Telephone Numbers:
Yolo County Parks Department: (916) 666-8115.
Yolo County Sheriff (Woodland): (916) 666-8282;
  toll-free dial "O" and ask for Enterprise 9-4099.

Logistics: The entire run is along Highway 16. The shuttle takes only a few minutes.

A million years ago, about 80 miles north of the Golden Gate, a volcano now called Mount Konocti (4200′) erupted and sent lava flowing southeast to block the upper watershed of a small river that ran south toward the Delta and the Bay. With time, the waters behind the volcanic dam rose high enough to spill over into the river canyon again. The river is Cache Creek—so named because Canadian trappers hid their pelts there in the 1840's—and the body of water created by the volcanic dam is Clear Lake. Unfortunately, now that so much waste has been spilled into the lake by surrounding settlements, its name is far from descriptive.

Still, while Cache Creek water is entirely undrinkable, it is pleasant enough for boating. Since 1914 a small dam at the upstream end of Cache Creek has held back water for summer releases to irrigated farms in the Sacramento Valley. These low flows are ideal for novices, including paying customers who guide their own small rafts provided by the river's only commercial outfitter. Summer weekends are crowded.

But Cache Creek is quite different in winter and early spring. After heavy rains, flows often exceed 5000 cfs—big water less than three hours from San Francisco. In very early spring (usually February) blooming almond orchards along lower Highway 16 make the drive to the river exceptionally pleasant. Geology buffs will enjoy looking at the tilted strata that form the rugged canyon walls: the Great Valley Sequence, ancient ocean beds that formed the edge of the North American continent some 70 to 150 million years ago. Highway 16 follows the entire Rumsey run, providing convenient vehicle access and making one-day trips based in the Bay Area or Sacramento feasible. Not far to the north are several hot springs that provide a relaxing end to a day on the river.

It is possible to run the entire Cache Creek canyon beginning at the dam at its upstream end, but the other stretches have problems. The first eleven-mile section below Clear Lake, called "The Jams Run," has difficult river access and a dangerous boulder-choked waterfall ("The Jams") about five miles below the dam. The second run, a scenic seventeen-mile stretch of Class II–II+ rapids, has dangerous brush in the river channel. The run begins where the Highway 20 bridge crosses

144

the North Fork of Cache Creek. Water is often skimpy after the rainy season ends, though Indian Valley Dam on the North Fork occasionally releases just enough water for boats to float the two miles or so down to the Cache Creek confluence.

Mile by Mile Guide

0   Put in on the left bank at the Yolo County Regional Park just downstream from the mouth of Bear Creek. Enjoyable Class II rapids begin right away. Boaters have sometimes put in a few hundred yards upstream, where Highway 16 leaves Cache Canyon and heads north up Bear Creek, but that spot is private property.

2.4   **TAFT'S TUMBLE (II +).** Just beyond a sharp left-hand bend, the river drops over a steep ledge.

2.7   ◆ *HAZARD* ◆ *PORTAGE* ◆ Low-water bridge across Cache Creek leads to Rayhouse Road (right bank). The bridge creates a dangerous river-wide reversal except at low flows, when it blocks the channel. Scout and portage on the right.

4.6   Highway 16 bridge across the river. Stop here to scout the next rapid (either bank).

4.7   **ROWBOAT (III).** Just below the bridge the river divides, then converges and drops down a chute cluttered with big rocks (holes at higher flows). High water in the 1980's rearranged the rapid slightly and made it a bit easier.

5.6   *RIVER ACCESS.* Haswell Boy Scout Camp (right bank). Some boaters take out here.

5.8   **ROCK GARDEN (II–III).** The river splits around an island just below a private home. The right channel once had a dangerous snag but is now an easy Class II ride. More adventurous boaters run the left channel, which plunges over a sharp, rocky drop. Scout on the right. Class I and II rapids to the take-out.

8.5   *TAKE-OUT.* Rumsey Bridge. Take out on the left, just above or just below the bridge.

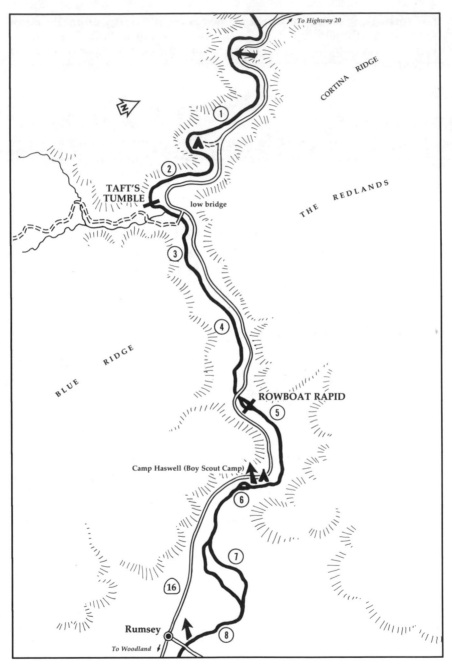

Cache Creek

Rancheria Creek

Mountain View Road to Hendy Woods State Park

Difficulty: II + .   **Length:** 13 miles.
Gradient: 25 ft./mi.   **Drainage:** 65 sq. mi. at put-in.
Season: December–early April except in dry spells. Rainy season run.
Runnable Levels: 150/250–2000 cfs.   **Elevation at Put-in:** 400'.
Flow Information: Not on flow phone. A very rough guess would be one fifth of the flow of the South Fork Eel at Leggett.
Scenery: Excellent.   **Solitude:** Excellent.
Rafts: Small rafts only below 600 cfs.
Kayaks: Excellent beginner and novice run. Weather is often cold, so add head protection and mittens or pogies to usual full wet suit.
Open Canoes: Technically suitable for intermediates, but they should be well prepared for the cold and capable of handling emergencies because of the run's isolation.
Special Hazards: When Rancheria Creek is runnable, days are short and weather is likely to be cold. Be prepared. Have warm, dry clothes available at the take-out.
Commercial Raft Trips: None.
Camping: The narrow stream bed offers few suitable spots for camping, but most boaters make this run in one day anyway. There is an excellent developed campground among first-growth redwoods at the take-out (Hendy Woods State Park). For warmer accommodations, try the restored Boonville Hotel at (707) 985-3478, or the Philo Motel—complete with hot tub—at (707) 895-3325. Call ahead and they'll warm up the hot tub for you.
Water: Clear except after rains, but not drinkable because of upstream grazing. Clear-running side streams should be drinkable; purify to be sure. Don't drink from Anderson Creek or Indian Creek, large tributaries that enter near the end of the run.
Maps: Ornbaun Valley, Boonville (USGS 15'); Mendocino and Lake Counties (AAA).
Auto Shuttle: 14 miles; 30 minutes. Paved roads.
Emergency Telephone Numbers:
  Mendocino County Sheriff (Ukiah): (707) 462-2951.

Logistics: Turn west off Highway 101 at Cloverdale and follow Highway 128 27 miles northwest to Boonville. Turn west onto Mountain View Road and follow it for 4.5 miles. Put in at the bridge across Rancheria Creek. To reach the take-out, return to Boonville, turn north on Highway 128, and turn left on Greenwood Road, about four miles beyond the hamlet of Philo. Take out either at the first bridge or at the upper end of the parking area just inside Hendy Woods State Park.

Rancheria Creek, only three hours north of San Francisco, is one of the most popular rainy-season runs in the state. The stream's low-lying headwaters (3000') are rarely fed by snow melt, but the watershed receives more than 50 inches of rain per year. Several small gorges with delightful but forgiving rapids are scattered along this scenic stretch of white water. This is the prosperous Anderson Valley, whose lush red-wood forests have given way to orchards and pastures. In Boonville some residents still speak the strange local dialect called "Boontling." ("Kimmies japin' broadies to the airtight" means "Men driving broad-horned cattle to the sawmill," according to a 1971 book on Boontling by Charles C. Adams.) Most of the first-growth redwoods have been logged, except near the take-out, but some younger redwoods stand here and there amidst the lush vegetation lining the banks of the stream.

Rancheria Creek is actually the upper half of the Navarro River, but the stream takes that name only toward the end of this run, after it is joined by the major tributaries of Indian and Anderson Creeks. The word "rancheria"—common throughout California—is the Spanish term for a collection of Indian dwellings.

Mile by Mile Guide

0   Put in at the bridge where Mountain View Road crosses the river.

2   Horse Creek enters on the left.

4.2   Cold Springs Creek enters on the left. Just downstream the river enters Big Canyon, which is actually rather small. This beautiful, narrow mini-gorge is sprinkled with enjoyable Class II rapids.

8   **THE CLASS III RAPID,** as boaters refer to it, begins at a sharp right-hand bend. The river drops quickly over ledges and around boulders. This is the most difficult rapid on the run, but it's really not quite Class III.

9.1   Ham Canyon Creek enters on the right. Beautiful cascades just up the creek.

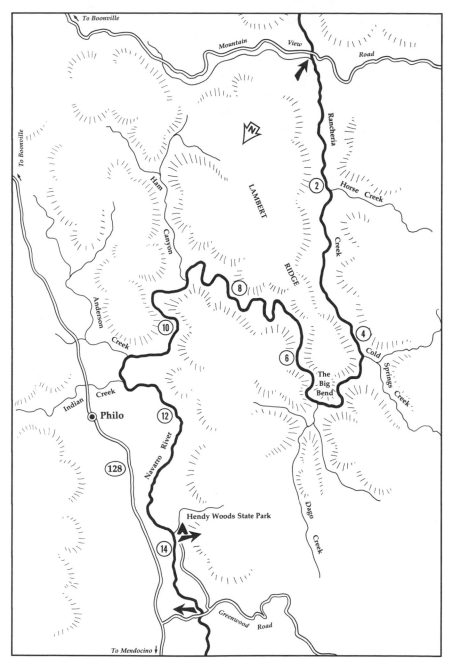

Rancheria Creek

10.8   Anderson Creek enters on the right. The canyon begins to open up. Class I rapids the rest of the way.

11   Indian Creek enters on the right. Rancheria Creek becomes the Navarro River. Pastures appear among the redwoods and the road approaches the river, though no vehicle access is available.

13   *TAKE-OUT.* Hendy Woods State Park. Parking area on the left bank provides a good take-out. A fine stand of first-growth redwoods is beyond the parking area.

14.8   *TAKE-OUT.* Greenwood Road bridge. Downstream, the Navarro River meanders through fifteen miles of second- and third-growth redwoods on the way to Dimmick State Park. This is a popular Class I wilderness canoe run in March and April.

Stony Creek

Fouts Springs to Diversion Dam

Difficulty: IV; III with a few portages.　　　**Gradient:** 70 ft./mi.

Length: 5 miles (or 3.5 miles from Middle Fork confluence).

Drainage: 32 sq. mi. at put-in; 102 sq. mi. at take-out.

Season: December–early April. A rainy-season run extended a few weeks by spring snow melt from an upper watershed well above 6000'.

Runnable Levels: 200/300–2000 cfs.　　　**Elevation at Put-in:** 1650'.

Flow Information: Not available by telephone. Stony Creek is usually runnable through March in average years, and into April in a wet spring. Flows are skimpy except after heavy rains.

Scenery: Excellent.　　　**Solitude:** Excellent below Middle Fork.

Rafts: Small rafts only below 600 cfs.

Kayaks: Excellent advanced run; intermediates might need to portage.

Open Canoes: Too tough except for experts, who might be able to navigate the run at low flows with a few portages.

Special Hazards: Scout the difficult and dangerous take-out before you put in. The current takes boats right to the brink of a filled-in diversion dam.

Commercial Raft Trips: None.

Water: Clear except after rains. Probably drinkable. Purify to be sure.

Camping: Forest Service campgrounds at put-in and take-out.

Maps: Stonyford (USGS 15'); Mendocino National Forest; Mendocino and Lake Counties, North Bay Counties (AAA).

Auto Shuttle: 5 miles; 15 minutes.

Emergency Telephone Numbers:
Mendocino National Forest (Stonyford): (916) 963-3128.
Colusa County Sheriff (Colusa): 911.

Logistics: At the town of Maxwell, 35 miles north of the intersection of I-5 and I-505, turn west and drive 23 miles to Lodoga. Turn right (east) to Stonyford, eight miles away; then turn west onto Fouts Springs Road. Three miles west of Stonyford, stop at a small campground on the right and scout the dangerous take-out just upstream from the dam behind the campground. Continue five miles west to the bridge across Miner Creek, half a mile upstream from its confluence with the South Fork of Stony Creek. Put in on the right bank of Miner Creek, or if the water is too low, follow the dirt road along the west bank downstream to the confluence with the larger Middle Fork.

Like its cousin Cache Creek, Stony Creek is a small river whose headwaters drain the eastern slope of the Coast Range north of Clear Lake. Just to the north and west are the upper reaches of the Eel's watershed on the wetter western slope. Stony Creek drops quickly from the twin peaks of Snow Mountain (7056' and 7040') and empties into the Sacramento.

Though Stony Creek's gradient is quite steep, at low and moderate flows the Fouts Springs run is a delightful blend of Class III and IV rapids in a small, isolated gorge. Like any small river with a narrow stream bed, Stony Creek is dangerous at higher flows. Since the river is runnable only when days are short and weather cool at best, the short float and easy shuttle are attractive features. This is one of the finest advanced and expert rainy-season runs in California.

The South Fork of Stony Creek and Miner Creek converge just downstream from the put-in. The flow doubles when the Middle Fork enters at mile 1.5 and increases again a quarter mile farther at the confluence with the North Fork. If the water level is low, or if dirt bikers are out in full force and you don't like the noise, put in at the mouth of the Middle Fork. Be alert for the potentially dangerous diversion dam at the take-out.

Mile by Mile Guide

0	Put in on the right bank of Miner Creek just downstream from the bridge. The flow will double at the South Fork. If even that isn't enough water, follow the dirt road down the left bank to the alternate put-in at the Middle Fork confluence.
0–1.5	Class II–III rapids.
0.5	Confluence of South Fork Stony Creek and Miner Creek.
1.2	**UNNAMED RAPID (IV)** laced with boulders and holes.
1.5	*RIVER ACCESS.* Middle Fork Stony Creek, which drains Snow Mountain, enters on the left and boosts the flow with its cold, clear water.
1.8	North Fork Stony Creek enters on the left. The road comes this far down the river, but access is better back at the Middle Fork confluence. The river turns to the east, enters a gorge, and drops 100 feet in the next mile. The rapids become more difficult.

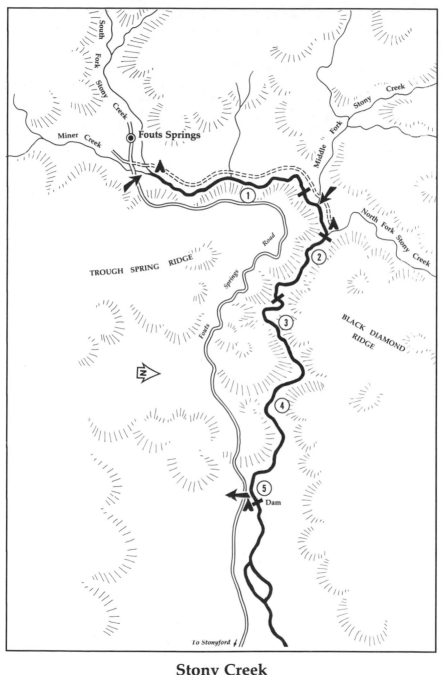

Stony Creek

1.9 **UNNAMED RAPID (IV).** A long cascade. Scout left.

2.6 **UNNAMED RAPID (IV)** at a blind left turn. Scout as best you can from the right.

3.5 Gorge opens up and rapids become easier.

5 *TAKE-OUT* ◆ *HAZARD* ◆ A dangerous take-out. To catch the eddy on the right, boats have to float within a few feet of the brink of a 40-foot waterfall over an old, silted-up diversion dam. Consider stopping upstream and lining the boats down.

Eel River

Eel River country is a land of heavy rain, floods, and slides. During the devastating "thousand-year" flood of December 1964, the Eel's peak flow at Scotia (upstream from the mouth of the Van Duzen River, a major tributary) was measured at 752,000 cfs. Its highest recorded flow is 35 per cent larger than the greatest ever measured on the Klamath, though it drains an area only a quarter the size of the Klamath's watershed.

Early river runners who knew the Middle and Main Forks of the Eel before 1964 have reported that the flood made both runs considerably easier by rearranging and silting up the rapids. Huge slides dumped countless tons of rocks and soil into the river channel. Years later, the Eel was still laboring to remove the immense gravel bars deposited by the flood. Rapid erosion is characteristic of the the North Coast mountain ranges, whose primary components are the weak rocks of the Franciscan Complex, fragments of sea bed scraped up onto the edge of the continental shelf. But there is little doubt that destructive logging practices, like clear-cutting entire hillsides, accelerated the process in this and other floods.

The main stem of the Eel* rises at the foot of Bald Mountain (6739′) in Mendocino National Forest and flows south for twenty miles before it swings northwest into its final path to the ocean. This curious drainage pattern, shaped like a fish hook, is repeated by the North and Middle Forks of the Eel. The upper sections of all these streams were already established 30 to 50 million years ago, flowing southward from the Klamath Range along a gently-sloping plain toward the sea, which covered the present Bay Area and Central Valley. In the past 5 to 10 million years, a northward-moving ripple of uplift has thrust the Coast Range above the sea and tilted the lower paths of the rivers, forcing them to turn west and northwest to find new outlets.

The Eel has long been a target of dam builders. Two are presently in place on the upper Eel: Scott Dam, which retains the waters of Pillsbury Reservoir, and Cape Horn Dam, from whose small Van Arsdale Reservoir a private utility diverts Eel River water into the East Fork of the Russian River via a pipeline driven through the intervening ridge. Beginning in April of most years, the Main Eel is reduced to a trickle while a steady flow is sent down the Russian. The Russian and Trinity River pipelines are examples of what water developers have in mind for the North Coast rivers in the future.

Doug Carson

156

In the 1960's the Army Corps of Engineers proposed a 730-foot-high dam on the Middle Fork of the Eel at Dos Rios to divert water into the Sacramento Valley for shipment farther south. With a capacity of 7.6 million acre-feet, Dos Rios Reservoir would have dwarfed Shasta (4.5 million acre-feet), presently the largest man-made lake in California. Meanwhile, the U.S. Bureau of Reclamation announced plans for a 553-foot-high dam on the Main Eel at English Ridge, downstream from Hearst, along with a pipeline to send water from the new reservoir to polluted Clear Lake. Critics commented that this means of cleaning up Clear Lake sounded about as efficient as running water from a garden hose into a dirty swimming pool.

As it turned out, Governor Ronald Reagan finally decided to oppose Dos Rios Dam and to support State Senator Peter Behr's tough version of a California Wild and Scenic Rivers Act, which became law in 1972. Both dam projects were eventually shelved. The law prohibits the construction of more dams or diversion structures, except for local needs, on most stretches of the Eel and a number of other Coast Range rivers. However, it provides for a review by March 1985 of needs for water supply and flood control** on the Eel. If the state Department of Water Resources recommends against more dams at this time, the Eel will probably be safe for another decade.

*The river was named in 1850 by the explorer Josiah Gregg after a member of his party successfully traded a broken skillet to local Indians for a mess of eels. The Indians called the river "Weeyot."
**Studies by the DWR have shown that even the huge Dos Rios Dam would scarcely have affected the level of the Eel downstream during the December 1964 flood.

Eel River

Pillsbury Run

Scott Dam (Pillsbury Reservoir) to Bucknell Creek

Difficulty: III +. **Gradient:** 30 ft./mi.

Length: 5.7 miles. Longer and shorter runs possible.

Drainage: 290 sq. mi. **Elevation at Put-in:** 1700'.

Season: December–April for rafts; nearly year round for kayaks. Low summer releases from Scott Dam begin in May and are usually close to 300 cfs. The river is sometimes too low even for kayaks in July and August.

Runnable Levels: 200/500–6000 cfs.

Flow Information: (916) 322-3327. Release from Lake Pillsbury.

Scenery: Excellent. **Solitude:** Very good.

Rafts: A rainy-season run. Upstream dams shut off much of the flow in April. Larger rafts need about 900 cfs; small rafts, about 500 cfs, though they can scrape down as low as 300 cfs with a few carries. Unseasonal rains in May and November sometimes bring the river back up to runnable levels.

Kayaks: Fine, technical low-water run down to 200 cfs. Narrow, rocky chutes require finesse to avoid broaching. For tough intermediates.

Open Canoes: Experts willing to portage several times can run the river at flows below 1000 cfs.

Commercial Raft Trips: None.

Water: Cloudy during rainy season; clear thereafter. Not drinkable. Few side streams, so carry your own water.

Camping: Primitive camping at the take-out. If you can stand to camp by a reservoir, there are Forest Service campgrounds around Pillsbury.

Maps: Lake Pillsbury (USGS 7.5'); Lake Pillsbury, Potter Valley (USGS 15'); Mendocino National Forest; Mendocino and Lake Counties (AAA).

Auto Shuttle: 6 miles; 15 minutes.

Emergency Telephone Numbers:
Mendocino County Sheriff (Ukiah): (707) 462-2951.
Mendocino National Forest (Upper Lake): (707) 275-2361.

Logistics: Turn east off Highway 101 just north of Ukiah at Calpella, follow Highway 20 five miles, and turn left (north) on Potter Valley Road, which runs along the East Fork of the Russian River. At the town of Potter Valley, turn right onto the Eel River Road and continue to the bridge across the Eel.

Roads run along both banks to Scott Dam, ten miles upstream. Put in at the Elk Mountain Road bridge across the Eel a mile downstream from Scott Dam, or at Benmore Creek (mile 0.6). The Bucknell Creek take-out (mile 5.7) is accessible only from the south (left) bank, so boaters usually take the south bank road and try to dodge the logging trucks that roar up and down it on weekdays. If you use the north bank road, the first take-out is the Eel River Road bridge, making the run nearly nine miles.

At this point, not far from its headwaters, the Eel River canyon is still quite narrow. The roads on both banks perch high above the stream bed most of the way, so the run has the feel of wilderness. From May through the summer and early fall, the Pillsbury run is a favorite of kayakers working on their technical skills. In winter and spring, when rain runoff swells the river, rafters and kayakers alike enjoy the good ride and the excellent scenery. Those who want a longer float can take out at the Eel River Road bridge near the top of Van Arsdale Reservoir (mile 8.8). For all runs below Van Arsdale, see the Dos Rios to Alderpoint section of the Eel.

Mile by Mile Guide

0	Elk Mountain Road bridge. Put in just upstream on the right bank.
0.6	*RIVER ACCESS.* Benmore Creek enters on the left. Alternate put-in.
0–1.5	Easy rapids. Erosion on the banks mars the scenery a bit.
1.5–1.8	A sharp left bend in the river announces four Class III rapids in quick succession, separated by short pools. The third rapid, called **Dennis's Menace**, is very difficult at high flows, when big holes appear.
1.8–4.4	Occasional Class II–III rapids. The canyon walls narrow beneath a wooded ridge.
4.5	**DOUBLE FALLS (III+).** Watch for a horizon line across the river at the end of a pool. Two steep, rocky drops at low flows; at higher flows, the drops merge. Scout on the right.
4.8	The canyon walls begin to open up, and the rapids ease.
5.7	*TAKE-OUT.* Bucknell Creek enters on the left. Take out just downstream on the left, or continue to the Eel River Road bridge (mile 8.8).

159

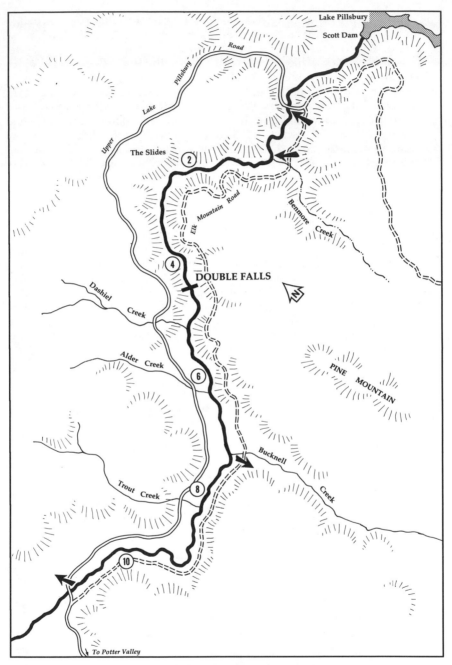

Eel River: Pillsbury Run

Eel River

Dos Rios to Alderpoint

Difficulty: II–III.   **Gradient:** 13 ft./mi.

Length: 46 miles; 3-5 days. Longer runs possible.

Drainage: 2107 sq. mi. at Fort Seward (6 miles below take-out).

Season: December–May. Days are cold and often rainy through March, so April and May are best. Upstream winds and skimpy dam releases make the going slow in the summer.

Runnable Levels: 500/800–20,000 cfs.   **Elevation at put-in:** 870'.

Flow Information: (916) 322-3327. Flow at Fort Seward.

Scenery: Excellent.   **Solitude:** Excellent.

Rafts: Upstream winds play havoc with rafts. For this reason, a minimum flow of 2000 cfs is recommended for raft trips. If flows are low, get an early start and cover most of your miles before afternoon winds blow you back upstream.

Kayaks: Good crafts to face the wind, but you'll have to pack light for such a long trip. This run is suitable for novices as long as they are accompanied by more experienced boaters.

Open Canoes: Excellent run for advanced canoeists and top-level intermediates at low flows, though several portages may be necessary. Canoes catch less wind than rafts and carry a lot more gear than kayaks, so summer runs are feasible.

Special Hazards: Isolated wilderness area. It's a long hike out in case of trouble. Watch for rattlesnakes.

Commercial Raft Trips: Usually offered only by a few outfitters based in the area, or by special charters. No list available.

Camping: Beautiful sandy beaches all along the river.

Water: Brown at high flows, clear at lower flows. Drinking the main river is not recommended, but side creeks are probably safe. Purify to be sure.

Maps: Dos Rios, Iron Peak, Updegraff Ridge, Lake Mountain, Jewett Rock, Alderpoint (USGS 7.5'); Laytonville, Spyrock, Kettenpom, Alderpoint (USGS 15'); Mendocino and Lake Counties, Northwestern California (AAA).

Auto Shuttle: 82 miles; 3 hours.

Emergency Telephone Numbers:
Mendocino County Sheriff (Willits): (707) 459-4652.
Humboldt County Sheriff (Eureka): (707) 445-7251.

Logistics: To reach the put-in at the confluence of the Middle and Main Forks of the Eel, drive 13 miles north of Willits on Highway 101 and turn east on Highway 162 (Covelo Road). The confluence and the hamlet of Dos Rios are about 15 miles up the road. Put in at a big gravel bar on the left bank of the Main Eel just above the confluence, or on the Middle Fork between the bridge and the confluence, or just downstream at Dos Rios.

To reach the take-out, return to Highway 101, either via Covelo Road or by means of a shorter dirt road from Dos Rios to Laytonville. Follow 101 north, exit at Garberville, and turn east onto Alderpoint Road. A bridge crosses the river 21 miles ahead, just beyond the small town of Alderpoint. If you don't have a four-wheel drive vehicle, you'll have to carry your gear from the right bank take-out up a fairly steep dirt road to the bridge. An easier take-out may be found half a mile upstream, where a dirt road runs south from Alderpoint to the left bank of the river.

The Eel is a river of contrasts. Its extensive watershed receives 50 to 90 inches of annual precipitation, almost entirely from November through April, and its winter flows commonly surpass 100,000 cfs during big storms. The awesome flood of late December 1964 was by far the biggest on any California river since stream flows have begun to be measured. Yet because of upstream dams, by late April only a tiny trickle of water meanders down the wide, gravel-choked bed of the main stem of the Eel. Now that the Trinity's situation has been partially rectified, the Eel may be the most flagrant example in the state of a major river in need of a higher guaranteed minimum flow. If the river below Dos Rios remains runnable through May, it is only because the undammed Middle Fork supplies sufficient water.

The Dos Rios to Alderpoint run is the heart of the Main Eel, with rugged scenery, fine beaches, and a sprinkling of good rapids. It has long been a classic spring trip for Sierra Club kayakers, who have floated the river over the Memorial Day weekend for the last twenty years. For longer runs, boaters can put in upstream at Van Arsdale Reservoir (eleven river miles to Hearst), Hearst (seventeen miles to Outlet Creek), or Outlet Creek (six miles to Dos Rios), adding more than 30 miles of Class II+ water. But these upper sections are dried up by dam diversions beginning in April of most years. Boaters can also float more Class I–II river at the lower end of this run by taking out at Fort Seward, six miles below Alderpoint, or at Eel Rock, twelve miles beyond Fort Seward. Better yet, combine the lovely Middle Fork of the Eel, also described in this guide book, with the Dos Rios to Alderpoint run for a 77-mile wilderness float.

Only two roads reach the river between Dos Rios and Alderpoint, but the tracks of the Northwestern Pacific Railroad follow the Eel from above Dos Rios to its mouth south of Eureka. Train traffic is extremely scarce and at times non-existent—the railroad has been trying to abandon the run, so far unsuccessfully—but the road bed provides a way out in case of emergencies, and the railroad mileage markers (included in the guide below) are a handy way of keeping track of your progress. Wintertime high water periodically rearranges the rapids of the Main Eel, so the following descriptions are brief and general.

Mile by Mile Guide

0	Confluence of Main and Middle Forks. See Logistics for put-ins. RR mile 165-166.
0–13	Easy rapids for the first thirteen miles.
2.5	USGS gaging station on the left.
5	Woodman Creek enters on the left.
12.7	Shell Rock Creek enters on the left.
13.3	**SPYROCK (III).** The rapid is at the base of Spyrock, a 600' spire on the right bank. Good side hike, but watch out for rattlesnakes. Spyrock Road leads from the left bank out to Highway 101—a long, twisting 15 miles—but may have locked gates and should be used for emergency access only. From here to mile 43.5 the rapids are more difficult.
17.6	**BLUE ROCK (III).** Blue Rock Creek enters on the left.
23	North Fork of the Eel enters on the right. By May there is little water, but some nice warm swimming holes remain. RR mile 188.
30	**ISLAND MOUNTAIN FALLS (III).** Possibly the biggest rapid on this run. The river drops through a cordon of huge boulders blocking the channel. Scout on the left. RR mile 194.
30.5	Railroad bridge. The river begins a long bend around the peninsula called Island Mountain while the railroad tunnels straight through it. A dirt road (private property; emergency access only) leads from the left bank to Bell Springs Road, which runs north-south between Highway 101 and the Alderpoint-Garberville Road.
33.5	**KEKAWAKA FALLS (III).** A long rapid best scouted on the right. Kekawaka Creek enters on the right five miles downstream. The name may mean "Frog Creek" in Lassik Indian dialect.
34	Railroad tracks appear again on river right.

39   **MILE 201 RAPID (III).** At high water this is the most difficult rapid on the river. The rapid is half a mile below RR mile 201.

43.5   Class I-I+ rapids the rest of the way.

45   Railroad bridge across the river.

46.5   *TAKE-OUT.* A dirt road connects the left bank with Alderpoint.

47   *TAKE-OUT.* A more difficult take-out is on the right bank just upstream from the bridge where Alderpoint Road crosses the river. Or continue downstream for more easy water and good scenery—to Fort Seward (6 miles) or Eel Rock (18 miles).

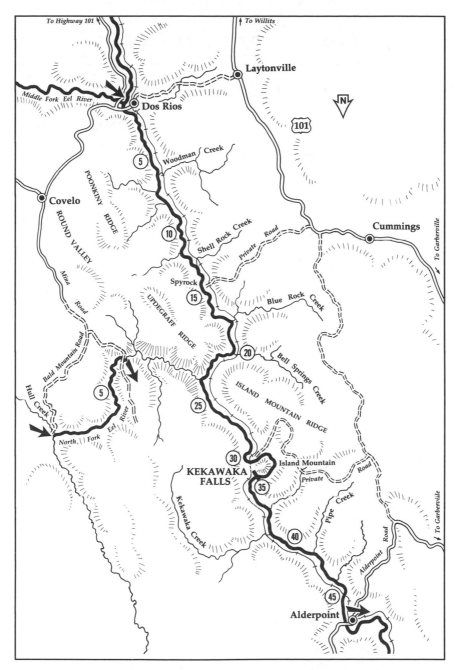

Eel River & North Fork Eel

North Fork Eel River

Hulls Creek to Mina Road

Difficulty: III.   **Length:** 8.4 miles.
Gradient: 33 ft./mi.   **Drainage:** 248 sq. mi. at Mina.
Season: December–April. Runnable into May in wet years.
Runnable Levels: 200/300–4000 cfs.   **Elevation at Put-in:** 1300′.
Flow Information: Not on flow phone. For a rough estimate, take two thirds of the flow of the South Fork Eel at Leggett.
Scenery: Excellent.   **Solitude:** Excellent.
Rafts: Small rafts only below 600 cfs.
Kayaks: A good intermediate run. Even novices can run it at low flows in the company of more experienced boaters.
Open Canoes: Advanced canoeists can run the North Fork at low flows with a few possible portages.
Commercial Raft Trips: None.
Water: Don't drink from the North Fork or Hull Creek. The few side creeks are probably drinkable. Purify to be sure.
Camping: Boaters usually run the North Fork in one day. There are no campgrounds near the river area, but there is a primitive campsite at the take-out (left bank, downstream from the bridge). Its legal status is unknown. A hotel/cafe in Covelo has inexpensive rooms.
Maps: Long Ridge, Mina (USGS 7.5′); Mendocino and Lake Counties (AAA).
Auto Shuttle: 15 miles; nearly 1 hour on a winding dirt road with some spectacular views. Vandalism has been reported at the put-in, so you may not want to leave vehicles there.
Emergency Telephone Numbers:
  Trinity County Sheriff (Weaverville): (916) 623-2611.
  Mendocino County Sheriff (Willits): (707) 459-4652.
Logistics: Follow Highway 101 12 miles north of Willits and turn east on Highway 162 (Covelo Road) to the town of Covelo, located in the beautiful Round Valley 29 miles ahead. Continue north beyond town on Mina Road, which becomes a well-maintained dirt road as it climbs out of the valley. The road forks 12 miles north of Covelo. The left fork, Mina Road, leads to the take-out five miles away. The right fork, Bald Mountain Road, eventually becomes Hull Creek Road and leads to the put-in about ten miles ahead. This road crosses private property, and the put-in may be on private property, so be courteous and ask permission where appropriate.

The North Fork Eel is a little-known river in a beautiful portion of the Coast Range between Round Valley and Six Rivers National Forest. The river's headwaters, twenty miles north of the put-in at Hull Creek, drain the southern end of the Mad River Ridge and the eastern slopes of Grizzly Mountain (5456'). Though the North Fork is basically a rain-fed river, some snow melt from its upper watershed—especially the Hull Creek drainage, whose highest points are above 6000'—prolongs its boating season several weeks beyond the end of the rainy season.

The run described below is a scenic wilderness float with several Class III rapids, most of which occur toward the beginning. It's difficult to determine your progress because few side streams enter, and there are no dramatic changes in the character of the river canyon. Though there are few significant rapids in the last half, fallen trees and slides could block the narrow stream bed, so boaters should remain alert.

Several miles below the take-out at Mina Road, the river carves its way through Split Rock Ridge, dropping more than 100 feet per mile on the last four miles of its plunge down to the Main Eel confluence. The few experts who have run this dangerous six-mile stretch, including co-author Jim Cassady, don't want to do it again.

Mile by Mile Guide
See previous river map.

0	Put in at the road's end on the left bank of the river, just downstream from the mouth of Hull Creek. Good rapids are scattered throughout the run, but more of the tougher ones (mainly Class III) occur in the first few miles. Always be alert for unexpected brush or changes in the rapids.
1.3	Round Valley Indian Reservation land on the left bank almost all the way to the take-out.
1.5	Lowsy Creek enters on the right.
2.5	**THE NARROWS (III). Recognition:** Small slide on the right bank alongside a pool above a right-hand bend. Scout from the right. **The rapid:** At the bend boats start down a rocky chute leading toward two big boulders. At higher flows the slot between the boulders is a vertical drop. At low flows rafts must be tipped on their sides to fit through it.
3.5	**UNNAMED RAPID (III).** A long boulder garden. Scout on the left and portage if necessary on either side.
6.5	Bear Canyon on the left.
8.4	*TAKE-OUT.* Downstream side of the Mina Road bridge (left bank).

Middle Fork Eel River

Black Butte River to Dos Rios

Difficulty: II–IV$_6$.   **Length:** 30 miles; 3 days (2 if you hurry).
Gradient: 20 ft./mi.   **Elevation at Put-in:** 1575′.
Drainage: 529 sq. mi. at put-in; 745 sq. mi. at take-out.
Runnable Levels: 400/700–10,000 cfs.   **Season:** March–May.
Flow Information: Not available on flow phone. As a rough guess, before the date (usually in April) when upstream dams cut off most of the Main Eel's flow, take half the flow of the Main Eel at Fort Seward. After that date, the Middle Fork provides 80 per cent or more of the flow of the Main Eel at Fort Seward.
Scenery: Excellent.   **Solitude:** Excellent.
Rafts: This would be a favorite spring run except for the big rapid, Coal Mine Falls, which most rafters should portage—not an easy task.
Kayaks: A fine wilderness kayak run. Advanced and expert kayakers often negotiate Coal Mine Falls successfully. Portage if in doubt. Intermediates and even novices can run the Middle Eel in the company of experts, but they should portage a few rapids.
Open Canoes: Advanced and expert canoeists can run the Middle Eel, but they should portage several rapids.
Special Hazards: (1) Coal Mine Falls. (2) The Middle Fork can rise in a hurry during heavy rains. Don't get caught on the river at high water. During the 1964 flood the Middle Eel peaked at 270,000 cfs! (3) Novice boaters should keep in mind that the isolation of this run and several very difficult rapids make it potentially a more dangerous river than the Class II–III rating of most of its rapids would indicate.
Commercial Raft Trips: Rare, but some companies occasionally offer runs, usually on a charter basis. For a list of outfitters, contact Bureau of Land Management, 555 Leslie, Ukiah CA 95842; phone below.
Water: Except for Mill Creek, which drains populated Round Valley, both the side creeks and the main river are probably drinkable. Purify to be sure.
Camping: Numerous sites along the river except in the vicinity of Coal Mine Falls.
Maps: Covelo East, Newhouse Ridge (USGS 7.5′); Eden Valley, Laytonville (USGS 15′); Mendocino National Forest; North Bay Counties and Northwestern California (AAA).

Auto Shuttle: 25 miles; 1 hour.

Emergency Telephone Numbers:

Mendocino County Sheriff (Willits): (707) 459-4652.

BLM (Ukiah): (707) 462-3873.

Logistics: To reach the take-out, turn east off Highway 101 some 13 miles north of Willits onto Covelo Road, which follows Outlet Creek and then the Main Eel for 16 miles to Dos Rios, a hamlet at the confluence of the Main and Middle Eel. Take out on a gravel bar on the left bank of the Middle Eel just downstream from the bridge. Look at the dirt road leading down to the take-out before you attempt it in your vehicle.

To reach the put-in, cross the bridge and continue to Covelo. One mile north of the little town, turn right on Mendocino Pass Road, which crosses the Middle Eel at its confluence with the Black Butte River some ten miles ahead. There are several possible put-ins; a good one is at a Forest Service campground on the Black Butte River just upstream from the confluence.

The Middle Fork of the Eel rises among 7000' peaks in the Yolla Bolly Wilderness, just south of the headwaters of the Mad and the South Fork Trinity. Like the Main Eel, the Middle Fork first flows south, then swings toward the Pacific. Unlike the Main Eel, the Middle Fork is still undammed, and its watershed is higher, so its boating season is later and longer than the Main Eel's.

The Middle Eel is one of the best long wilderness runs in California. It can be combined with the Dos Rios-Alderpoint section of the Main Eel for a major float 77 miles in length. Only the difficult passage at Coal Mine Falls, a major obstacle that is often portaged, keeps the Middle Eel from becoming popular.

For the first 24 miles river runners enjoy scenic rolling hills and moderate Class II rapids; then the river changes character, and boaters must face several big rapids. Just above the confluence with the Main Eel at Dos Rios, the river drops through a steep-walled three-mile gorge. If the Army Corps of Engineers had had its way, the Dos Rios High Dam would have flooded this gorge and more than 30 miles of the canyon upstream.

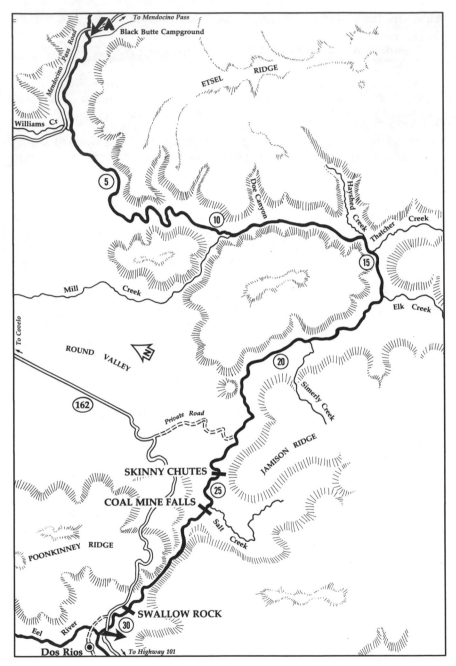

Middle Fork Eel River

Mile by Mile Guide

0   Confluence of the Middle Eel and the Black Butte River. There are several possible put-ins. A good one is at the Forest Service campground on the Black Butte just upstream from the confluence.

0–24   Class II rapids for the first 24 miles. A good current helps boaters make time.

10.1   Mill Creek enters on the right. A dirt road across private property leads out of the canyon from the right bank. For emergency use only.

14.2   Hayshed Creek enters on the left. Nice swimming holes up the creek.

14.7   Thatcher Creek enters on the left.

16   Elk Creek enters from a large valley on the left.

23   Levi Ranch (private property) has a dirt road out of the canyon from the right bank. For emergency use only (with permission).

24.6   **SKINNY CHUTES (IV). Recognition:** The rapid is just downstream from a heavily eroded, rocky area on the right bank. Scout both sections of the rapid from either bank before running any of it. **The rapid:** Rocks and boulders are everywhere. The right side becomes an unrunnable sieve. There are no clean routes.

25.2   Salt Creek enters on the left. A long Class III rapid follows, then the big one.

25.8   ◆ *POSSIBLE PORTAGE* ◆
         COAL MINE FALLS (V–VI). Recognition: Big boulders and a horizon line across the river. The left bank shows scars from the old mine. Scout and portage along either bank. Neither is easy. **The rapid:** Big boulder-choked drops over landslide rubble in the river channel. Boats must move quickly from one side to the other or face disaster. Kayaks usually fare better because of their greater maneuverability (as would self-bailing rafts). The portage is difficult, tempting many rafters to run the rapid against their better judgment. Consequently, the river has claimed lots of equipment at this spot.

26.2   The river enters a deep gorge.

29.8   **SWALLOW ROCK (IV).** Houses appear along the right bank as the road approaches the river, and a huge boulder blocks the main channel. The chute to its right ends in a nasty hole with a rock just downstream.

30.2   *TAKE-OUT.* Gravel bar on the left bank downstream from the bridge. This is one of the put-ins for the Dos Rios–Alderpoint run. The Main Eel confluence is just ahead.

I love springtime boating, but you have to watch out for high water. On several memorable occasions I've been caught on a rising river with no way out but downstream. A few years ago our small party camped overnight in the wilderness section of the South Fork American below Lotus and was surprised by a big rainstorm. The river was flowing about 4000 cfs when we went to bed and about 20,000 when we got up. The South Fork Gorge run was an amazing experience at that level.

The first time it happened we weren't prepared. I had invited four college buddies on a spring break float down the Middle Fork of the Eel in March 1974. We paddled a flimsy old "Hypalon" and failed to bring wet suits. The river was high, and it drizzled the night before the put-in. But the weather cleared, allowing us to cover a dozen miles the first day. The second day we had to float in the rain. We camped a few miles above Coal Mine Falls. About bedtime it started to pour, and it kept up until dawn. We staggered out of our tents the next morning to find that the water level had risen four feet. The rock to which we had tied our boat was under water, and I had to swim out to get the line before the raft worked loose. And so we set out downstream.

Skinny Chutes and the Class III rapid below Salt Creek were big but washed out, and we got down them without any trouble. But suddenly Coal Mine Falls was upon us, and there was no place to stop upstream—not an eddy in sight, just swift, muddy currents racing along the foot of a cliff. We had no choice but to head straight down the rapid. The first hole filled our wobbly raft to the brim. When we tried to straighten the boat, three wooden paddles broke. Fortunately for us, by then the boat was too heavy to flip, and we managed to hang on through the whole foaming ride. No one had to swim. When we finally got the raft to shore, we hiked back upstream and stared in amazement at the rapid we had blundered through.

—Spreck Rosekrans

South Fork Eel River

Branscomb and Tenmile Creek Runs

Branscomb or Tenmile Creek to Big Bend

Difficulty: IV–V.   **Gradient:** 35 ft./mi.

Length: 16 miles. Longer runs possible, but no shorter runs.

Drainage: 44 sq. mi. at Branscomb; 244 sq. mi. at Leggett, 5 miles downstream from Big Bend.

Elevation at Put-in: 1380′ at Branscomb.

Season: December–early April. Rainy season only. Even during the winter, if it hasn't rained recently, the South Fork may be too low to run.

Runnable Levels: 900/1200–8000 cfs at Leggett. Flow at Branscomb is about a quarter of the flow at Leggett. If you plan to put in at Tenmile Creek, the minimum flow at Leggett is 1500 cfs for kayaks and 2000 or more for rafts.

Flow information: (916) 322-3327. Flow at Leggett.

Scenery: Excellent.   **Solitude:** Excellent.

Rafts: Need a minimum flow of 1200 cfs at Leggett to put in at Branscomb and 2000 cfs to put in on Tenmile Creek. Small rafts only at flows below 1800 (Branscomb put-in) or 3000 (Tenmile Creek put-in). All flows refer to Leggett.

Kayaks: The South Fork Eel is one of California's finest rainy-season runs for expert kayakers. Advanced kayakers can run it at moderate flows if they are accompanied by experts familiar with the river.

Open Canoes: Not recommended, although it has been done (by seasoned experts at low flows). Downstream from Big Bend is an excellent Class II run suitable for intermediate canoeists.

Special Hazards: In 1982 a huge tree blocked the river a few miles downstream from the put-in. It may be gone, but another may have lodged somewhere else. Be alert. Days are short when the river is running, so get an early start and be prepared for cold weather.

Commercial Raft Trips: Rare, but some outfitters will book special charters.

Water: Cloudy during and immediately after rains; green otherwise. The South Fork, Tenmile Creek, and Rattlesnake Creek are probably not drinkable. Other side streams probably are. Purify to be sure.

Camping: Good campsites may be found in the first mile or two below Tenmile Creek, and toward the end of the gorge, in the last few miles above Rattlesnake Creek. Campsites are scarce in the middle of the gorge. Off-river camping is available at a roadside rest area on Highway 101 about half way between the Tenmile Creek put-in and Leggett. At the take-out, Big Bend Lodge offers food, drink, and overnight accommodations in a lovely riverside setting. See the mile guide below for details.

Maps: Leggett, Lincoln Ridge, Tanoak Park [for Tenmile Creek] (USGS 7.5'); Mendocino and Lake Counties (AAA).

Auto Shuttle: 40 miles; over 1 hour (Branscomb put-in). 12 miles; 20 minutes (Tenmile Creek put-in).

Emergency Telephone Numbers:
Mendocino County Sheriff (Willits): (707) 459-4652.

Logistics: To reach the Branscomb put-in, follow Highway 101 24 miles north of Willits to Laytonville, turn west on Branscomb Road, pass through the hamlet of Branscomb, cross the South Fork, and turn north on Wilderness Lodge Road. Just before the end of the road, about three miles farther, look for the next to last house on the right — the one with abalone shells lining the fence. It belongs to Betty Barnes, who allows boaters to put in on her land and even to camp there. Call ahead for permission — (707) 984-6632 — and if possible bring her something for her hospitality. Alternate put-ins of uncertain legal status are at the bridge where Wilderness Lodge Road crosses the river, or farther upstream at the Branscomb Road bridge. Please respect property rights. To put in on Tenmile Creek, follow 101 about seven miles north from Laytonville. Put in just below the gaging station where the creek begins to turn away from the highway.

To reach the take-out, exit 101 at Cummings, about seven miles south of Leggett, and follow the Drive-Thru Tree Road (old Highway 101) for three miles. At the Big Bend Lodge sign, turn left onto a one-mile dirt road that leads to the lodge and the river. There is a small take-out fee unless you stay at one of the lodge's pleasant, secluded cottages. (Big Bend Lodge, PO Box 111, Leggett, CA 95455; phone (707) 984-6321.) The next take-out — a mediocre site — is five miles downstream on the left bank, just upstream from the Highway 1 bridge across the river at Leggett.

The tiny watershed of the South Fork Eel, squeezed between the ocean and the Main Eel, is fed entirely by rainfall (80 inches annually) and ground water. Because its headwaters a few miles upstream from Branscomb are at only 4000', snow melt is negligible. The South Fork rises quickly and drops quickly, offering boaters only limited opportunities to enjoy it at its best. But the river is less than four hours north of San Francisco, so rafters and kayakers from the Bay Area can schedule trips on short notice when conditions are right. River runners should keep an eye on the weather and arrive a day or two after a big storm has passed through the area. The South Fork will still be up but running green and fairly clear.

Rainy-season river runners with the necessary skills should not miss the exciting gorge of the South Fork Eel. Those who put in at Branscomb, where the river is hardly larger than a creek, will enjoy six miles on a sparkling green stream winding through an intimate little canyon. Only a few big redwoods, notably those in the Nature Conservancy grove on Elder Creek*, have escaped the loggers, but the banks are lined with pine, Douglas fir, hemlock, oak, and madrone, and the scenery is fine all the way. The only difficult passage is a major rapid just above the Tenmile Creek confluence.

Another way to run the South Fork is to put in on Tenmile Creek where it leaves the highway and float six miles down to the river. The two runs are equal in length. The scenery along the creek is less impressive, but the Tenmile Creek run has the advantage of a much shorter shuttle entirely along Highway 101. It also has a lot more tough white water than the Branscomb run. Tenmile Creek is laced with Class IV rapids, especially in the last mile above its confluence with the South Fork. The creek carries less water than the river, so when the creek is high enough to run, the river itself may be very high indeed. The Tenmile Creek run is definitely for experts only in kayaks or self-bailing rafts.

The South Fork changes character where Tenmile Creek meets the river. Ahead is a rugged seven-mile gorge strewn with exhilarating Class IV and IV+ rapids and one bigger one that is usually portaged. The river rejoins the outskirts of civilization below Rattlesnake Creek, where Highway 101 perches precariously above the right bank.

Downstream from the Big Bend take-out, the South Fork Eel flows peacefully through its narrow canyon past magnificent giant redwoods in the Standish-Hickey State Recreation Area and Smithe Redwoods State Reserve. Boaters can continue their float another nine miles down to Redwood Flat, or even farther (Class II).

*Just downstream from the Branscomb put-in is Elder Creek, a rare protected area where the public can see a bit of the South Fork Eel as it was before miners, loggers, and developers arrived. The creek's watershed is owned by the Nature Conservancy, a non-profit conservation organization which buys and holds wilderness lands threatened by encroaching civilization until the government gets around to protecting them. Advance permission to hike on the Nature Conservancy's Northern California Coast Range Preserve is required. If you're already in Eel River country, call (707) 984-6653. Otherwise contact the West Coast office at 425 Bush St., San Francisco, CA 94105; phone (415) 777-0541.

Mile by Mile Guide

Branscomb Run

0	Put in near the end of Wilderness Lodge Road or at the bridge upstream (see Logistics). Please respect private property rights.
0–6	Class II rapids and a continuous drop in the river bed for the first six miles. The only big rapid is just above Tenmile Creek. Almost immediately, the river enters the Nature Conservancy's Northern California Coast Range Preserve along the watershed of Elder Creek. See above for details.
1.2	◆ *HAZARD* ◆ Elder Creek enters on the right. A big Ponderosa pine may still block the river below Elder Creek.
6	**TENMILE CREEK RAPID (IV).** Just above the mouth of Tenmile Creek, which enters on the right, is a steep, boulder-choked drop. Scout—and portage, if you don't like its looks —on the right.

Tenmile Creek Run

0	Put in on the right bank of the creek just below the gaging station.
0–4	Just below the put-in, Tenmile Creek bends left and away from the highway. The first four miles are fairly easy, with Class III and occasional Class IV rapids as the creek winds through open grazing country.
4–6	The creek's gradient steepens as it drops toward the South Fork confluence, and Class IV and V rapids come in quick succession. Most are long boulder gardens. In the last mile Tenmile Creek drops 100 feet.

South Fork Gorge

(Branscomb and Tenmile Creek Runs)

6	At the confluence of the South Fork Eel and Tenmile Creek is a large pool. Downstream, the river drops through a series of small, steep gorges for the next eight miles. Tenmile Creek usually adds considerably to the flow, so boaters must contend with more powerful currents. Of the dozen or more major rapids, most unnamed, only a few are listed below.

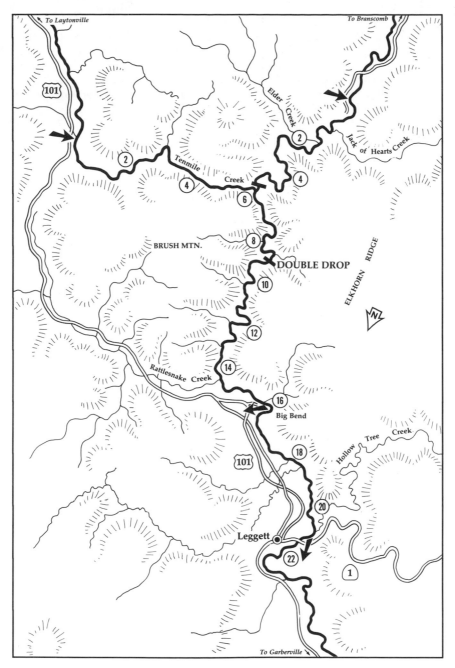

South Fork Eel River

9   ♦ *POSSIBLE PORTAGE* ♦
      DOUBLE DROP WHERE SLOTS DON'T MATCH (V–VI).
      Below a good-sized pool in a relatively straight stretch of river,
      the current pours over two successive drops. The rapid's
      name describes the boater's problem accurately enough. At
      lower flows, this rapid should definitely be portaged (right
      bank). At higher flows, some boaters run the rapid after
      scouting on both sides. No guarantees.

10.5   **THE HOLE THAT ATE CHICAGO (IV–V).** The river curves
      left through some tricky, boulder-studded drops, then
      plunges into a big hole with a rock just downstream. At high
      flows the hole becomes a monster. Scout on the left.

14.4   Private summer camp (left bank). The gorge begins to open
      up.

14.8   Rattlesnake Creek enters on the right, and the highway
      appears far above the river. Just downstream is the Hermitage
      (guarded private property) on the right. Emergency river
      access only with permission.

16   *TAKE-OUT.* Big Bend. Take out at Big Bend Lodge (right
      bank) for a small fee (see Logistics for details). Boaters may
      also continue downstream for more pleasant Class II rapids,
      require a flow of only 400 cfs at Leggett and can be negotiated
      through April in most years. A mile below Big Bend, Grizzly
      Creek Falls drops dramatically into the river. The next take-
      out is five miles below Big Bend, just above the Highway 1
      bridge at Leggett. This take-out (left bank) involves carrying
      gear up to the road. If you float past Leggett, you will enjoy
      the giant redwoods of the Standish-Hickey State Recreation
      Area (left bank). There is a good take-out nine miles below Big
      Bend at Redwood Flat. Take out at a mini-park on the right
      bank where the highway comes close to the river. Here the big
      trees are part of the Smithe Redwoods State Reserve.

Redwood Creek

Tall Trees Run

Lacks Creek to Orick

Difficulty: I–IVp. **Length:** 25 miles; 2–3 days.

Gradient: 30 ft./mi. (first half); 10 ft./mi. (second half).

Drainage: 278 sq. mi. at Orick. **Elevation at Put-in:** 480'.

Season: March–early May. Basically a rainy season run, but some snow melt from its 5000' headwaters extends the season a bit.

Runnable Levels: 400/600–3000 cfs at Orick.

Flow Information: (707) 443-9305. Flow at Orick.

Scenery: Excellent except for the extensive logging scars, now slightly overgrown, in the first 11 miles.

Solitude: Excellent.

Rafts: Small rafts under 900 cfs.

Kayaks: A warm-weather trip in plastic boats during May would be a joy, even if the flow is so low you have to bump, scrape, and carry.

Open Canoes: Experts who like secluded wilderness and who are willing to portage a few rapids will find this a marvelous low-water run.

Special Hazards: High water during the winter of 1982-83 rearranged Redwood Falls (mile 12.3) into a death trap. A portage is just barely possible, but it would be by far the worst in this guide book, and failure to stop in time could be disastrous. **We therefore recommend that boaters avoid this run** until the river moves the furniture around again. See the mile guide below for details. For updated information contact the Chief Ranger at Redwood National Park (address and phone below).

Commercial Raft Trips: Outfitters have run Redwood Creek in the past, but no commercial floats are scheduled while the death trap at Redwood Falls remains. For updated information and a list of outfitters, contact Chief Ranger, Redwood National Park, 1111 Second St., Crescent City, CA 95531; phone below.

Water: Don't drink from Redwood Creek. Side streams are probably OK. Purify to be sure.

Camping: Good campsites are rare the first nine miles because of extensive logging, but they are more plentiful farther downstream.

Maps: Coyote Peak (USGS 15'); Rodgers Peak, Orick (USGS 7.5'); Six Rivers National Forest; Redwood National Park; Northwestern California (AAA).

Auto Shuttle: 70 miles; 2 hours.

Emergency Telephone numbers:
Redwood National Park (Crescent City): (707) 464-6101.
Humboldt County Sheriff (Eureka): (707) 445-7251.
Six Rivers National Forest (Willow Creek): (916) 629-2118.

Logistics: Ten miles north of Eureka, turn off Highway 101 onto Highway 299. About 18 miles later, just beyond Lord Ellis summit, turn north on Bair Road. Cross Redwood Creek, turn left onto Stover Road, and follow it to the end. If you want to put in at Stover Ranch, ask permission first. The people at the ranch have always been hospitable toward river runners in the past; please be considerate of them. Otherwise find a suitable, legal spot somewhere upstream. To reach the take-out, drive north on Highway 101. One mile north of Orick, turn right on Bald Hills Road and almost immediately right onto a short dirt road leading down to the take-out.

Along the banks of the lower portion of Redwood Creek stand the tallest known trees in the world. The magnificent giant redwoods *(Sequoia sempervirens)* live as long as 3000 years, and some stand well over 300 feet tall. Not long ago their thick groves extended all the way up to Lacks Creek and beyond. But many fell during a race between timber companies and conservationists—a race that continued beyond 1968, when the federal government included 12,000 acres along Redwood Creek's lower watershed in Redwood National Park but left upstream trees open to exploitation.* The protected area was almost doubled in size ten years later, but too late: by then loggers had cleared the giants from both banks for miles below Coyote Creek, the upstream limit of the newly expanded park.

The dozen or so miles of virgin redwood that remain along the lower stretch of the river are among the most spectacular sights in this guide book, and for that reason Redwood Creek may one day become a classic spring wilderness run. Unfortunately, that day has been postponed by the transformation of Redwood Falls during the wet winter of 1982-83. After the next significant flood, perhaps as soon as next year, it may be transformed again. Until then, though, **boaters are urged not to attempt this run.** (See Special Hazards, above.)

Redwood Creek drains a narrow watershed between the Mad River on one side and the Trinity and the Klamath on the other. The region receives an average of more than 70 inches of precipitation annually. As with most small Coast Range rivers, the best time to run Redwood Creek is a couple of days after a good spring storm, when the stream is still up and when another big storm isn't on the way. Though most of the rapids are not difficult, the area is fairly remote, and the hazard of freshly downed trees is increased because upstream logging has left so many wooden carcasses along the banks. Though some new undergrowth has sprung up in the last few years, for the first eleven miles the river banks still show signs of the rush to cut the big redwoods before Congress could act to save them.

*This political struggle was the occasion of then-Governor Reagan's infamous alleged remark, "If you've seen one [redwood], you've seen 'em all."

Mile by Mile Guide

0	Stover Ranch (private property; permission to launch required). Put in at a large bar just upstream from Lacks Creek. If permission cannot be obtained, find a legal spot upstream.
0–10	The river drops swiftly through tight Class II and II+ rapids that require some maneuvering. Be alert for brush and snags.
4	Panther Creek enters on the left, just downstream from a logging bridge across the river. Like others in the area, it is a fine specimen of redwood construction.
6.2	Coyote Creek enters on the right, with its own redwood bridge just up the creek from its mouth. The boundary of Redwood National Park is just downstream.
7.2	Devil's Creek enters on the left as the river bends right.
9	Good campsites become more frequent from here on.
10–13	Three miles of Class III–IV rapids and a very hazardous portage at Redwood Falls.
11	Original boundary of the national park in 1968. First-growth redwoods begin to appear.
12	Class IV boulder garden spells trouble because it leads directly to Redwood Falls. Stop well upstream to scout (right bank). Walk all the way to Redwood Falls.
12.3	♦ *HAZARD* ♦ *PORTAGE* ♦ **REDWOOD FALLS (U)**. Also called **Rocky Gap**. Before the winter of 1982-83, a calm pool preceded a straight, unobstructed twelve-foot vertical drop that could be portaged without undue difficulty. By spring 1983, however, the pool had disappeared. Instead, a long, technical Class IV boulder garden led directly to the lip of a cascade choked with downed trees and undercut rocks. Worst of all, it would be easy to enter the rapid by mistake and to be swept into the falls.

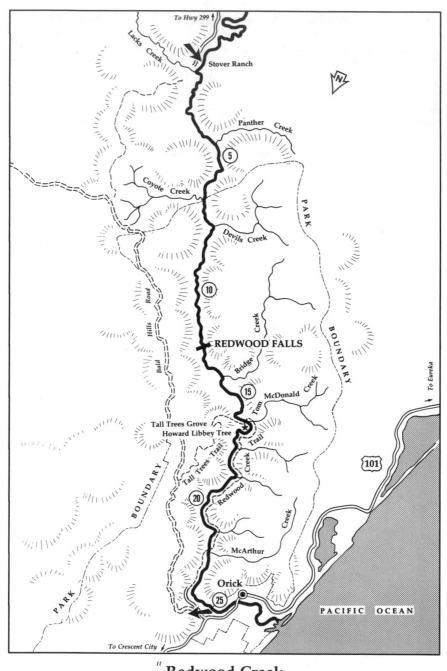

To Hwy 299

Stover Ranch

Lacks Creek

Panther Creek

⑤

Coyote Creek

PARK

Devils Creek

Creek

⑩

BOUNDARY

REDWOOD FALLS

Bridge

Bald

Hills Road

⑮ McDonald Creek

Tom

Tall Trees Grove
Howard Libbey Tree

Tall Trees Trail

Trail

Creek

101

BOUNDARY

⑳

Redwood

Creek

To Eureka

McArthur

PARK

Orick

㉕

PACIFIC OCEAN

To Crescent City

" **Redwood Creek**

In April 1983 we were rafting Redwood Creek, and about mile 12 we started looking for the landmark we remembered from the year before: a small slide on the right with a cliff below it, right at the lip of the falls. Unfortunately, there is a similar spot half a mile upstream, and I mistook it for the real one, thinking the falls had been washed out by winter floods. Then we started into a technical boulder garden I didn't remember, and we began to get suspicious. We managed to catch an eddy and walked downstream for a look at what may be the ugliest tangle of snags and rocks I've ever seen. Redwood Falls had been completely transformed.

The portage took three hours. We lined boats down the right side until the cliff blocked our way. Then we had to set up a line across the river to keep the boats from drifting downstream while we ferried across. Blow it and you die. We made the final carry on the left. I don't plan to run this river again until Mother Nature does a bit of redecorating. But I expect Redwood Creek to be runnable again in the future, and that's why I wanted to put it in this guide book.   —Jim Cassady

13	The river's gradient slackens, and only Class I rapids remain. But the biggest redwood groves are still ahead.
14	Bridge Creek enters on the left.
16.5	Tall Trees Grove (right bank), just upstream from a right-hand bend. With so many huge trees around, the grove is not all that easy to pick out from the river, so look for Tom McDonald Creek entering on the left and signs of a low-water trail on both banks. Downstream, the left bank has been logged. In the grove, clearly marked by signs, is the 368-foot Howard Libbey Tree, tallest in the world.
21.8	McArthur Creek enters on the left, and the Redwood Creek Trail crosses the river.
25	*TAKE-OUT.* A dirt road reaches the right bank several hundred yards upstream from the Highway 101 bridge.

Sacramento River

Box Canyon Dam to Shasta Reservoir

Difficulty: III–IV₅.   **Elevation at Put-in:** 3000′.

Length: 36 miles; 2–3 days. Shorter runs possible.

Gradient: 53 ft./mi. overall; 100 ft./mi. first 2 miles.

Drainage: 135 sq. mi. at put-in; 425 sq. mi. at take-out.

Season: April–mid-June. Hard-core boaters who don't mind cold weather can run the river from November or December on.

Runnable Levels: 200/300–3000 cfs at put-in. Toward the end of the run, the flow is usually two to three times greater.

Flow Information: (916) 322-3327. Release from Siskiyou.

Scenery: Very good.

Solitude: Good except in the Dunsmuir area, even though the highway and the railroad follow the river.

Rafts: The put-in just below Box Canyon Dam is very difficult. An alternate put-in is at Stink Creek, but launching here means missing two miles of excellent Class IV white water. (Small rafts only for the upper two miles.)

Kayaks: Advanced and expert run, though strong intermediates could run most sections at flows below 750 cfs with a few portages.

Open Canoes: Not recommended. Top experts could manage at very low flows (below 500 cfs) with several portages.

Commercial Raft Trips: One- and two-day trips. For a list of outfitters, contact Shasta-Trinity National Forest, PO Box 319, Mount Shasta, CA 96067; phone below.

Water: Clear and cold but not drinkable. Side creeks entering Box Canyon from the right and creeks on both sides below Dunsmuir may be drinkable. Purify to be sure.

Camping: Riverside camping is fine when the stream bends away from the highway and the railroad. Noisy trains are frequent at night. Developed Forest Service campgrounds at Sims Flat (mile 22) and Pollard Flat (mile 31.1).

Maps: Weed, Dunsmuir, Lamoine (USGS 15′); Shasta-Trinity National Forest; Northwestern California (AAA).

Auto Shuttle: 35 miles; 1 hour.

Emergency Telephone Numbers:
Siskiyou County Sheriff (Yreka): 911.
Shasta County Sheriff (Redding): 911.
Forest Service (Mount Shasta): (916) 246-5222.

Logistics: Follow Interstate 5 to the small town of Mount Shasta, 63 miles north of Redding. Take the Central Mount Shasta exit and follow the signs to Lake Siskiyou, veering right off South Old Stage Road to reach the reservoir. The put-in on the left bank about a quarter of a mile downstream from Box Canyon Dam is very difficult; boats must be lowered on lines the last 50 feet down to the river. To find this put-in, scout the maze of dirt roads on foot to find the dead-end spur road that will get you closest to the river. (The most direct route is four-wheel drive only.) A fisherman's trail leads from the end of the spur across a cobblestone slope, back toward the dam, and down to the river.

To reach an easier put-in at Stink Creek (mile 2), continue south on South Old Stage Road, jogging right across the railroad tracks. Turn right on Cantara Road, which turns into a dirt road as it descends into the canyon. Much of the property along the river is privately owned. Put in near the gaging station on the left bank, just upstream from the mouth of Stink Creek, which enters on river right.

To reach the take-out by car, exit I-5 at Dog Creek Road about four miles north of Lakehead. Turn left almost immediately onto Fender Ferry Road (dirt), which crosses the railroad, then the river. A poor road leads to the take-out just downstream from the bridge.

Only a dozen miles south of Mount Shasta, where Box Canyon Dam blocks its course, the Sacramento is just a small mountain river, not the enormous valley waterway it becomes as it makes its way south toward the Delta and San Francisco Bay. Nor is the Sacramento a Sierra river, though it eventually carries most of the runoff from that great range. The Sacramento rises on the eastern slopes of the Trinity Alps not far from the headwaters of the Trinity and the Shasta. It becomes a big river only after it is joined by the McCloud and the Pit.

These three streams converge north of Redding, but their confluences have been buried beneath the waters of the state's largest reservoir (4.5 million acre-feet) since 1949, when the Bureau of Reclamation completed massive Shasta Dam, a concrete gravity barrier 600' high and 880' thick at its base. Shasta produces electrical power and serves as the main storage area for summer irrigation water shipped south from the Delta to San Joaquin Valley farmers via the Delta-Mendota Canal, the federal twin of the California Aqueduct.

Upstream is a dam that should never have been built. The Sacramento flowed free above Shasta Lake until 1969, when the Siskiyou County Water District completed Box Canyon Dam. Because California has more than 1200 man-made lakes, and because the biggest, Shasta, is nearby, Siskiyou Reservoir has generated only a fraction of the tourist and recreational activity its proponents promised. It was proven in 1974 that Box Canyon Dam is far too small for flood control, when the downstream town of Dunsmuir suffered the worst inundation in its history. Finally, in 1984 Siskiyou County began to retrofit the dam to generate electricity which will be sold at wholesale prices to a private utility company.

Still, there is some of the Upper Sacramento left to enjoy between Siskiyou and Shasta Reservoirs. The rapids are good and the scenery is impressive, though solitude is minimal because Interstate 5 and the Southern Pacific Railroad tracks run alongside much of the way. The advantage is that there are numerous alternate river access points along the Upper Sacramento—far more than are listed in this guide—so boaters can run the entire river or choose the part that suits them.

The most popular sections are the first six miles (Class IV) from Box Canyon Dam to above Dunsmuir and the last fifteen miles (III–IV) from Sims Flat to Dog Creek. But the middle stretch between Castle Crag and Sims Flat (miles 12.8–21.8) has much to recommend it, including fine views of Mount Shasta and Class III–IV rapids, with a bigger one at Mears Creek. Running through the Dunsmuir area is much less scenic, though the nearly continuous Class III rapids allow little time for gazing at the town from the river.

Mile by Mile Guide

0	Lower boats down to the left bank of the river about a quarter mile below Box Canyon Dam (see **Logistics**).
0–2	Box Canyon. Nearly continuous Class IV rapids. Watch for downed trees across the narrow, rocky stream bed. Stop to scout whenever possible.
2	*RIVER ACCESS.* Stink Creek enters on the right. River access via Cantara Road. A much easier put-in, especially for rafts, but you miss what remains of Box Canyon. Downstream the rapids ease a bit, with longer pools between the drops.
2.4	First railroad bridge across the river. The tracks bend through the long Cantara Loop to gain elevation as they seek a way out of the steep-walled canyon.
3.2	Big Canyon Creek enters on the left, just downstream from another railroad bridge. In case of emergency, you can hike out of the river canyon via the railroad tracks and a trail that leads downstream to Shasta Retreat.

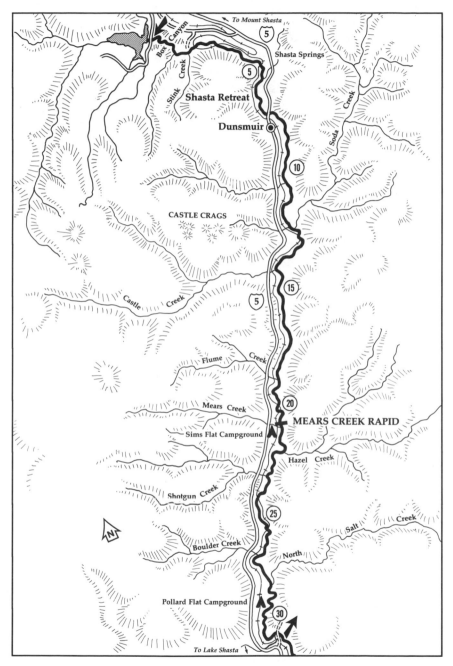

Upper Sacramento River

4.7   Foot bridge across the river.

5.4   Railroad bridge.

5.5   Mossbrae Falls, fed by springs, on the left.

6.2   *RIVER ACCESS.* Bridge. Shasta Retreat and the beginning of civilization are just downstream on the left bank.

6.2–12.8 Less scenic stretch as the river passes through the Dunsmuir area. Water quality declines, though it still looks good. Numerous Class III rapids in this stretch.

12.8   Castle Crags, towering over the right bank, is a spectacularly eroded collection of granite peaks and pillars.

12.8–21.9 Numerous Class III–IV rapids. This guide mentions only a few. A bigger one is at Mears Creek (mile 21).

16.4   Flume Creek enters on the right.

19.9   Railroad bridge and tunnel.

20.3   Railroad bridge.

21   **MEARS CREEK RAPID (V).** Upstream from the mouth of Mears Creek, which enters from the right, are three difficult drops down obstructed chutes. Scout and portage on the right.

21.8   Sims bridge. Better river access downstream.

22   *RIVER ACCESS.* Sims Flat, a developed Forest Service campground, offers good vehicle access on the left bank. The most popular run on the Upper Sacramento begins here.

22–32   Numerous Class III–IV rapids. Wider stream bed and more powerful currents.

22.1   Hazel Creek enters on the left.

23.5   Shotgun Creek enters on the right.

24.7   Railroad bridge.

26.1   Railroad bridge.

27.7   Gibson bridge crosses the river.

29.8   Railroad bridge.

31.1   Pollard Flat, a developed Forest Service campground on the right bank. Class II–III rapids the rest of the way.

32.6   Slate Creek enters on the right.

36   *TAKE-OUT.* Dog Creek enters on the right. Take out at a gravel bar on the left bank just downstream from Fender Ferry Road bridge, across from the mouth of the creek. The upper reaches of Shasta Reservoir are just downstream.

Trinity River

The Trinity, the Klamath's largest tributary, rises some twenty miles west of Mount Shasta. Nearby are the headwaters of the Sacramento, the Shasta, and the Scott. The Trinity runs first south, then west and north, looping around the snow-covered peaks of the Trinity Alps. By the time it joins the Klamath at Weitchpec, the Trinity has become a big river on a stately march through a lush, green canyon.

Though the countryside is rugged and forbidding, the river—called the "Hoopa" by local Indians—has been the scene of intense human activity since the middle of the last century, when it became known as the Trinity because a pioneer mistakenly thought it flowed into Trinidad Bay. The same man who misnamed the river, Pierson B. Reading, found gold along the Trinity in July 1848, only six months after Marshall's discovery of the precious metal at Sutter's Mill on the American. By 1851 10,000 men were mining the Trinity and its side creeks. Huge placer operations left mountains of rock tailings, many still visible along the upper Trinity in the Junction City area. Then came a long era of hydraulic mining, when high-pressure hoses washed away entire mountainsides in pursuit of the precious metal. Dredging operations around the turn of the century reworked the stream bed. As a result, the Trinity has been transformed by mining more than any other river in the Coast Range. The runs recommended in this guide are downstream from most of the damage.

The river has also been hard hit by modern water projects. The biggest is Trinity Dam, an earthfill barrier northeast of Weaverville completed by the Bureau of Reclamation in 1960. Its reservoir, now called Clair Engle Lake, is California's third largest (2.5 million acre-feet) and can hold two years of runoff from the Trinity's upper watershed of 700 square miles. Just downstream, smaller Lewiston Dam diverts 80 per cent of this water through a tunnel into Whiskeytown Reservoir, on a tributary creek of the Sacramento. The water eventually winds up on irrigated farms in the Central Valley.

Until January 1981, these dams reduced flows on the Trinity to a mere 150 cfs ten months of the year—far too little for downstream fish populations and water quality. At that time a decision by outgoing President Carter's Interior Secretary, Cecil Andrus, required the dams to release a minimum of 300 cfs year round, 450 in June and September, and 500 in July and August, except in critically dry years. So far this schedule is still in effect.

The Trinity drains the drier countryside of the eastern Coast Range and remains a small river from its headwaters all the way to the mouth of its North Fork, except where dams turn it into reservoirs. Still, the upper Trinity offers a dozen miles of Class III–III+ white water above Clair Engle Reservoir and 37 miles of Class II–II+ river between Lewiston and the North Fork. The latter section is a popular run for advanced open canoeists in the summer.

The Trinity is at its best downstream, where the river leaves behind the worst scars of the gold-mining era and flows through wetter country. Canyon Creek and the North Fork Trinity drain the southern slopes of the Trinity Alps, adding considerably to the main river's flow. Soon the canyon narrows, the vegetation becomes lusher, and the rapids grow more difficult. The first run recommended in this guide begins here, at the mouth of the North Fork. Farther west the river changes again as it slices through the Ironside Mountain Batholith, a massive granite intrusion formed 150 million years ago. This is Burnt Ranch Gorge, eight miles of Class V white water in a steep-walled canyon inaccessible except by boat. Below Hawkins Bar is the Lower Trinity, a scenic, easy float past the mouth of the South Fork, through the Hoopa Indian reservation, and on to the Klamath confluence at Weitchpec.

Expert canoeist in difficult drop. *Keith Miller*

Trinity River

North Fork Confluence to China Slide

Difficulty: III+ to mile 5.2; II+ thereafter.

Length: 25 miles. Longer and shorter runs possible.

Gradient: 17 ft./mi.   **Drainage:** 1440 sq. mi. at take-out.

Season: Year round. Best in late spring and summer.

Runnable Levels: 300/500–8000 cfs.   **Elevation at Put-In:** 1390'.

Flow Information: (916) 322-3327. Roughly 60 per cent of flow at Hoopa.

Scenery: Very good.

Solitude: Fair. Highway 299 is alongside most of the way.

Rafts: Small boats only below 1000 cfs.

Kayaks: Excellent river for learning to kayak. World of Whitewater Kayak School is located at Big Flat; address: PO Box 708, Big Bar CA 96010; phone: (916) 623-6588.

Open Canoes: Intermediates can handle the river below Big Flat (mile 5.2) at flows below 1000 cfs. Advanced canoeists can run the first five miles at low flows with a few portages. There is an easier canoe run upstream, between Lewiston and the mouth of the North Fork.

Commercial Raft Trips: One- and two-day trips. For a list of outfitters, contact Shasta-Trinity National Forest, Big Bar CA 96010; phone below.

Water: Usually clear but not drinkable. Some side creeks are probably OK. Purify to be sure.

Camping: Developed Forest Service campgrounds at the Pigeon Point put-in, Big Flat (mile 5.7), Big Bar (8.4), and Hayden Flat (17.1). There are plenty of suitable sites along the river as well. Choose the left bank, away from the highway, for more privacy.

Maps: Helena, Hayfork, Hyampom, Ironside Mountain (USGS 15'); Shasta-Trinity National Forest; Northwestern California (AAA).

Auto Shuttle: 24 miles; 30 minutes.

Emergency Telephone Numbers:
  Shasta-Trinity National Forest (Big Bar): (916) 623-6106.
  Trinity County Sheriff (Weaverville): (916) 623-2611.

Logistics: The put-in just downstream from the mouth of the North Fork Trinity, Pigeon Point Campground, is about 80 miles east of Arcata and 15 miles west of Weaverville on Highway 299. Easy shuttles up and down the highway.

This stretch of the Trinity has good scenery and more rapids than the Lower Trinity below Burnt Ranch Gorge. Frequent vehicle access to the river makes it possible to break up the run at many different points—far more than those indicated in this guide. Most rapids can be seen from the highway.

Mile by Mile Guide

0   Pigeon Point Campground, just downstream from the mouth of the North Fork Trinity, is the most convenient put-in site. There are plenty of alternate put-ins both upstream and downstream.

2.2   **THE SLOT (III).** Also called **Z-Drop.** Above 1200 cfs the reversal at the bottom becomes so big that many boaters will want to portage.

2.5   Eagle Creek enters on the left.

3.2   **HELL HOLE (III+).** A steep vertical drop. Washed out at flows above 1500 cfs.

5.1   **FISH TAIL (III).** A boulder garden. Rapids ease below this point.

5.2   *RIVER ACCESS.* Big Flat Campground on the right. A popular take-out for those who want to run only the more challenging upper section.

6.3   Big Bar Creek enters on the left.

7   Skunk Point Picnic Area (right bank).

8   Bridge across the river. Big Bar Campground is on the left, a short distance up the road and away from the river. Forest Service ranger station on the right, across the highway.

10.3   White's Bar Picnic Area (right bank).

13.5   French Bar. The river bends right around a peninsula. From the highway you can see the tunnel dug through the peninsula by gold miners in an attempt to divert the river and mine its bed. Big French Creek enters from the right at the tip of the peninsula. A Class II+ rapid begins just below its mouth.

14.7   Highway leaves the river, returning a mile downstream.

16.9   Hayden Flat Campground (right bank).

18.2   The Trinity enters a mini-gorge with two Class II+ rapids, and the highway leaves the river for a short distance.

21.8   Foot bridge across the river.

23.6   *TAKE-OUT.* Cedar Flat. Take out on the right bank just above the highway bridge across the river.

25   *ALTERNATE TAKE-OUT.* China Slide Dump (left bank). A less inviting take-out, but the very last one before Burnt Ranch Gorge, an extremely difficult stretch for experts only at low flows. The side road to this take-out veers off Highway 299 shortly after the highway begins to climb above the river.

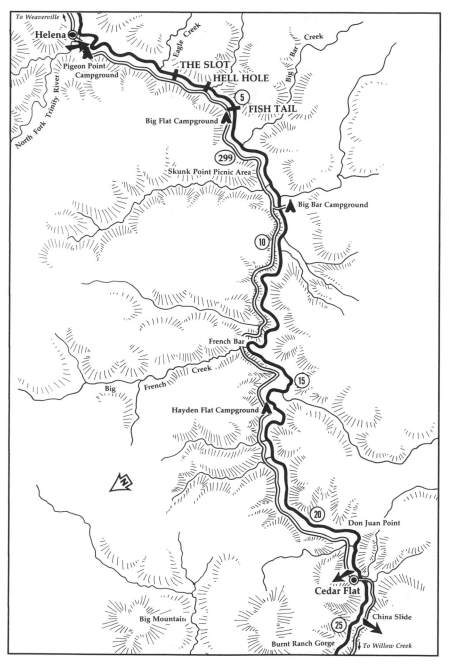

Trinity River

Trinity River

Burnt Ranch Gorge

China Slide to Hawkins Bar

Difficulty: V.   **Length:** 8.5 miles.

Gradient: 45 ft./mi.; 100 ft./mi. between miles 1.5 and 3.5.

Drainage: 1440 sq. mi. at put-in.   **Elevation at Put-in:** 900'.

Season: Summer, after high water. **Runnable Levels:** 300/500–3000 cfs.

Flow Information: (916) 322-3327. Two thirds of the flow at Hoopa.

Scenery and Solitude: Excellent. Highway 299 is too high above the left bank to be noticed.

Rafts: Self-bailing rafts preferred but not absolutely necessary since there are pools between the drops. Late-summer flows below 800 cfs make small rafts essential.

Kayaks: A great expert run.   **Open Canoes:** No.

Commercial Raft Trips: One- and two-day trips for experienced passengers. For a list of outfitters, contact Big Bar Ranger District. See previous section of Trinity River.

Water: Don't drink water from the river or from side creeks entering from the left. Right-bank creeks should be OK. Purify to be sure.

Camping: Gray's Falls and Burnt Ranch Falls Campgrounds (Forest Service) on Highway 299. It's not advisable to carry camping gear down the river.

Maps: Ironside Mountain, Willow Creek (USGS 15'); Trinity National Forest; Six Rivers National Forest; Northwestern California (AAA).

Auto Shuttle: 10 miles; 15 minutes.

Emergency Telephone Numbers: See previous section.

Logistics: Burnt Ranch Gorge is about 60 miles east of Arcata and 40 miles west of Weaverville on Highway 299. To reach the put-in, turn north off the highway toward China Slide Dump and follow the road to its end by the river; or put in just upstream from Cedar Flat bridge, just off the highway a mile and a half upstream. To reach the take-out, turn north off the highway onto a dirt road just west of Hawkins Bar Trailer Park and follow it to the river access point.

Not too many years ago most boaters considered Burnt Ranch Gorge unrunnable. Only a few kayakers did more than peer down at the river from the highway far above. A hair-raising story about a run down this stretch in Dick Schwind's pioneering guide book, *West Coast River Touring* (1974), concluded with a kayaker's fatal heart attack and an admonition that this section of the Trinity was unsafe for boating.

Since then, white water sport has changed. This eight-mile slice of the Trinity is now considered one of the best expert runs in California — and not just by kayakers. After a raft trip down Burnt Ranch Gorge led by Jim Cassady and Bill McGinnis in July 1982, McGinnis's company Whitewater Voyages (El Sobrante) became the first outfitter here in 1983. Now other professional rafters also offer trips down this Class V pool-and-drop river.

Though the overall gradient is moderate, the run is laced with major rapids and is definitely for experts only. Help is hard to come by since few trails penetrate the sheer walls of the canyon. Don't hesitate to portage the biggest rapids, and don't make the mistake of attempting Burnt Ranch Gorge at high water. Wait for low summer flows, when Lewiston Dam far upstream furnishes most of the water (minimum releases of 500 cfs in July and August and 450 in June and September). The actual flow in Burnt Ranch Gorge will be somewhat higher because of tributaries downstream from the dam.

Mile by Mile Guide

0	China Slide. Put in here or at Cedar Flat, a mile and a half upstream. In 1890, following heavy rains, a huge landslide half a mile long and 1000 feet wide broke loose from the south wall of the canyon, killed two Chinese miners, and temporarily blocked the river, backing water twelve miles up the Trinity.
0.3	**CHINA SLIDE RAPID (IV).** Just around the first left-hand bend in the river is a shallow, rocky chute requiring tight maneuvering. More difficult for rafts.
0.5	**PEARLY GATES (IV+).** An eight-foot drop announces the beginning of Box Canyon. Scout on the right.
1.5	**TIGHT SQUEEZE (IV+).** House-sized rocks block the river and permit only a cramped run along the right wall. Scout on the left.
1.5–3.5	The river drops 200 feet in two miles. Scout whenever possible.
1.8–2.5	Two unnamed Class IV+ rapids in this stretch should be scouted.

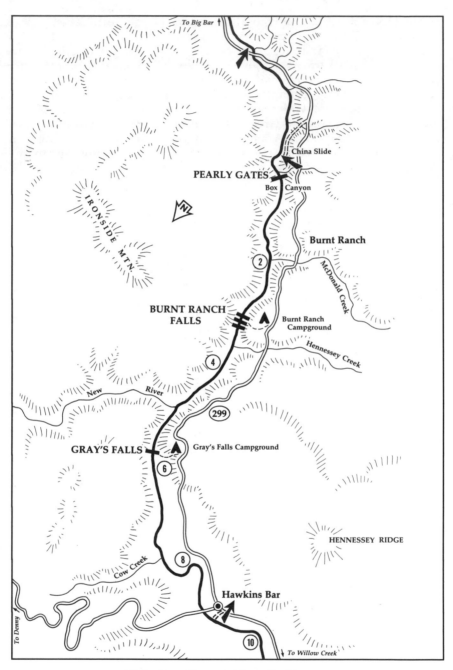

Trinity: Burnt Ranch Gorge

2.7 **UPPER BURNT RANCH FALLS (V–VI).** Also called **Jaws**. A simple chute leads to three monoliths blocking the river. Boaters have successfully run the ten-foot falls between the two left-hand boulders. Depending on the flow, the slot is five to seven feet wide. Scout and portage on the left.

3 **MIDDLE BURNT RANCH FALLS (V).** Just below the upper falls, the river surges down a jumbled slide with an overall drop of twenty feet. Scout on the left. Downstream, a trail leads from the left bank up to Burnt Ranch Campground and the highway.

3.1 **LOWER BURNT RANCH FALLS (V–VI).** Probably the most difficult rapid in Burnt Ranch Gorge—which means one of the toughest in the state. A frightening hole is followed by a vicious boulder maze. The rapid is a bit more runnable below 1000 cfs. Most boaters should choose the portage on the left, even though it's a hard one.

3.3 **HENNESSY FALLS (V).** At the end of a long pool the river drops down a right-left zigzag.

3.5 **ORIGAMI (V).** Rafts that get caught in the turbulent holes at the bottom of this rapid could be folded like Japanese paper. Above 1200 cfs a sneak route appears on the left and should be used. Scout left.

3.8 **TABLE ROCK (IV–VI).** A dangerously undercut flat rock waits at the bottom of a chute. Below 1000 cfs the slower current allows boaters to move right of the rock. At higher flows consider the easy portage on the left.

5 The New River enters from the right. The mouth of its canyon, crossed by a foot bridge, affords a spectacular vista from the highway above.

6 **GRAY'S FALLS (V).** Scout from the left bank to find a runnable route through large boulders blocking the river. The trail to Gray's Falls Campground leads up from the left bank.

6.1–8.5 Only Class II rapids from here to the take-out.

8.5 *TAKE-OUT.* Take out on the left at the Hawkins Bar River Access downstream from the Hawkins Bar Bridge. This is the put-in for the Lower Trinity run.

Lower Trinity River

Hawkins Bar to Weitchpec

Difficulty: II$_3$.

Length: 39 miles. Shorter runs possible.

Gradient: 10 ft./mi.

Elevation at Put-in: 500'.

Drainage: 1700 sq. mi. at put-in; 2865 sq. mi. at take-out.

Season: Year round. Best in summer—hot weather and warm water.

Runnable Levels: 400/700–15,000 cfs.

Flow Information: (916) 322-3327. Flow at Hoopa.

Scenery and Solitude: Good; excellent in wilderness sections. The highway is usually nearby but rarely obtrusive.

Rafts: Because upstream winds can be a problem on summer afternoons, rafts fare better at flows over 2000 cfs.

Kayaks: Excellent beginner's run at low summer flows.

Open Canoes: The Lower Trinity is one of the finest intermediate and advanced canoe runs in the country. Guided canoe trips are offered by California Rivers, PO Box 468, Geyserville, CA 95441; phone (707) 857-3872.

Commercial Raft Trips: One- to three-day floats may be offered at the Trinity River Rafting Center (see mile 18.4 in the guide below).

Water: Clear and warm in the summer, but not drinkable. Avoid side creeks in the open valley sections. Purify to be sure.

Camping: Good on-river camping in the wilderness sections. There is a developed Forest Service campground, Tish Tang (mile 22.7), and a private campground at mile 18.4 (see guide below).

Maps: Willow Creek, Hoopa (USGS 15'); Six Rivers National Forest; Northwestern California (AAA).

Auto Shuttle: 32 miles; 1 hour.

Emergency Telephone Numbers:
Six Rivers National Forest (Willow Creek): (916) 629-2118.
Trinity County Sheriff (Weaverville): (916) 623-2611.
Humboldt County Sheriff (Eurkea): (707) 445-7251.

Logistics: The put-in at Hawkins Bar is at a Forest Service river access point about 10 miles east of Willow Creek on Highway 299. Turn north onto a dirt road just west of the trailer park. The take-out at Weitchpec is 22 miles north of Willow Creek on Highway 96. Shuttles are quick and easy.

Here in the western part of the Coast Range the Trinity has become a large river. Its lush mountain setting is much like that of the Lower Klamath. This is a classic summer run for boaters who like Class II white water with their scenery. There are several wilderness sections where the highway and other traces of civilization disappear: from Hawkins Bar to the mouth of the South Fork (miles 0–8.4); from Riverdale Park to Tish Tang Campground (miles 18.4–22.9); and from Hoopa to Weitchpec (miles 30.9–39). Around mile 23 the river enters the Hoopa Valley Indian Reservation, at 93,000 acres the largest in the state. Because of upstream winds, the Lower Trinity is less popular with rafters than with kayakers and canoeists. If you want to run a shorter stretch, be sure to pick one of the wilderness sections.

Mile by Mile Guide

0   Hawkins Bar River Access is also the take-out for the Class V run through Burnt Ranch Gorge just upstream.

0–8.4   Frequent Class II–II+ rapids provide the best white water on the Lower Trinity. The highway is well above the river, and the canyon is deep and virtually inaccessible except by boat.

7.2   Bridge across the river. Hamlet of Salyer high above the left bank. River access is difficult at best.

8.4   *RIVER ACCESS.* South Fork of the Trinity enters on the left, adding considerably to the flow. The stream bed grows, too. River access on the left bank just above the confluence via a trail leading up to Highway 299. At this point the river canyon begins to open up. For almost 30 miles—until the last rapid in Weitchpec Gorge—the Trinity is easy Class I–II.

13.7   Bridge across the river. Poor river access. Town of Willow Creek on the left.

14.2   *RIVER ACCESS.* Big Rock. Vehicle access on the left bank next to the gravel pit and airstrip.

18.4   *RIVER ACCESS.* Riverdale Park and Trinity River Rafting Center on the left, just downstream from the mouth of Coon Creek, which enters on the right. Address: Star Route 5, Willow Creek CA 95573; phone (916) 626-3485. Camping and river access for small fees.

19–23   A beautiful gorge with the highway far away.

19.8   Horse Linto Creek enters on the right. The name of the creek, pronounced "hahs-LIN-tun" by local residents, is derived from Haslintah or Haslinding, a Hoopa village that once stood here.

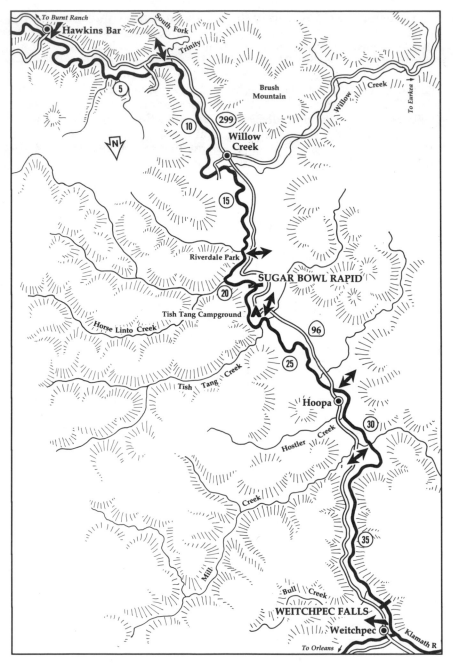

Lower Trinity River

21	**SUGAR BOWL RAPID (II+).** A small ledge. Scout on the right. Sugar Bowl Ranch is just downstream in a clearing on the left.
22.9	Tish Tang Campground on the left, just upstream from the mouth of Tish-Tang-a-Tang Creek on the opposite side. Good river access via a large gravel bar next to the campground. A closer approximation of the name of the Hoopa village that stood here would be "Tish-Tong-a-Ting."
23–39	Hoopa Valley Indian Reservation, home both to the Hoopa, who lived along the Trinity, and the Yurok, who lived along the lower Klamath and the coast. The two small tribes traded with each other and shared religious beliefs. See the chapter on the Klamath River. The lovely Hoopa Valley is rich in timber, minerals, fishing, and agriculture.
28.2	*RIVER ACCESS.* Highway 96 bridge across the river. Good access just downstream on the left.
29.5	*RIVER ACCESS.* Hostler Creek enters on the right.
30.9	*RIVER ACCESS.* Mill Creek enters on the right.
33	The Trinity enters Weitchpec Gorge, a spectacular canyon with the road far up on the wall. With one exception, the rapids are only slightly more difficult.
37.2	Bull Creek enters on the right.
38.4	**WEITCHPEC FALLS (III).** The rapid changes from year to year, and its difficulty varies with the flow. Scout on either side, and portage on the right if necessary.
39	*TAKE-OUT.* Just above the Klamath confluence on the right bank of the Trinity, a steep trail leads up to the hamlet of Weitchpec. An alternate take-out requires boaters to make a strong ferry across the Klamath to its right bank, where there is vehicle access on Martin's Ferry Road. This move is difficult when the Klamath is high.

South Fork Trinity River

Highway 36 to Low Level Bridge Site

Difficulty: Vp. **Length:** 48 miles; 3–7 days. Shorter runs possible.

Drainage: 208 sq. mi. at put-in; 880 sq. mi. at take-out.

Elevation at Put-in: 2300'. **Gradient:** 37 ft./mi.

Season: April–May. Runnable into late June in wet years.

Runnable Levels: 400/600–4000 cfs at take-out.

Flow Information: Not on flow phone. For a rough estimate, take one quarter of the flow of the Trinity at Hoopa. (916) 322-3327.

Scenery: Excellent. **Solitude:** Excellent.

Rafts: Any rafter who takes on this run must be a wilderness nut who doesn't mind several long, difficult portages. Seasoned experts only. Pack light.

Kayaks: A marathon trip; pack light. Experts only. Portage when in doubt.

Open Canoes: No, unless you're an expert willing to undertake countless portages. But there is a nice eight-mile Class I stretch between the take-out and the confluence with the Main Trinity.

Special Hazards: Very difficult rapids and tough portages just below Winton Flat (mile 22.5) and in the Big Slide area (mile 31.1). Portages in other stretches aren't so hard.

Commercial Raft Trips: None.

Water: Clear except after heavy rains. Probably drinkable above Hyampom; use side streams thereafter. Purify to be sure.

Camping: Superb campsites with sandy beaches all the way. Developed Forest Service campgrounds at the put-in and at mile 30.9.

Maps: Pickett Peak, Hyampom, Willow Creek, Pilot Creek (USGS 15'); Shasta-Trinity National Forest; Six Rivers National Forest; Northwestern California (AAA).

Auto Shuttle: 100 miles via Douglas City; 145 miles via Eureka. Several hours either way.

Emergency Telephone Numbers:
Trinity County Sheriff (Weaverville): (916) 623-2611.
Shasta-Trinity National Forest (Hayfork): (916) 628-5227.

Logistics: The put-in is at the Forest Service campground at Forest Glen, where Highway 36 crosses the river 63 miles east of Highway 101 and 70 miles west of Red Bluff. To reach the take-out, turn south off Highway 299 about eight miles east of Willow Creek onto South Fork

Road (just east of the bridge across the South Fork). Stay on the main road for 6.8 miles, then take a right-hand fork down to the river and the site of a washed-out bridge. The only other good river access for vehicles is in Hyampom Valley (miles 25–30). Poor access, in case of emergency, may be found at Klondike Mine (mile 4.4), Oak Flat (mile 20.4), Underwood Creek (mile 35.9), and Surprise Creek (mile 42). There are two long shuttle routes: (1) nine miles east of Forest Glen, turn north onto Highway 3, then turn west on Highway 299 at Douglas City; (2) drive west to Highway 101, north to Eureka, and east on 299.

The South Fork Trinity rises on the northern slopes of the Yolla Bolly Mountains, whose tallest peaks approach 8000 feet and retain their snow cover well into the summer. The river flows northwest, parallel to and just east of South Fork Mountain, a 35-mile long ridge that marks the geological boundary between the ancient Klamath Mountains and the much newer Coast Range. Much of its watershed has been logged, but few of the scars are visible from the river, which is one of the most scenic streams in California.

Like the Eel, the South Fork Trinity flooded in December 1964, and its stream bed is still partially choked by boulders and slides moved by the record rain runoff of that very wet year. The lower part of its canyon is strewn with numerous sand and gravel deltas that provide excellent campsites.

In spite of its moderate gradient, the South Fork Trinity has plenty of very difficult, boulder-strewn rapids. The most challenging sections include the first four miles, the stretch just below mile 22.5, and the first seven miles of the run below Big Slide Campground (mile 30.9). Because of its relatively short season, remote location, and tough white water, few boaters know this river. We're not sure that anyone has floated the run described below in one continuous trip.

You don't have to travel to Peru, Zimbabwe, or Papua New Guinea to run a remote, exotic river. You only have to penetrate one of the most isolated sections of the Coast Range and run the South Fork of the Trinity. Keep in mind, however, that this is an expedition for teams of experts only.

Every time I get into South Fork Trinity country, I think that making this entire run would be the experience of a lifetime. I've floated all of it, but only one stretch at a time. The river flows through a rugged canyon as beautiful as any I've ever seen. The rapids are fantastic—a challenge to any boater in the world. But I have to admit that running a river this difficult and this remote is demanding. Some of the portages are very hard. Road access is skimpy, and the shuttles are long. Yet I always come back happy.   —Jim Cassady

Mile by Mile Guide

0	Put in on the right bank at Forest Glen Campground just east of the Highway 36 bridge. *ALTERNATE PUT-IN.* For a warm-up, put in 1.5 miles upstream. The one big rapid in this stretch can be run or portaged easily. To get there, drive south on a Forest Service road that intersects the highway a mile east of the bridge.
0–4	The gradient averages 90 feet per mile for the first four miles. Class V rapids come in clusters. You may want to portage some of the steepest drops. The carries are relatively easy.
4.4	Emergency vehicle access via Klondike Mine Road, which leads from a point several hundred yards above the left bank back to Highway 36, 2.5 miles west of the put-in bridge. A trail connects the road with the river. Poor road; four-wheel drive only when wet.
4.4–22.5	The river's pace slackens. A long stretch of Class II and III.
11.6	Plummer Creek enters on the right.
20.4	*RIVER ACCESS.* Oak Flat. A dirt road on the right (St. John Road) leads from the river north to Hyampom Road, two miles east of Hyampom. Driving from the river to Hyampom, bear left at the intersections; driving the other way, bear right.
21.5	Butter Creek enters on the right.
22.5	◆ *HAZARD* ◆ Winton Flat. A cabin on the left bank warns boaters that a difficult section of the South Fork canyon is just ahead. Steep Class VI drops are strewn with dangerous undercut rocks. Long portage. There is emergency river access at the cabin across private property. Ask permission.
25	The river canyon opens up into Hyampom Valley. Class I drifting for the next five miles. "Pom" meant "land" in the Wintu Indian tongue, but no one is sure what "Hyam" denoted—probably something good, since the Hyampom Valley is a splendid mountain setting. Jedediah Smith and a small party were the first white men to explore the rugged South Fork Trinity country in 1827. The Hyampom Trail connected the Hayfork Valley to the east with Humboldt Bay and Eureka.
26	Hayfork Creek, the South Fork's major tributary, adds significantly to the flow as it enters on the right. Just downstream is the small town of Hyampom (right bank) with some amenities: grocery store, restaurant, and bar. A possible put-in or take-out for shorter trips.

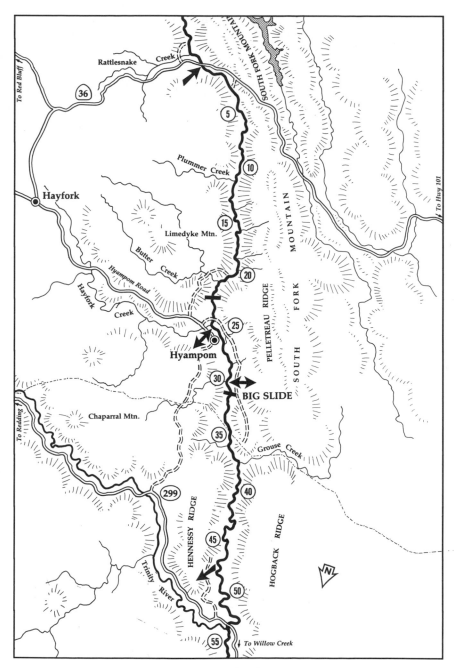

South Fork Trinity River

29.3   The canyon walls narrow as the river leaves Hyampom Valley, but the rapids remain easy for another mile and a half.

30.9   *RIVER ACCESS.* Big Slide Campground (left bank). The last good river access point before the take-out—and a warning of the falls ahead. To reach the campground, cross to the left bank of the river at Hyampom and turn north onto Lower South Fork Road.

31.1   ◆ *PORTAGE* ◆
BIG SLIDE FALLS (VI). Fearsome chutes across landslide debris with boulders the size of trucks. Scout and portage on the left. You may choose to shorten the carry by lining or running certain sections of the rapid.

31.5–34.5 Class III–IV rapids except for one big Class V–VI drop about a mile and a half below Big Slide Falls.

33   ◆ *POSSIBLE PORTAGE* ◆
UNNAMED RAPID (V–VI). The river turns left, then right as it drops down a bedrock staircase. The major problem is a dangerous undercut rock squarely in the center at the bottom of the rapid. Scout and portage (an easy carry) on the right.

34.5   POWER LINE FALLS (V). **Recognition:** Power lines appear on the hills ahead. Scout on the right. **The rapid:** The river divides as it passes through a boulder field, then drops over a wide ledge choked with big rocks. Some boaters have negotiated a tricky S-turn on the far right side of the ledge. At higher flow a sneak route appears even farther right. After a short pool below Power Line Falls, expect several Class IV and V rapids in succession.

35   Power lines across the river. High atop the left bank is Manzanita Ranch.

35.9   Underwood Creek enters on the right. There is a foot bridge just downstream. On the left, a precarious road—for emergency access only—comes fairly close to the river. To reach this spot, follow Lower South Fork Road six miles beyond Big Slide Campground (see above, mile 30.9), pass under the power lines, and take the second right (Gates Road) down toward the river.

37.3   Grouse Creek enters on the left.

37.7   UNNAMED RAPID (V). After a left-hand bend, the river drops down a 200-foot-long chute cluttered with big boulders and fearsome holes. Scout and portage either side.

37.8   For the next several miles the river winds through a deep, lush canyon festooned with hanging gardens. Rapids are Class III–IV.

42   *RIVER ACCESS.* Downstream from the mouths of Coon Creek and Surprise Creek, which enter from the right, a cable crosses the river to a lone house on the left. The canyon begins to open up slightly. Poor vehicle access via South Fork Road.

45.8   **THE THREE BEARS (IV). Poppa Bear** and **Momma Bear** just downstream require tricky maneuvering around big boulders. **Baby Bear** (mile 46.4) is a wrap rock that is hard for rafts to miss at low flows.

48   *TAKE-OUT.* The remains of a washed-out low-water bridge announce the take-out on the right. Or continue eight miles downstream to the confluence with the Main Trinity at Salyer —a beautiful Class I float.

Skilled teamwork in a C-2.

R. Valentine Atkinson

Salmon River

Forks of Salmon to Somes Bar

Difficulty: V; II–III above mile 4.3 and below mile 14.

Length: 19 miles; 2–3 days. Longer and shorter runs possible.

Drainage: 490 sq. mi. at put-in; 750 sq. mi. at take-out.

Season: April–June. **Gradient:** 31 feet/mile.

Runnable Levels: 300/500–5000 cfs. **Elevation at Put-in:** 1200'.

Flow Information: (707) 443-9305. **Scenery:** Excellent.

Solitude: Very good. The road is usually so high above the river that boaters hardly notice it.

Rafts and Kayaks: The gorge is for experts only. Intermediates can handle the upper four miles and the last five miles, as well as the last six miles of the South Fork above Forks of Salmon (Class III; not included in this book). There is a kayak school two miles downstream from the put-in at Otter Bar Lodge, Forks of Salmon CA 96031; phone (707) 442-3712.

Open Canoes: At low flows, advanced and expert canoeists can try the stretches recommended above for intermediate rafters and kayakers, although the six-mile stretch on the South Fork may be too difficult.

Commercial Raft Trips: One- to four-day trips (sometimes including the Ikes Run on the Klamath). For a list of outfitters, contact Klamath National Forest, 1312 Fairlane Road, Yreka CA 96097; phone (916) 842-6131.

Water: Clear, cold, and usually drinkable. Purify to be sure.

Camping: Scarce in the gorge (miles 5–14). The road is close to the river at Butler Creek (mile 10.5), so one possibility is to leave the boats there and camp elsewhere—for example, at Nordheimer Flat or Oak Bottom Campground (mile 15.7).

Maps: Forks of Salmon (USGS 15'); Klamath National Forest; Northwestern California (AAA).

Auto Shuttle: 17 miles; 30 minutes.

Emergency Telephone Numbers:
Siskiyou County Sheriff (Yreka): 911.
Forest Service (Ukonom Ranger Station): (916) 469-3331.

Logistics: To reach the take-out, drive 50 miles east of Eureka on Highway 299, turn north on Highway 96 at Willow Creek, and continue 47 miles north to Somes Bar, where the Salmon meets the Klamath. Turn right on the Salmon River Road. See mile by mile guide for details on the take-out. The put-in is at the little town of Forks of Salmon, 17 miles up this road.

The Salmon rises in the Salmon-Trinity Alps Primitive Area, one of the most isolated regions in the state, at the base of Sawtooth, the only glacier in California's Coast Range. The "Cal Salmon"—so called to distinguish it from the better-known Salmon River in Idaho—is a charter member of the state Wild and Scenic Rivers System as well as one of the finest white water runs in the country. Until a few years ago, only a few kayakers had boated this river. Tom Foster and his company Sierra Whitewater (Springfield, Oregon) pioneered rafting here, and several other professional organizations quickly followed. But the river is never crowded.

Boaters soon find themselves in an intimate, steep-walled gorge where sparkling green waters splash through an exhilarating series of Class IV and V rapids separated by deep, quiet pools. Heavy precipitation —80 inches a year on the average—encourages the growth of lush forests along the river and feeds the brilliant side creeks that often drop down spectacular cascades into the main stream. Even in June, storms can move in quickly, so always bring wet suits. The run can be extended by putting in at Methodist Creek on the South Fork, six miles above Forks of Salmon, and by running the Ikes section of the Klamath and taking out near Orleans.

Mile by Mile Guide

0   There is a good put-in at a gravel bar just downstream from the school in Forks of Salmon.

0–5   The river meanders through five miles of scenic open country and easy Class II–III rapids.

4   The road crosses from the right to the left bank of the river just above Crapo Creek.

4.3   *RIVER ACCESS.* Nordheimer Creek enters on the left. Nordheimer Flat Campground is just downstream on the left.

5   **BLOOMER FALLS (III–IV).** During the 1964 flood, a landslide blocked the river at this point, backing up a lake behind the debris. When a channel was dynamited, Bloomer Falls—one of the most dangerous rapids in the state—was created. An expert kayaker drowned here in 1982 when the big reversal at the bottom of the falls dashed him against the right-

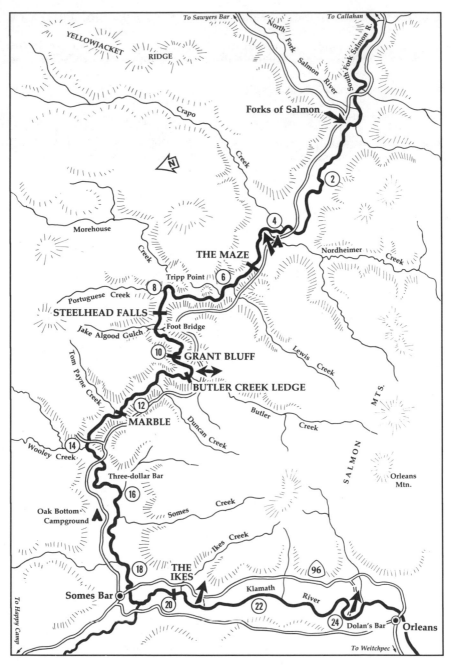

Salmon River

hand wall and knocked him unconscious. In August 1983 the state Department of Fish and Game dynamited the falls again —officially, to provide a better path for salmon swimming upstream to spawn, but probably to alleviate the danger as well. Thus a man-made Class V–VI rapid has become a man-made Class III–IV. Scout on the left.

5.1   **THE MAZE (IV +).** A long, nearly continuous zigzag through rocks and boulders deposited by a slide during the 1964 flood.

6   **LEWIS CREEK FALLS (IV +).** Lewis Creek enters on the left. The river turns sharply right and piles up against a rock. This is the beginning of the Salmon River gorge.

6.5   Morehouse Creek enters on the right.

6.8   **AIRPLANE TURN (IV +).** The river turns right and drops down a channel obstructed by large boulders. Look for a runnable chute on the left.

8   Portuguese Creek enters on the right.

8.5   **STEELHEAD FALLS (V).** Also called **Cascade.** The river plunges through a boulder maze. There are several channels, but no easy ones. Scout from the left.

8.7   **CATARACT (IV +).** Also called **Achilles Heel.** Another boulder-choked drop, but the passages are easier. Scout from either side.

9.2   Foot bridge across the river.

10   **GRANT BLUFF (V).** Also called **Freight Train.** A high bluff on the left bank marks the halfway point where this long, difficult rapid turns sharply left. You can see the rapid from a turn-out atop the bluff. Just upstream, a big hole (called **Last Chance**) guards the entrance to the rapid. The hole gets worse as the water level rises. At high flows most boaters avoid this stretch of river and put in downstream at Butler Creek.

10.5   ♦ *POSSIBLE PORTAGE* ♦ *RIVER ACCESS.*
    BUTLER CREEK LEDGE (V–VI). Butler Creek enters on the left, and the road comes close to the river. The rapid consists of a huge river-wide ledge and a reversal that surfs boats into a big wrap rock just below. There is a tiny runnable slot at the far left side of the ledge. At higher flows you can miss the rapid by taking a side channel even farther left. Consider portaging if this chicken route is unavailable.

10.6   **DOUBLE HOLE (IV +).** Two big drops right below Butler Creek Ledge.

11.1   **THE FIN (IV +).** Also called **Fish Ladder.** An eight-foot drop followed by a hard left turn. The rapid can be seen from the road.

211

11.6   Duncan Creek enters on the left. The road is close by.

12.8   **MARBLE RAPID (IV +).** A fairly long, complex maze of boulders (holes at higher flows) begins just after a sharp right-hand bend. Routes depend on the water level. Scout from the left. There is a large limestone cave on the left bank just below the rapid.

13   Tom Payne Creek enters on the right.

14   Wooley Creek, one of California's finest salmon streams, enters on the right. The gorge begins to open up. Class II–III rapids the rest of the way to the Klamath.

14.2   Bridge across the river. The road is close by for the next four miles, providing boaters with several spots to take out or put in.

15.7   *TAKE-OUT.* Oak Bottom Campground (Forest Service) on the right. Many boaters take out here.

16-18.5   *TAKE-OUT.* Find a spot before the road leaves the river. There is only poor river access from mile 18.5 to the confluence. You can also float a five-mile stretch of the Klamath (see the section on the Ikes run).

19   Klamath confluence. Somes Bar is on the hill between the Highway 96 bridge and the confluence.

Scott River

Canyon Entrance to Klamath River Confluence

Difficulty: IV–V (III below mile 18).

Length: 21.5 miles; 2 days. Shorter runs possible.

Gradient: 52 ft./mi.   **Drainage:** 800 sq. mi. at Scott Bar.

Season: April–late June.   **Elevation at Put-in:** 2600'.

Runnable Levels: 400/600–3000 cfs.   **Flow Information:** (707) 443-9305.

Scenery: Very good.   **Solitude:** Very good.

Rafts: Rapids are nearly continuous, so at higher flows rafters must avoid swamping and blundering downstream out of control (or use self-bailing rafts).

Kayaks: Most of the canyon can be scouted from the road. Select a section that suits your skills.

Open Canoes: At low flows, expert canoeists can run the 3.5-mile section from Scott Bar to the Highway 96 bridge. Farther upstream, in the picturesque Scott Valley, open canoeists can find more than 30 miles of runnable river.

Commercial Raft Trips: Usually two-day trips. For a list of outfitters, contact Forest Service, 1215 S. Main, Yreka, CA 96097; phone number below.

Water: Because of upstream cattle grazing, it's best not to drink the river. Side creeks are usually OK. Purify to be sure.

Camping: Forest Service campgrounds along the river.

Maps: Scott Bar, Seiad Valley (USGS 15'); Klamath National Forest; Northwestern California (AAA).

Auto Shuttle: 20 miles; 40 minutes.

Emergency Telephone Numbers:
Siskiyou County Sheriff (Yreka): 911.
Klamath National Forest (Yreka): (916) 842-2741.

Logistics: To reach the take-out at the Klamath confluence, drive 35 miles west on Highway 96 from Interstate 5 north of Yreka. To reach the put-in, turn south on the Scott River road and drive some 20 miles. There are a number of possible put-ins upstream from the Kelsey Creek bridge.

The Scott drains the east side of the Marble Mountain Wilderness and the northern and eastern slopes of the Trinity Alps, with headwaters at about 8000 feet. Because it is in the partial rain shadow created by these mountains, Scott River country is drier than the area around the Salmon River, and the Scott's season is usually a bit shorter than the Salmon's. Above the town of Callahan the Scott is steep, but it then slows down as it passes through the wide Scott Valley. Ten miles west of Fort Jones the river plunges into a deep canyon some eighteen miles long—the site of the run described below—before opening up again at Scott Bar. The river and the valley are named for John Scott, who discovered gold here in 1850.

Long a run known solely to a few expert kayakers, the Scott has only recently begun to receive attention from rafters. The first regular commercial raft trips began in 1983. The upper three miles are less ferocious (Class III–IV) and the final section of 3.5 miles from Scott Bar (mile 18) to the Klamath confluence is Class II–III, but most of the Scott canyon is for experts only. Rapids are almost continuous, with only short pools separating the sharp, boulder-choked drops. Between Indian Scotty Campground (mile 4.6) and Tompkins Creek (mile 10.2) the gradient averages 90 feet per mile.

Mile by Mile Guide

0	Choose a put-in site from the many good possibilities between the canyon entrance and the gaging station on the right bank, just where the rapids begin.
0–3.5	Class III and moderate Class IV rapids.
3.5	Jones Beach Picnic Area (right bank). Below this point the rapids become more difficult.
4.6	Indian Scotty Campground (right bank). Steep gradient and extremely tough rapids for the next six miles. This guide lists only the biggest ones.
5.8	**BOULDER CREEK FALLS (V–VI).** Huge boulders block the river. You may find a runnable channel between the boulders on the far right, but at most flows you must finish on the left. Scout from the right bank. The road is close by, so a portage is also possible.
6	**CANYON CREEK RAPID (IV–V).** Immediately below the big rapid, the river bends right and plummets down several hundred yards of churning foam. Canyon Creek enters on the left.
6.7	Spring Flat Campground (right bank).

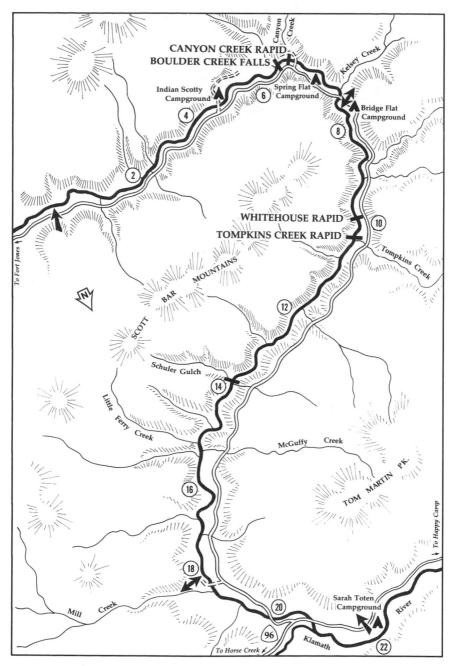

Scott River

7.5   *RIVER ACCESS.* Kelsey Creek enters on the left, and the road crosses the river. Vehicle access on the left, just below the bridge. Take out here if you don't want to float all the way to Scott Bar. For the next three miles, river access is difficult even though the road is not far away. The rapids come in quick succession.

10   **WHITE HOUSE RAPID (V).** Nearly a mile downstream from Middle Creek, which enters from the left, the Scott plunges through a boulder sieve and into a river-wide reversal. Scout from the right bank. A white house between road and river serves as a landmark. A turnout just upstream from the house offers a good view of the rapid.

10.2   **TOMPKINS CREEK RAPID (V).** The next rapid after **White House** is a 200-yard conglomeration of rocks and holes just upstream from the mouth of Tompkins Creek, which enters from the left. Scout on the right. The road begins to climb away from the river at this point, and the rapids become only slightly easier.

13.6   **SCHULER GULCH RAPID (V).** The river bends left as Schuler Gulch enters from the right. Scout this long rapid from the right. Downstream, the canyon begins to open up and the rapids slacken a bit.

18   Scott Bar. A sandy beach on the right, upstream from the bridge, offers a convenient take-out (or put-in for those who don't want to run the Class IV–V section). A dirt road leads from the beach up to the main road.

18–21.5   The river continues to drop, but the gravel bar rapids are only Class II and III.

21.5   *TAKE-OUT.* Highway 96 bridge and Klamath River confluence. You can take out at the bridge or continue downstream on the Klamath to another take-out at Sarah Totten Campground (left bank).

Klamath River

Among California's rivers, the Klamath is second in size only to the Sacramento. The river's course was well established some 10 million years ago, before the last major uplift of the Klamath Mountains and the emergence of the Coast Range. Its enormous watershed begins just east of Crater Lake in Oregon. From Klamath Lake and Lake Ewauna the river runs southwest through high desert country, cutting through the Cascade Range where the Upper Klamath white water run is located. The river crosses the border northeast of Yreka and continues across northwestern California toward its junction with the Trinity near the town of Weitchpec. Here, the Klamath turns northwest, flows through the Coast Range, and finally empties into the Pacific south of Crescent City. Between the Cascades and the Coast Range, the mountains are named for the river. The Klamath Mountains actually include several ranges: the Siskiyous, the Salmon Mountains, the Marble Mountains, the Scott Bar Mountains, and the glaciers and 8000-foot peaks of the Trinity Alps.

Klamath—or Tlamatl, a closer approximation of the word's original pronunciation—meant "swiftness" in Chinook and was applied to a tribe of Modoc Indians which lived along the upper reaches of the river. Several other groups of Indians lived along the Klamath: the Shasta, whose home was between Jenny Creek and Seiad and up the Scott Valley; the Karok (whose name means "upstream"), who dwelled along the river between Seiad and Weitchpec and up the Salmon River; and the Yurok ("downstream"), who lived between Weitchpec and the mouth of the Klamath.

The life of these Indian tribes, who depended primarily on the plentiful salmon and steelhead for subsistence, was profoundly disrupted after 1850 when gold-seeking whites overran their remote homelands. Dam building, dredging, and other mining operations dumped tons of rock and dirt into the river and cut the fish off from some of their best spawning grounds. The native population dropped sharply.* In 1917 the completion of Pacific Power and Light's Copco Dam and hydroelectric plant just south of the Oregon border blocked the upper reaches of the Klamath and drastically altered the river's flow. The plant's "peaking power" schedule called for alternating high and low releases that often left fish high and dry and made sport and commercial fishing much more dangerous.

217

Since then things have improved. In 1924 California voters passed an initiative to protect the rest of the fishery by prohibiting dams on the Klamath downstream from its confluence with the Shasta River, 175 miles from the Pacific and about twenty miles below Copco. In the fifties the state Department of Fish and Game began to tear down abandoned mining dams, break up log jams, and construct fish ladders around natural obstacles. The program reopened hundreds of miles of streams where adult salmon and steelhead can spawn and where fry still too small for the journey to the sea can grow unmolested. Finally, in 1961, PP&L built Iron Gate Dam about six miles downstream from Copco to smooth out the upper dam's irregular releases. Iron Gate also produces power and has a fish hatchery. Below Iron Gate the Klamath runs unimpeded to the Pacific.

Upstream, however, the river is controlled by Oregon dams— especially John Boyle Power Plant, just above the Upper Klamath white water run—and threatened by yet another hydroelectric project. The proposed 120-foot-high dam at Salt Caves (mile 8.7) would flood four miles of the canyon upstream and divert water into a penstock, drying up four more miles downstream. The project would destroy the Upper Klamath white water run and finish the job of reducing the entire river north of the Oregon border to a series of reservoirs and pipes.**

*For more on the Klamath and its human history, as well as a detailed mile by mile guide to the river, see J.M. and J.W. Quinn, *Handbook to the Klamath River Canyon* (Educational Adventures, PO Box 445, Redmond, OR 97756).
**For current information, contact the group organizing opposition to the dam: Save Our Klamath River, PO Box 1956, Klamath Falls, OR 97601.

Upper Klamath

Hell's Corner Run

John Boyle Powerhouse to Copco Lake

Difficulty: IV + .   **Length:** 11 or 17 miles; 1 – 2 days.
Gradient: 40 ft./mi.   **Drainage:** 4080 sq. mi. at put-in.
Season: April – October except for several weeks in July, when the powerhouse is closed for maintenance. The river is often too low for rafts—and marginal for kayaks—in June, when dam-controlled flows are kept around 600 cfs.
Runnable Levels: 500/800 – 5000 cfs. When one generator at Boyle Powerhouse is in operation, the flow is usually about 1700 cfs—typical summer conditions. When both generators are running (winter, spring, sometimes fall), the flow rises to about 3000 cfs. Higher flows occur only on the rare occasions when upstream reservoirs are full or during major storms.
Flow Information: (916) 322-3327; (800) 547-1501.
Elevation at Put-in: 3300′.
Scenery: Very good.   **Solitude:** Very good.
Rafts: Abrasive volcanic rocks in the river bed are hard on tubes and floors.
Kayaks: Advanced and expert boaters only.
Open Canoes: Not recommended. At 1700 cfs (one generator) the river is probably too rough even for top experts.
Commercial Raft Trips: One- and two-day trips. For a list of outfitters, contact BLM, 3040 Biddle Road, Medford, OR 97501; phone below.
Water: Carry your own. The river is brown, polluted, and unsafe to drink. No usable side streams, either.
Camping: Most boaters on overnight trips camp within the first five miles of this run, where a dirt road follows the river, and send their gear out by car before entering the gorge. There are some good wilderness campsites for those willing to carry gear. Topsy Campground, on Topsy Road just off Highway 66, is not far from the put-in and can be convenient for the night before the float.
Maps: Surveyor Mountain, MacDoel (USGS 15′); Klamath National Forest; Northeastern or Northwestern California (AAA).
Auto Shuttle: 40 miles; 1.5 hours.

Emergency Telephone Numbers:
BLM (Medford): (503) 776-4190.
Siskiyou County Sheriff (Yreka): 911.

Logistics: To reach the take-out, follow Interstate 5 a dozen miles north of Yreka and turn east at Henley or Hornbrook. Turn left (east) at Ager onto Ager-Beswick Road. About 15 miles farther, where the Klamath flows into the upper reaches of Copco Reservoir, look for the take-out at Fishing Access 1 (mile 17). If you choose to cut your run by six miles, continue upstream. Just before the road leaves the river near the Oregon border, turn left to the upper take-out at the BLM River Access site (mile 11). Do not use any other river or fishing access sites; they are reserved for fishermen.

To reach the put-in, you can (1) drive west along the north side of Copco Lake, turn north at Copco onto a dirt road, and turn east on Oregon Highway 66 some 10 miles farther; or (2) return to Interstate 5, turn north, then turn east at Ashland onto Highway 66. The first route is the shortest and easiest. The much longer second route is appropriate only when the unpaved road is very muddy, requiring four-wheel drive vehicles. (There is a third route—continuing upstream on Ager-Beswick Road, which becomes Topsy Road—but it is very rough and slow and definitely not recommended.) Highway 66 crosses the Klamath six miles west of Keno. An unpaved road intersects the highway west of the river and leads down to John Boyle Powerhouse on the right bank of the Klamath. The put-in, several hundred yards downstream from the powerhouse, is identified by a sign. Scout the last 50 yards of road leading to the river before you start down.

Only a few years ago the Upper Klamath was known only to a private river runner from Oregon, Jack LeRoy. In 1979 Dean Munroe, head of Wilderness Adventures of Redding, floated the river and passed the word that the "Hell's Corner Run" was comparable to the Tuolumne. (Munroe invented the name "Hell's Corner," wrote a song about the river, and christened most of the rapids as well.) Within a couple of years, dozens of outfitters were applying for commercial permits.

The Upper Klamath flows through a rugged high desert canyon cut into volcanic rocks. The river is on the Pacific Flyway, a major migratory route for a great variety of birds. Boaters may see blue and green herons, bald and golden eagles, falcons, ospreys, cormorants, Canadian geese, numerous species of river birds, and even pelicans. Along the way they can stop to look at the remains of old mines, ranches, and mills. Even in the late summer and early fall, when most Sierra rivers are marginally runnable at best, the Upper Klamath's dam-controlled flows provide more than enough water to swamp your boat. Except for the section of river described here, the entire Klamath north of the Oregon border has been dammed, and if the developers have their way, this stretch will also be destroyed by the Salt Caves Dam project.

The Upper Klamath is for advanced and expert boaters only. A concentrated dose of tough rapids waits in a five-mile gorge just north of the Oregon-California border. When both generators are running and the river is flowing at 3000 cfs or more, action is fast and furious. Lower flows aren't so easy, either. The sharp volcanic rocks cluttering the river bed are unforgiving to boats and swimmers alike. The river water is turgid brown and polluted. Be sure to carry plenty of drinking water.

Mile by Mile Guide

0	A sign directs boaters to the put-in several hundred yards downstream from the powerhouse. The last stretch of road down to the river is very bad; look at it before you descend.
0 – 5.7	Easy rapids—none above Class III—for nearly six miles. Numerous river access points.
1	Campsite on right bank, just downstream from a Class III rapid, **Osprey**, where the river splits around an island.
2.5	*RIVER ACCESS.* BLM campsite on right bank. A good alternate put-in.
4–5.7	Good campsites on both sides of the river. A dirt road follows the river along the right bank to mile 5.7. There are a few good campsites in the following five-mile gorge, and after that land on both sides of the river is privately owned.
5.5	Frain Ranch (left bank), built by an early settler in the nineteenth century on the site of an old Indian village. Ranch buildings and Indian artifacts are worth a stop.
5.7–11	Upper Klamath gorge. Only the biggest rapids are listed below. Gradient steepens to 75 feet per mile for nearly four miles beginning with Caldera.
5.7	**CALDERA (IV+).** As the canyon walls pinch together, the river drops down a 100-yard, boulder-choked chute. Scout from the left bank.
6.9	**SATAN'S GATE (III+).** A sharp right turn into a series of drops around and over boulders. Catch an eddy at the bottom left to scout the next rapid.
7.2	**HELL'S CORNER (IV+).** Walk the entire length of this sinuous 600-yard rapid before you run it. Watch out for a sharp submerged rock about fifteen yards off the right bank near the top of the rapid. The river bends first left, then back

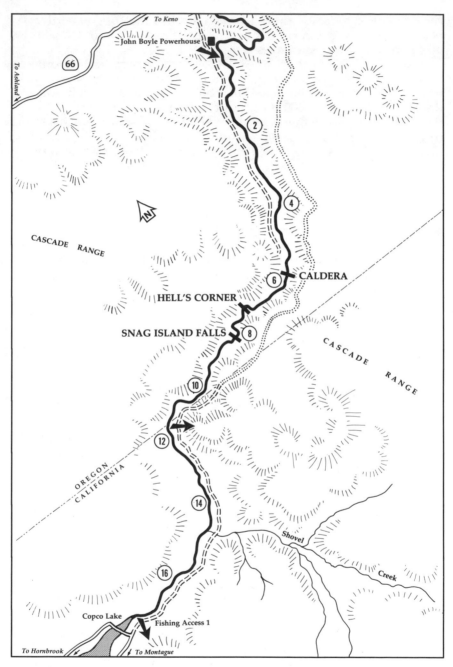

Upper Klamath River

to the right, but the current sweeps boats left toward impassable boulders. Boaters try to stay right and catch an eddy before the river swings left again into its final drop, called **The Dragon**. The teeth of the beast are two submerged rocks at the bottom. Though it is still tough, Hell's Corner has been easier since the high waters of winter 1981-82 removed a wrap rock about halfway down the rapid.

8.2   **AMBUSH (IV).** Upstream, the current picks up speed as it splits around a shallow island. The ambush is just downstream, where the river turns right and several wrap rocks block the center and left. Stop well upstream to scout (right bank).

8.7   Salt Caves (left bank). A 120-foot high dam proposed for this site would flood four miles of river canyon upstream and dry up four more miles of the river below this point.

9.9   **SNAG ISLAND FALLS (IV).** The river splits around an island. Take the right channel, but hug its left side. The right side of the right channel turns into an unrunnable sieve. This is the last big rapid in the gorge.

11   *RIVER ACCESS.* California-Oregon border. The state line is marked by the remains of a bridge. If you want to stop here, take out at the BLM access site on the left bank just downstream.

11 – 17   A scenic, pleasant stretch of river with a few Class III drops over old diversion dams. The canyon opens up and ranches appear. Almost all the land is privately owned, so don't try to take out.

13.8   Shovel Creek enters on the left, just upstream from Klamath Hot Springs, a nineteenth-century health resort built on the site of Beswick, an old stop on the stage line that once ran along the Topsy Grade. The big hotel burned down in 1915.

14   Indian Caves (right bank).

14.5   Nineteenth-century log chute on the right bank is half a mile long and drops more than 800 feet. Logs were floated down to Klamathon, just east of Hornbrook.

17   *TAKE-OUT.* Take out at Fishing Access 1 (left bank), or float less than half a mile downstream to an improved take-out at the Copco Lake Store (small fee).

Klamath River

Sarah Totten Campground to Weitchpec

Difficulty: II–IIIp.   **Gradient:** 14 ft./mi.

Length: 100 miles. Longer and shorter runs possible.

Season: Year round.   **Runnable Levels:** 300/500–50,000 cfs.

Flow Information: (916) 322-3327. Flow at Orleans.

Drainage: 6940 sq. mi. at put-in; 8480 at Orleans; 11,600 at Weitchpec.

Scenery: Very good.   **Elevation at Put-in:** 1600'.

Solitude: Very good. Highway 96 follows the river but is usually high on the bank and far enough away that boaters rarely notice it.

Rafts: A good river for boats of every size, from inflatable kayaks to Havasus. Larger rafts are recommended for higher flows (10–15,000 cfs and up), especially for the Ikes.

Kayaks: At lower summer flows, the Klamath is a good run for novice kayakers; in spring and early summer, it provides a good introduction to big water for intermediates.

Open Canoes: Only at 2000 cfs and below. Intermediates and advanced open canoeists should try the easier stretches of the Klamath to be sure they can handle the hydraulics before testing the Class III sections. Even at lower flows late in the summer, the tougher rapids can easily swamp or capsize a canoe.

Commercial Raft Trips: One- to seven-day floats. The most popular trips last two or three days and extend from Happy Camp to somewhere below Ukonom Creek. Guided floats in small inflatable kayaks and fishing trips in hard-hulled drift boats are also offered. For a list of outfitters contact Klamath National Forest, 1312 Fairlane Road, Yreka, CA 96097; phone below.

Water: Don't drink the main river, but the numerous side creeks are normally drinkable. Purify to be sure.

Camping: Numerous developed and primitive campsites along Highway 96. Boaters seeking more privacy camp on the bank away from the road.

Maps: Seiad Valley, Happy Camp, Ukonom Lake, Dillon Mountain, Orleans, Forks of Salmon, Hoopa (USGS 15'); Klamath National Forest; Northwestern California (AAA).

Auto Shuttle: 95 miles; 2.5 hours (Sarah Totten Campground to Weitchpec, one way).

Emergency Telephone Numbers:
   Klamath National Forest (Yreka): (916) 842-6131.
   Siskiyou County Sheriff (Yreka): 911.
   Humboldt County Sheriff (Hoopa): (916) 625-4231,
      or ask Operator for Enterprise 1-8601.
Logistics: You can reach Highway 96 either by turning west off Interstate
   5 about eight miles north of Yreka, or by following Highway 299 east
   from Arcata or west from Redding and turning north at Willow
   Creek. Highway 96 follows the river, so river access points are nu-
   merous.

The Klamath is the longest river in this guide book. By the time it
reaches Sarah Totten Campground, the put-in for the 100-mile run
described below, the river drains an area the size of New Jersey. At
Weitchpec, the take-out, its heavily forested watershed is almost twice as
large. Well known for its salmon and steelhead fishing, the Klamath is
truly a year-round river—though it should be avoided during heavy
winter rains, when it becomes a raging torrent. Even during summer
1977, at the worst point of California's most recent severe drought, the
river was still runnable.

This run can be extended to 184 miles by putting in just below Iron
Gate Dam, 48 miles above Sarah Totten, and by floating 36 miles below
Weitchpec to Klamath Glen, only a few miles above the river's mouth.
The first 18 miles below Weitchpec (to the end of Martin's Ferry Road) are
especially scenic and make a rewarding float. But these additional
sections have their problems. The upper stretch above Sarah Totten
consists of Class I and II rapids through a drier and less scenic part of the
Klamath canyon. As the river approaches the Pacific, its watershed
becomes wetter and its forests lusher. Below its confluence with the
Trinity downstream from Weitchpec, however, the Klamath turns northwest into strong prevailing winds—particularly tough for rafts—and
Class III rapids soon give way to less interesting Class I and II. The
shuttle to Klamath Glen is a long one.

For these reasons, the 100 miles between Sarah Totten and Weitchpec offer the best combination of white water, scenery, and convenience.
Because Highway 96 is nearby—though usually unobtrusive—and river
access points are frequent, boaters can tailor the length and difficulty of
their trips to suit their tastes and capabilities. Many will choose to begin
below Happy Camp (mile 35). Plan on taking out several miles above Ishi
Pishi Falls (mile 76). You can put in a mile downstream to run the Ikes.
The Ikes run may also be tacked on to the end of a Cal Salmon float.

Mile by Mile Guide

0	Sarah Totten Campground provides easy river access. The mouth of the Scott River is a mile upstream (left bank).
1	**HAMBURG (III).** Large boulders obstruct the channel just after the river turns sharply right. The town of Hamburg (left bank) was as important a mining center as Happy Camp in the last century. Before the miners arrived, there was a sizable Indian camp a short distance up Mack Creek, near the present cemetery.
3.5	Negro Creek, formerly known by a cruder name, enters on the right. A hydraulic mine operated on river right and a placer mine on river left.
4.7	O'Neil Creek enters on the left. Forest Service campground above the highway (left bank).
8.6	Walker Creek enters on the left. Old mining sites on both banks.
9.1	Seiad Valley, about two miles long and a mile wide, begins where the Klamath flows under the Highway 96 bridge. Its name, of Indian origin but uncertain meaning, is pronounced "sigh-ADD" and was spelled "Sciad" in earlier days.
14.2	Portuguese Creek enters on the right. Old mining sites on both banks.
15.2	Fort Goff Creek enters on the right. There is an old cemetery and a Forest Service campground nearby.
16.5	**UPPER SAVAGE (III +).** Holes and boulders block the river channel. Look for sneak routes on the left and right.
17.5	**OTTER'S PLAY PEN (III).** Big slabs of rock divide the river.
18.8	Thompson Creek enters on the right. An old mining camp called Nolton stood here in the last century. Legend has it that the first "Bigfoot" was sighted near here by Chinese workers.
18.8–34.8	Class I rapids for the next sixteen miles.
22	Joe Miles Creek enters on the left.
23.8	China Creek, site of an old placer mine, enters on the left.
30.2	Site of old Muck-a-Muck Mine (right bank).
34.8	Happy Camp (right bank), population 800, is still the largest town along the Klamath. As its name indicates, gold miners found what they were looking for as well as a place to live. In late December 1964 flood waters isolated Happy Camp from the outside world for ten days.

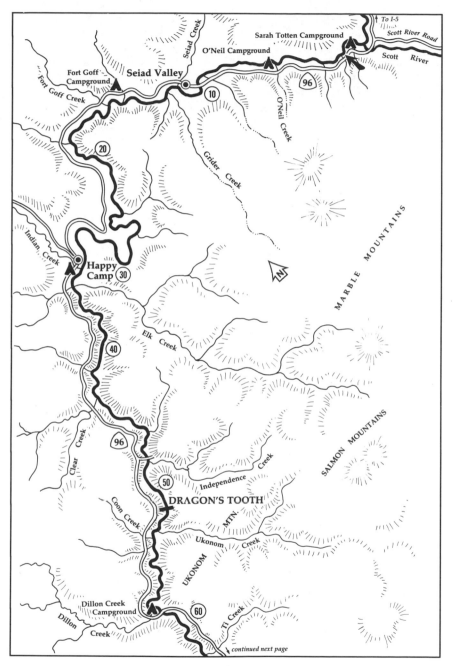

Klamath River

Open canoes: experts only below Happy Camp.
The river changes character here. A bit upstream from Happy Camp the Klamath turns south, the canyon walls rise, the forests become thicker, side streams and underground water add to the flow, and the rapids grow more difficult.

35.8   *ALTERNATE PUT-IN.* Curley Jack Creek enters on the right. Most commercial rafters as well as many other boaters begin their trips at the Forest Service campground on the left bank, opposite the creek's mouth. To reach Curley Jack Campground, cross to the left bank of the Klamath at Happy Camp and turn right.

38.9   **KANAKA CREEK RAPID (III).** Also called **Rattlesnake**. A big hole just to the right of two big rock islands is usually runnable. (No guarantees.)

39.5   **DEVIL'S TOENAIL (III).** A boulder bar with a big rock at the main drop. Scout from the right bank.

41.4   Buzzard Creek enters on the left. Creek water may be chemically polluted from old mining operation.

43.1   Clear Creek enters on the right. **For the next three miles, both banks are ceremonial grounds sacred to the Karok Indians.** Every year the Karok hold their World Renewal Ceremony here. During this five-week period, which varies from summer to summer according to their lunar timetable, no camping is allowed, and boaters are asked to respect Karok beliefs by avoiding any stops along the banks.

46   Ferry Point. Travelers on the old trail from Crescent City to Scott Bar crossed the river by ferry here and then traversed the Marble Mountains, which lie to the east between the watersheds of the Klamath and the Scott.

47.6   Just before Independence Creek enters on the left, the Klamath passes under a highway bridge, another old ferry site.

51.2   **DRAGON'S TOOTH (III +).** Also called **Little Blossom**. The best route through the big boulders littering the river bed takes boats directly toward the tooth, a pointed boulder below the main drop. Kayaks have an easier time avoiding the rock than rafts and drift boats. Scout from the right bank.

53   Ukonom Creek, named after a Karok chief, Yukhnam, enters on the left. The side hike here is one of the finest in California. Three quarters of a mile up the creek is spectacular Twin Falls. The campsite at the creek's mouth is much sought after by boaters. River access for vehicles 0.7 miles downstream (right bank).

Twin Falls, Ukonom Creek. *Whitewater Voyages*

54.5	Cottage Grove (right bank), an old mining town, was founded in 1852. What remained of it was swept away by the 1964 flood.
58.5	*RIVER ACCESS.* Dillon Creek enters on the right. Forest Service campground.
59.3	Highway bridge.
59.6	Blue Nose, an abandoned open pit mine, on the left.
61.3	*RIVER ACCESS.* Persido Bar (left bank). Name derived from Patsiluvra, a Karok settlement a few hundred yards upstream.
64.3	Eyese Bar (right bank) was the site of the Rood Gold Mine. A local story tells of gold coins buried here and never found. The name is pronounced "EYE-ease" and is derived from Ayiis, a Karok village.
68.8	Horseshoe Bend.
70.2	Highway bridge across river.
71.4	Another highway bridge. Get ready to take out.
72.4	*TAKE-OUT.* **Green Riffle**, a Class I rapid, is the last take-out above Ishi Pishi Falls, 3.6 miles downstream. Vehicle access on left, a quarter of a mile above the mouth of Reynolds Creek, via a dirt road leading up to the highway. The portage at Ishi Pishi is long and difficult, so don't miss this take-out.
75.8	Sites of two old Karok Indian camps, Kot-e-meen on the left and Ishi Pishi on the right. Kot-e-meen was the largest Karok settlement and a meeting ground for important religious rites. These days the Karok observe their annual ceremonies upstream near Clear Creek. The original site of Kot-e-meen is now occupied by a fishing lodge.
76	◆ *PORTAGE* ◆ **ISHI PISHI FALLS (VI).** Don't attempt this long, rocky, dangerous chute. A few daredevils have run it, but it's a far better idea just to take pictures. The portage (left bank) isn't easy, but it is recommended if you fail to take out upstream. Ishi Pishi means "end of the trail" to the Karok; the name celebrates their arrival at this, their new home, after a long migration across the ocean. Some Indians still fish here in the old style with nets on long handles. Somes Bar and Ukonom Ranger Station are above the highway on the left bank.
76.4	Sugarloaf Mountain (left bank), called "Auich" by the Karok, was for them a sacred peak; souls of the dead climbed to its top and departed for their next lives. Early in the century a mining company blasted a 1700-foot-long tunnel through the

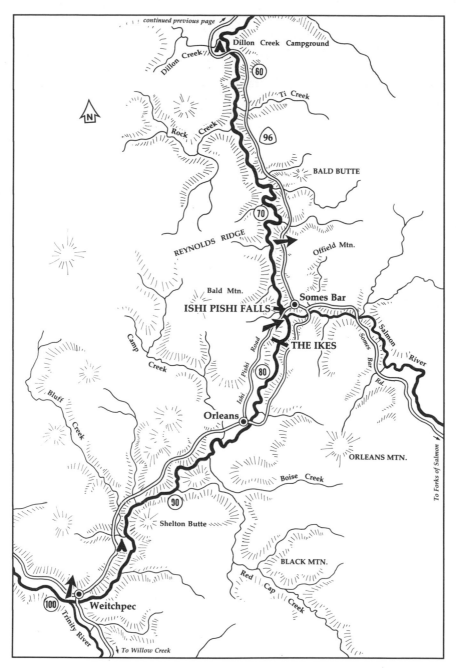

Klamath River

base of the mountain and planned to divert the river through it, mine the river bed, and then erect a hydroelectric dam. But California voters outlawed more dams on the Klamath in 1924, and the tunnel was left high and dry.

76.8   *RIVER ACCESS.* Salmon River enters from the left, just downstream from the highway bridge. Put in under the bridge on the right bank of the Klamath or upstream on the Salmon (see chapter on that river). Watch out for the strong eddy fence where the currents of the two rivers meet.

77.5   **THE IKES. Little Ike (II–III)**, with a big rock outcropping in the middle of the river, warns boaters that **Big Ike (IV–V)** is just ahead. Above 12,000 cfs Big Ike is a Class V rapid much like Crystal in the Grand Canyon: the powerful currents of a large-volume river sweep boats directly toward a fearsome hole in the center of the channel. Big Ike is easier at lower flows when boats can reach sneak routes on the right. Scout from the left bank when the river is high and from the right at lower flows.

77.9   Ikes Creek enters on the left. Named for Little Ike, the son of a Karok chief in the 1850's.

78   **SUPER IKE (III–IV)**. More difficult at lower flows, where there is a sharp drop over a ledge. At higher flows the rapid is a series of big standing waves.

82.2   *RIVER ACCESS.* Dolan Bar (left bank).

83.8   Town of Orleans (right bank, just downstream from the highway bridge) was originally named New Orleans Bar in 1850. The town served as county seat of remote Klamath County from 1855 until 1876, when the county was abolished and its territory divided between Siskiyou and Humboldt. Until a wagon road was finally put in around the turn of the century, Orleans was accessible only by horse and pack train.

93.2   **BLUFF CREEK RAPID (III +)**. A large river-wide ledge at the mouth of Bluff Creek, which enters from the right. Scout left.

99.8   *TAKE-OUT.* The Trinity River, the Klamath's largest tributary, enters from the left. River access on the right bank just downstream from the confluence. The town of Weitchpec is half a mile upstream (right bank) on the site of an old Indian village. The Indian word "Weitspek" or "Weitspus" may have meant "confluence." Downstream, the river widens and the rapids are easier, but upriver winds grow stronger. Highway 96 crosses the Klamath and follows the Trinity upstream to the town of Willow Creek, while Highway 169 accompanies the Klamath northwest another 18 miles.

Smith River

In the far northwestern corner of the state is a pristine jewel of a river, the Smith,* whose branches drain the western slopes of the Siskiyou Mountains in California and southern Oregon. The various forks of the Smith make up the only complete river system in the state left entirely undammed. How long it will remain relatively untouched is far from certain, but for the present this remote little river complex is one of the best on the West Coast, combining remarkable scenery with a variety of white water to suit every boater's taste and skills.

Smith River country is the closest thing in California to a rain forest. Its small watershed, wettest in the state, averages around 100 inches of precipitation annually, producing lush vegetation all along the river above the high-water mark. Except right after rainstorms, the Smith runs crystal clear. The fishing is excellent, too.

The Smith River region may not be safe much longer. Some pre-glacial (two million-year-old) tropical soils in the area are rich in nickel, chromium, and cobalt. Cal Nickel, a Canadian corporation, has applied for permission to strip-mine Gasquet Mountain, between the North Fork Smith and Hardscrabble Creek (a tributary of the main Smith), and to build three dams on the creek to provide water for the mining operation. Critics point to potential consequences including more erosion, air and water pollution, and even acid rain.

This guide concentrates on three runs: the North Fork, a Class IV wilderness float; the main Smith (Class II – III) along Highway 199 from Gasquet to the South Fork confluence; and the South Fork, a Class III run with an unobtrusive road usually high on the canyon wall. The main Smith and the South Fork change character abruptly a mile above their respective take-outs, ending in steep little gorges strewn with Class IV – V rapids. Only experts should attempt Oregon Hole and South Fork Gorges. In each case, however, alternate take-outs enable river runners to avoid these sections if they wish.**

*The river is named for Jedediah Smith (1799-1831), the legendary explorer who was the first white man to find a route through the Wyoming Rockies (South Pass), to traverse the Mojave Desert, to cross the Sierra Nevada, and to reach Oregon overland.

**In addition to these three runs, boaters may continue another ten miles downstream from the South Fork confluence along the edge of first-growth redwoods in Jedediah Smith State Park. Finally, highly skilled white water explorers may want to try the relatively uncharted upper reaches of the North Fork, Middle Fork, Siskiyou Fork, and South Fork.

North Fork Smith River

Low Divide Road to Middle Fork Confluence

Difficulty: IV.
Length: 13 miles. No shorter runs.

Gradient: 44 ft./mi.
Drainage: 157 sq. mi. at take-out.

Season: November–May. Boating season can be lengthened or short-ened by several weeks in years of heavy or light snowfall. Heavy rains, which occasionally occur in the off-season, bring the river up to runnable levels for the next few days.

Runnable Levels: 200/400–4000 cfs.
Elevation at Put-in: 880′.

Flow Information: (916) 322-3327. As a rough guide, take a quarter of the flow at Jedediah Smith State Park.

Scenery: Excellent.
Solitude: Excellent.

Rafts: Small rafts only under 700 cfs.

Kayaks: Plastic boats could scrape down at 200 cfs, effectively extending the boating season into June. Carry a spare paddle; it's a long walk out.

Open Canoes: No—though some day top experts will probably run it.

Commercial Raft Trips: None at present. For updated information, contact Gasquet Ranger District, Six Rivers National Forest, PO Box 228, Gasquet, CA 95543; phone below. This office manages all forks of the Smith.

Water: Crystal clear, even after rainstorms—perhaps due to the lack of logging. As drinkable as wilderness water can be. Purify to be sure.

Camping: Good sites on the river except in the numerous small gorges. An excellent two-day run if the weather isn't too cold.

Auto Shuttle: 34 miles (21 on a winding dirt road); 1.5 to 2 hours.

Maps: Gasquet, Crescent City (USGS 15′); Six Rivers National Forest; Northwestern California (AAA).

Emergency Telephone Numbers:
Six Rivers National Forest (Gasquet): (707) 457-3131.
Del Norte County Sheriff (Crescent City): 911.

Logistics: To reach the put-in, drive about eight miles east of Crescent City on Highway 199, turn left on Highway 197, follow it 2.5 miles and turn right on Low Divide (Wimer) Road. Veer right eight miles later at the intersection with Rowdy Creek Road and continue thirteen more miles to the put-in at the bridge across the North Fork.

The take-out is just above the confluence of the North Fork and the Middle Fork. Turn north off Highway 199 at Gasquet, about 20 miles

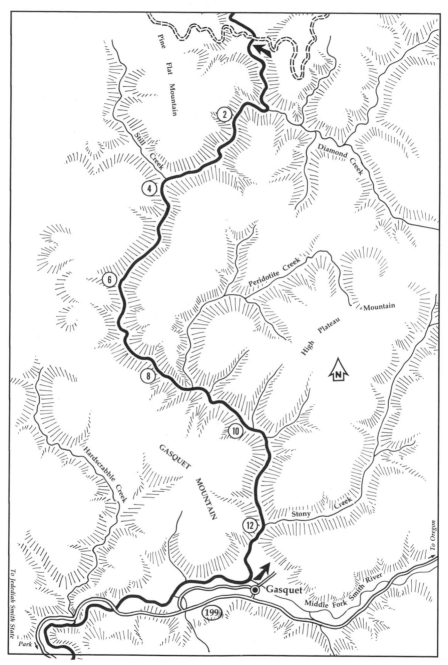

North Fork Smith River

east of Crescent City, and cross the Middle Fork. A trail leads from a turnout on the north side of the bridge down to the confluence of the North and Middle Forks. For other take-outs downstream, see the next run (Gasquet to South Fork Confluence).

The North Fork Smith is one of the loveliest wilderness white water runs in the country, but because it is so remote and because summer flows are too low, it is rarely floated. It is even more a rainy-season river than the other forks of the Smith because its upper watershed (well below 5000') is more than a thousand feet lower. The North Fork Smith rises in southern Oregon near the headwaters of the Chetco River, and not far from the drainages of the Illinois and the Rogue. The put-in is just a few miles south of the Oregon-California border, deep in a virgin forest.

Much of the North Fork's watershed is underlain by large fragments of ocean crust that have been scraped up and molded by the thrusting edge of the continent. Because the rocks and the clay soil formed from this old crust are deficient in certain trace elements, the trees are stunted and of little economic value. Consequently, the North Fork has never been logged. But the proposed Cal Nickel strip mine on Gasquet Mountain, part of the North Fork's drainage, would alter the landscape dramatically.

The guide below offers only very general information about the run. The North Fork canyon is laced with small gorges and plenty of Class III and IV rapids. Stop to scout when you can't see a clear route. Remember that winter floods can rearrange rapids and lodge fallen trees across the river.

Mile by Mile Guide

0   Low Divide Road Bridge. Put in on the left bank.

1.3   Diamond Creek, the North Fork's largest tributary, enters on the left. A few hundred yards downstream the river enters the first and probably the most difficult of some half dozen small gorges.

3.4   Still Creek enters on the right. Good campsite. Another gorge begins less than a mile downstream.

8.5   Peridotite Creek enters on the left as the river turns left.

11.7   Stony Creek enters on the left.

13   *TAKE-OUT.* Confluence with the Middle Fork, which enters from the left. Take out on the left just above the confluence. A trail leads up to the road. Or continue downstream on the main Smith.

Smith River

Gasquet to South Fork Confluence

Difficulty: II – III first six miles; IV – V in mile-long Oregon Hole Gorge.

Length: 7.7 miles. Shorter runs possible.

Gradient: 28 ft./mi.   **Drainage:** 287 sq. mi.

Season: November–May or June, and after heavy off-season rains.

Runnable Levels: 250/450–5000 cfs.   **Elevation at Put-in:** 310'.

Flow Information: (916) 322-3327. Roughly half the flow at Jedediah Smith State Park.

Scenery: Excellent.   **Solitude:** Good. Highway 199 is usually nearby.

Rafts: At moderate flows this is a fine training run for novices, as long as they take out above the gorge. Small rafts only below 700 cfs.

Kayaks: Good novice run above the gorge.

Open Canoes: At low flows the first six miles make a good run for advanced canoeists.

Special Hazards: Oregon Hole Gorge. Experts only below mile 6.2.

Commercial Raft Trips: None. See North Fork Smith.

Water: Clear, clean, and probably drinkable. Purify to be sure.

Camping: Panther Flat, a Forest Service campground, is two miles up Highway 199 from the put-in. For a few dollars more, camp among the redwoods at Jedediah Smith State Park, three miles downstream from the take-out.

Maps: Hiouchi (USGS 7.5'); Gasquet, Crescent City (USGS 15'); Six Rivers National Forest; Northwestern California (AAA).

Emergency Telephone Numbers: See North Fork Smith.

Auto Shuttle: 8 miles; 15 minutes.

Logistics: The put-in for this run is the take-out for the North Fork Smith at Gasquet. See that chapter for directions. To reach the take-out above Oregon Hole Gorge, drive about six miles west of Gasquet on Highway 199 and find a turnout near Caltrans highway marker 9.09. A short trail leads down to the river. Experts running the gorge can take out just downstream from the South Fork Road bridge across the main river. Vehicle access is via either of two rough dirt roads: one begins at the intersection of the highway and South Fork Road, the other intersects South Fork Road several hundred yards downstream from the bridge across the Smith.

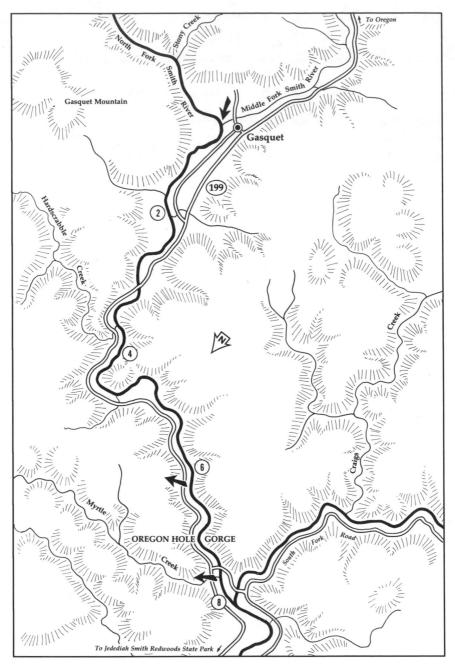

Smith River

The Smith River proper begins here, at the confluence of the North and Middle Forks. Though Highway 199 is alongside, the canyon remains beautiful. This is a lovely setting for low-water floats in late spring and early summer, but most boaters should take out above the difficult section known as Oregon Hole. The Class IV–V rapids in this little gorge look much smaller from the highway than they do at river level. Downstream from the South Fork confluence is another section not featured in this guide, ten miles of Class I–II river along the edge of first-growth redwoods in Jedediah Smith State Park.

Mile by Mile Guide

0	Confluence of North and Middle Forks. Put in on the left bank of the North Fork just upstream from the confluence. This guide does not list specific rapids. Scout carefully. The most difficult passages cannot be seen from the highway.
0–1.6	A beautiful section away from the highway. There are a few houses above the left bank.
1.6	Highway returns to the river.
2.6	Highway bridge across the river.
3.7	Hardscrabble Creek enters on the right. Cal Nickel has planned three dams on this creek to serve its proposed strip mine.
4.6	Highway leaves the river, returning just above the gorge.
6.2	*ALTERNATE TAKE-OUT.* To avoid running the gorge, take out on the right bank. A short trail leads up to the highway. Experts only downstream.
6.6	The river enters narrow, steep-walled Oregon Hole Gorge (IV–V).
7.7	*TAKE-OUT.* South Fork Road bridge across the river. Take out just downstream on either bank.

South Fork Smith River

South Fork Road Bridge to
Smith River Confluence

Difficulty: III first 12 miles; IV–V in mile-long South Fork Gorge.

Length: 13 miles. Longer and shorter runs possible.   **Gradient:** 35 ft./mi.

Drainage: 291 sq. mi. near take-out.   **Elevation at Put-in:** 550'.

Season: October to mid-June. Summer rains can raise the South Fork to runnable levels for a few days.

Runnable Levels: 250/450–5000 cfs.

Flow Information: (916) 322-3327. Roughly half the flow of the Smith at Jedediah Smith State Park.

Scenery: Excellent.

Solitude: Very good. Road is usually high above the river.

Rafts: First-rate intermediate run at moderate and low flows. Small rafts only under 800 cfs.

Kayaks: Plastic boats can scrape down as low as 250 cfs.

Open Canoes: Advanced canoeists could attempt this run—with several portages—at 700 cfs and lower.

Special Hazards: South Fork Gorge (IV–V). Experts only below mile 11.6.

Commercial Raft Trips: None. See North Fork Smith.

Water: Crystal clear and probably drinkable. Purify to be sure.

Camping: Fine beaches for camping along the river. Big Flat, a developed Forest Service campground, is just upstream from the put-in. Camping for a fee at the state park three miles below the take-out.

Maps: Hiouchi (USGS 7.5'); Gasquet, Crescent City (USGS 15'); Six Rivers National Forest; Northwestern California (AAA).

Auto Shuttle: 13 miles; 40 minutes.

Emergency Telephone Numbers: See North Fork Smith.

Logistics: Three miles east of Jedediah Smith State Park, turn south off Highway 199 onto South Fork Road and follow it about 13 miles upstream. Put in at the bridge across the river. For those not running South Fork Gorge, the take-out is reached via a trail from a turnout beside South Fork Road near Caltrans marker 2.05. Those running the gorge may choose among several take-outs. There are two possible access points at the new bridges around miles 6.3 and 6.6. Another take-out, a difficult one, is on the right bank of the South Fork just downstream from the South Fork Road bridge near mile 11.6, just above the gorge and the confluence with the main Smith.

Easier take-outs may be found at the state park campground, two miles downstream, or at the Highway 199 bridge a mile and a half farther.

Though not as pristine as the North Fork, the South Fork Smith and its watershed have been only slightly affected by man. Here and there a logging road testifies to our civilization's presence; otherwise, the river canyon is much as it has been for thousands of years. All that could change if the proposed Gasquet-Orleans Road becomes a reality. Timber interests want a paved route to connect Elk Valley Road, in the Klamath drainage, with the watershed of the South Fork Smith. In addition to bringing in its wake extensive logging, the road would cut across lands sacred to local Indians.

Boaters on the South Fork can enjoy nearly a dozen miles of exhilarating Class III white water before they approach South Fork Gorge, a mile of Class IV–V rapids for experts only. Other boaters should scout the upstream take-out (mile 11.6) carefully and memorize landmarks so they won't miss it.

This guide does not list individual rapids among the numerous Class II–III passages on the South Fork. Most are technical boulder gardens at low and moderate flows. You can see the rapids in South Fork Gorge from the road above, but they look deceptively small from a distance. Remember that minor variations in the flow can produce dramatic changes in rivers with narrow stream beds. Be alert for brush and snags in the channel, especially after winter rains and floods.

Mile by Mile Guide

0	Put in at the South Fork Road bridge, 12.5 miles from Highway 199.
2.7	Gordon Creek enters on the right.
5.2	Rock Creek enters on the left.
6.3, 6.6	New bridges across the river.
8.5	Coon Creek enters on the right.
11.5	Craigs Creek enters on the right. A take-out is just downstream.
11.6	*ALTERNATE TAKE-OUT.* Take out on the left, where a trail leads up to the road. If you miss it, you must run the gorge.
12	Entrance to South Fork Gorge (IV–V).
13	*TAKE-OUT.* South Fork Road bridge across the river marks the end of the gorge. The confluence with the main Smith is just downstream. Take out on the right just beyond the bridge if you don't mind scrambling up a steep trail to the road. There are easier take-outs at the State Park campground three miles downstream and at the Highway 199 bridge four miles downstream.

241

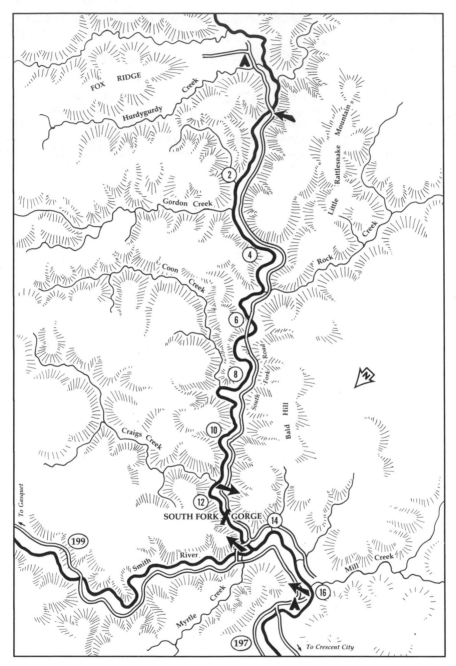

South Fork Smith River

More California Rivers

Madcap Adventures and Quiet Floats

San Joaquin

Difficulty: III–IV.   **Length:** 6 miles.

The San Joaquin is one of the state's biggest rivers. Its 1600-square-mile watershed in the southern Sierra begins at over 14,000' and includes several glaciers. But the private utilities PG&E and Southern California Edison harnassed most of the San Joaquin before the days of river running. Twelve powerhouses and nine reservoirs leave little of the river for us. The most frequently boated stretch is north of the town of Auberry, between Redinger Powerhouse and the top of Kerckhoff Reservoir. The season is short; upstream dams release sufficient flows only after upstream reservoirs are full—usually in late spring.

West Walker

Difficulty: V.   **Length:** 11 miles. Frequent road access.

The West Walker has the toughest runnable white water on the eastern slope of the Sierra Nevada. The gradient is over 100 feet per mile. The run begins above 6000' at the Highway 395 bridge a couple of miles north of the junction with Highway 108 (15 miles east of Sonora Pass) and ends at Eastside Road near the little town of Walker. Experts only, and only at flows between 700 and 2000 cfs. The West Walker's season is similar to that of the nearby East Fork Carson.

North Fork Stanislaus

Difficulty: IV–V.   **Length:** 4 miles.

This increasingly popular run, just south of Highway 4, begins at Board's Crossing and ends at Calaveras Big Trees State Park. The small stream drops at 70 feet per mile through a lovely canyon and is usually runnable into June, though the relatively high elevation means cold water all the time and cool weather at least until late April. If upstream reservoirs are enlarged as planned, they may eventually release flows sufficient for boating year round. The dam builders give and the dam builders take away.

For other boatable white water and extensions of the 45 featured river runs, see the essays and mile by mile guides in the individual river chapters.

North Fork Mokelumne.

Difficulty: V.   **Length:** 12 miles.

This beautiful wilderness stretch is runnable only when upstream Salt Springs Reservoir is full and the diversion to Tiger Creek Powerhouse has taken its share. In "average" years runnable flows usually last from mid-May to late June. In dry years the river never becomes runnable at all. Runnable levels range from 300/600 to 3000 cfs. High water is very dangerous. The run begins at the Bear River confluence with Class III–IV rapids and becomes gradually more difficult. There are a number of Class V passages in the last four miles. The final rapid, Mokelumne Falls (VI), is the toughest. Just downstream is an abandoned diversion dam that can be run on the far left—but be sure to scout it. The flat water of Tiger Creek Reservoir follows. Take out on the right above the powerhouse and carry gear to the parking lot.

South Fork American (Kyburz to Riverton).

Difficulty: IV–V.   **Length:** 7 miles. Frequent road access.

Upstream from the better-known Chili Bar section, the South Fork American plunges down a series of much more challenging rapids alongside Highway 50. Continuous white water and few eddies make this a run for advanced and expert boaters only, and even they should stay away at flows above 2500 cfs. Expect runnable flows throughout the spring and into June.

The put-in is below Kyburz, about 1.5 miles downstream from the confluence of the South Fork and the Silver Fork. Boaters face continuous Class V rapids for the first 1.5 miles, while the river drops at a rate of 120 feet per mile. Then the action tails off to Class III–IV. Just upstream from the take-out, the South Fork has cut a steep chute (Class IV–V) through sharp rocks where a big landslide blocked the highway and temporarily plugged the river in 1983. Take out on the right just upstream from the highway bridge at the town of Riverton.

Boaters can extend the Kyburz run by continuing 3.5 miles downstream through a Class III–IV gorge away from the highway. Take out at the Peavine Ridge Road bridge. Below Peavine Ridge Road the South Fork roars down an extremely steep Class VI gorge known by the suicide-tinged title of the "Golden Gate Run." Several miles have a gradient in excess of 200 feet per mile.

Bear River

Difficulty: II–Vp.   **Length:** Up to 11 miles.

The small Bear River watershed is squeezed between the canyons of the North Fork American and the South Fork Yuba near Interstate 80. Experts can put in at the Highway 174 bridge for two miles of Class IV–V rapids and several portages. The next access point is where Ben Taylor Road reaches the river. From here to Combie Road (on Combie Reservoir), boaters can expect 9 miles of Class II water with an occasional Class III passage. Within this section is a two-mile stretch from Bear River Campground to Dog Bar Road which is an excellent run for novice kayakers and intermediate open canoeists. Inner-tubers like it in the summer. Except during the short spring runoff, flow on the Bear is usually below 400 cfs, making it suitable only for plastic kayaks, durable open canoes, and inner tubes.

South Fork Yuba

Difficulty: IVp.   **Length:** 14 and 4.5 miles. Runs can be combined.

These two runs through the lovely canyon of the South Yuba have sufficient water only during spring snow melt. Much of the river's flow is diverted from Spaulding Reservoir through a tunnel into the Bear River drainage. In dry years the South Fork Yuba may never be runnable at all.

The first and longer stretch begins at the Washington bridge and ends at Edwards Crossing north of Nevada City. Near the end, about half a mile below Humbug Creek, the river drops over a dangerous 12-foot waterfall that should be portaged on the left. There is little warning of this falls, so be alert. The second run continues from Edwards Crossing 4.5 miles downstream to the Purdon Road bridge. There is one Class V rapid, followed by an old diversion dam that should be portaged.

McCloud River

Difficulty: III.   **Length:** 10 miles.

The McCloud drains old volcanic peaks near Mount Shasta. The porous volcanic rock soaks up rain and melted snow like a sponge, then releases it, often via springs, at a fairly steady rate. Consequently, the McCloud's flow is much more constant than those of most other rivers, rarely flooding or drying up. Make sure you put in downstream from two falls near Fowler's Campground—a big one just upstream, and a smaller one just downstream. Don't worry if the flow is skimpy; a mile downstream, Big Springs adds 500 to 1000 cfs.

The scenic 10-mile run from Fowler's Campground (reached by turning off Highway 89 seven miles east of McCloud) to Tarantula Gulch

245

(off Squaw Valley Road on McCloud Reservoir) has attracted considerable attention in the last couple of years. All the land on both sides of the river from just below the put-in to the reservoir is owned by the Hearst Corporation, and the Hearst family has a palatial retreat, Wyntoon, on the bank upstream from the reservoir. So far the landowners have been unable to prevent public boating on the river, but no stops are allowed along the banks.

Experts might want to tackle a more difficult (Class IV–V) run from McCloud Dam to Gilman Road on the upper reaches of Shasta Reservoir. An even more challenging route is to float Squaw Valley Creek down to its confluence with the McCloud—a Class V stretch with some waterfalls that must be portaged. Both of these runs have very short spring seasons because of upstream hydroelectric diversions.

San Lorenzo

Difficulty: IV.   **Length:** 6 miles.

Bay Area boaters like this little stretch of white water from Felton to Santa Cruz because it drops through a lovely narrow canyon in Henry Cowell State Park. It is runnable only for a few days after heavy rains. Brush and newly-downed trees are major hazards. Advanced and expert boaters only.

Noyo

Difficulty: II–III.   **Length:** 20 miles.

How about a gorgeous run through an isolated canyon with a train ride for a shuttle? Board the Skunk Railroad with your equipment at Fort Bragg, the take-out, at 9:50 a.m. and arrive at Northspur, the put-in, at 11:00 a.m. You should plan on spending at least one night on the river. Expect Class II and III rapids the first eight miles, and Class I and II thereafter. The stream bed is very narrow, so only small rafts should be used. Kayakers and canoeists won't be able to use the train for their shuttle, since at present the railroad won't carry their rigid boats. (For updated information, contact Skunk Railroad, PO Box 907, Fort Bragg, CA 95437; phone (707) 964-6371.)

Rivers of the Central Coast Range

Five rainy-season rivers drain the 160,000-acre Ventana Wilderness just east of Big Sur. The **Big Sur River** is the only one which runs toward the west. Between Pfeiffer Big Sur State Park Campground and its mouth, the Big Sur is only Class II, but there are bigger rapids in the small gorge just upstream from the campground (accessible only by trail). The other four flow toward the east. The **San Antonio, Carmel,** and **Arroyo Seco** are Class II–III, though Arroyo Seco has an experts-

246

only gorge (accessible only by trail) upstream from Arroyo Seco Campground. The **Nacimiento** is also Class II–III except for the unrunnable gorge called the "The Shut-In" in the Hunter Leggett Military Reservation. Stay away from the "The Shut-In."
Warning: Beware of unknown little creeks that swell during heavy rains. They become death traps where the uninformed and the unprepared drown. Never take on an obscure stream without scouting it first on foot.

When I lived in Long Beach and didn't have time for the three-hour drive to the Kern, I sometimes got desperate for white water. I would haul out my kayak and scrape down streams like Sespe Creek, Piru Creek, the Santa Ana, several forks of the San Gabriel, Malibu Creek, and Santa Margarita Creek. I even ran a section of the Los Angeles River, beginning at Willow Street in Long Beach, where the concrete channel ends and a long rapid leads almost to the ocean. I can't recommend these adventures. Usually, these little streams are dry, so dangerous brush grows right in the channels and creates a deadly hazard when they rise following big rainstorms. Stay away. To find a real river, you have to head north.
—Jim Cassady.

The Lay of the Land

Geology of California River Country

Imagine a California 200 million years ago that was more water than land. The coast line ran north through what became the southern Sierra Nevada, then northeast into present-day Nevada and Idaho. An imposing range of volcanoes stretched up the coast and out to sea, into the present Klamath Mountain region. Since that time the North American plate has drifted slowly westward for thousands of miles, riding over the ocean crust, scraping up a small part of it as a bulldozer blade scrapes up dirt, and shoving most of it downward, beneath the plate's leading edge. The land mass of California and the rest of western North America gradually grew—"accreted"—as this process continued over tens of million years.

Between 200 and 80 million years ago, California passed through the first of three long periods of volcanism, caused in part by frictional heat radiated upward from the subducted ocean crust as it was thrust deeper and deeper beneath the edge of the continental plate. During this first period the site of today's southern Sierra, the oldest part of the range, was a volcanic plateau underlain by huge bodies of granite called "plutons." These blobs, often ten miles or more in diameter, originated as magma (molten rock beneath the surface) at a depth of 50 to 100 miles. Beginning more than 200 million years ago, the still molten plutons pushed up toward the surface. Some of the magma escaped in volcanic eruptions as lava (molten rock above the surface), but most of it slowly came to rest and froze five to ten miles deep.

This granite and the surrounding metamorphic rocks which it invaded make up the basement rock of the Sierra Nevada. Granite predominates in the southern Sierra and becomes less prominent to the north, where metamorphic rocks like schist and slate are found more frequently. The Klamath range, which was once an extension of the Sierra, continues this trend. There, granite bodies are only islands in a sea of metamorphic rocks.

As the magma cooled, especially in the region of today's central and northern Sierra, veins of gold-bearing quartz formed within the metamorphic rocks which the granite had invaded. Eventually, uplift and erosion removed the overlying volcanic rocks and exposed the ore on the surface.[1] Then, for millions of years, an ancient generation of rivers cut into the rock and carried away fragments of its precious secret, depositing much of the quartz and gold in their stream beds.

This chapter was written in collaboration with Richard Ely.

The thin layer of rocks scraped up from the ocean crust by the continental plate was folded, faulted, jumbled, and stacked up, eventually to emerge from the sea as a line of islands where our present Coast Range stands. The much larger portion of ocean crust thrust downward ("subducted") was melted or slowly transformed by heat and pressure into metamorphic rock. Later, uplift and erosion exposed some of these metamorphosed rocks at the surface, where they commonly alter into serpentine. They underlie much of today's Klamath Mountains and parts of the central and northern Sierra Nevada, especially in the foothill regions. Many of the boulders that obstruct today's river channels and form white water rapids are fragments of these metamorphic formations.

By the end of the first volcanic period, some 80 million years ago, the coast had moved westward to a line roughly along the eastern edge of today's Great Valley. California's oldest rivers had already settled into drainage patterns running north-northwest to south-southeast along the structural grain of the volcanic chain. The Kern, at the extreme southern end of the Sierra, still follows this old route, and portions of other rivers like the San Joaquin and the Tuolumne also reflect it, but subsequent volcanic activity has profoundly disrupted the old pattern to the north. Then, about 50 million years ago, the infant Sierra Nevada began to rise and tilt toward the west, causing some of the rivers to seek more direct westward channels toward the sea. The most important traces of these rivers, from the human point of view, are the ancient buried river beds filled with gold-bearing gravel that are sometimes exposed high on the walls of today's Sierra river canyons from the Tuolumne north.[2]

The old drainage pattern was disrupted again when most of these rivers were buried by the second and third major episodes of volcanic eruptions. In the second period, between 33 million and 20 million years ago, the present Sierra range consisted of hills and low mountains, and the line of active volcanoes was well to the east, in what is now Nevada. Major eruptions transformed the landscape north of the divide that now separates the watersheds of the Tuolumne and the Merced.

While the southern Sierra remained relatively unaffected, north of the Merced great volumes of volcanic ash were carried west by the rivers, filling existing river channels to the brim and covering all but the highest hills. These rivers rose near the present Nevada-California border, or even farther east, and meandered across this vast, westward-sloping plain of volcanic debris toward a bay covering today's Central Valley. Their drainage patterns were similar to the eventual courses of our modern Sierra rivers. When the eruptions ceased, most of this volcanic material was eroded and removed over the next few million years.

During the third volcanic epoch, which lasted from 15 to about 4 million years ago, the center of activity moved to an area just east of the present Sierra crest, from Mono Lake north. From time to time lava and volcanic mud flows filled the river channels, forcing the rivers to move laterally (north or south) to find unobstructed paths.[3] Table Mountain, which marks a 10 million-year-old route which the Stanislaus once took, is the best example of such a formation. Over millions of years, the walls of this old lava-filled valley have eroded away, leaving exposed the more resistant river of frozen basalt. This volcanic era continues today, in an intermittent fashion, in the Cascade Range just to the north.[4]

Around the onset of the third volcanic period, 10 to 15 million years ago, the modern Sierra Nevada began to be lifted up like a great cellar door hinged on its western edge. This uplift—stronger than the uplift 50 million years ago—began on the southern end of the range and moved slowly north.[5] As the mountain range rose and steepend, the pace of erosion quickened, and the rivers carved their canyons with increasing speed and force. All the river canyons of the central Sierra north of the Merced, as well as the deep inner gorges of the southern Sierra rivers, have been cut in the last 10 to 15 million years.[6] In the northern Sierra, where the uplift began several million years later, the river canyons are even younger—less than 4 million years old.

The Sierra Nevada actually ends somewhere in the northern part of the Feather River watershed. At that point the Sierra basement rocks disappear under a range of young volcanoes culminating in Lassen Peak (10,457'), last active between 1914 and 1921, and a vast surrounding sea of volcanic debris. This is the southern end of the Cascade Range, which runs northward through Oregon and Washington. To the northeast is the high Modoc Plateau, a region of relatively young volcanic rocks broken by numerous north-trending fault scarps, where today's Pit River has its headwaters.[7] The Pit flows southwest through a gap which may mark the spot where the Klamath Mountains once joined the northern Sierra. The Klamaths were pulled away sometime in the last 40 million years.

The land mass that became the Klamath Mountains is about as old as the one that became the northern Sierra. Some of the rocks in the Klamaths date back more than 400 million years. But like the Sierra Nevada, the Klamath Mountains assumed their present form during periods of uplift beginning within the last 50 million years and continuing today. The rivers of the old rolling plain that developed into the Klamaths radiated out to the west and south from the core of the range. During the most recent geological era, say the last 5 million years, the drifting edge of the continent has lifted the Coast Range out of the sea and into the paths of the rivers, while fault movements along the western edge of the plate have pulled their mouths to the north.

Since then, volcanism in California has declined. Center stage has been taken by crustal movement along the faults parallel to the line where the continental and oceanic plates collide. Chief among these is the San Andreas Fault, whose western side has moved northward so rapidly that rocks which were near the Mojave Desert 10 million years ago can now be found 200 miles north. (Movement along the fault still averages two inches a year, a very rapid rate.)

The Coast Range north of San Francisco Bay is made up some of California's youngest mountains, lifted up from the sea in the last 2 to 5 million years. Their rivers are also among the newest in the state, though some (from the Trinity north) have their upper drainages in the much older Klamath Mountains. South Fork Mountain, a 35-mile long ridge that runs from southeast to northwest and separates the watersheds of the South Fork Trinity and the Mad Rivers, follows the geologic dividing line between the Klamaths and the Coast Range.

To the north and east of this line, in the Klamaths, most of the rocks are older, harder types like granite and foliated schist. Banks erode more slowly than those in the Coast Range, and the rivers carry less silt. To the west and south of this line, the Coast Range rivers cut through the weak rock formations of the Franciscan Complex, the name given to the material accreted onto the continent as it overrode the sea floor. Banks made of these weak rocks constantly collapse, and rainy-season landslides dump countless tons of rock, gravel, and soil into the stream beds. The Eel River is legendary for the amount of silt it carries. High water periodically changes the rapids of all rivers, but in the Coast Range this phenomenon occurs much more frequently.[8]

1. Granite is legendary for being a hard rock because it weathers slowly when exposed to water and air. But when it is buried beneath thick, moist soils, chemical weathering causes it to erode quickly.

2. Gold in California is found in these buried river channels, in the quartz veins of the Mother Lode, and in modern stream beds where contemporary rivers have eroded these two older sources.

3. One of these flows may have helped to sever the Tuolumne from the Stanislaus. The two rivers may once have joined about ten miles west of Sonora, near the present junction of Highways 108 and 120.

4. Recent stirrings in the Mammoth Mountain area indicate that central California volcanoes should not be considered entirely dormant. The birth of the volcano that became Mammoth Mountain cut the San Joaquin River off from its ancient headwaters in the Mono Lake basin about a million years ago or less.

5. The southern Sierra is the oldest part of the range and has the highest peaks— above 14,000' in the Kings and Kern watersheds. In the central Sierra (Stanislaus watershed) the tallest peaks are 11,000', and in the northern Sierra (Feather River drainage), where the uplift has been least, the summits are below 8000'.

6. Along the Forks of the Kern white water run, traces of 4 million-year-old lava flows can be seen within a hundred feet of the present river bed. That means that almost the entire depth of the Kern's imposing canyon had already been cut by the river when those flows occurred.

7. The Pit traces the path of what might be called the ancestral Sacramento, another of California's oldest rivers. Though officially the Pit is a tributary of the Sacramento, that relationship has more to do with the vagaries of naming parts of the landscape than with topography and geology. Realistically, the Pit is the main stem of the Sacramento, and the upper Sacramento is its west fork. But if we were always so logical, the Mississippi would be the Missouri.

8. Gravel bar rapids, where the river pools up before finding a narrow path across a small natural dam, are found on all rivers, but they are especially characteristic of the coastal streams. As their name implies, the rocks that make up gravel bar rapids are not very big, so they are also the easiest rapids for the river to change at high flows. Bigger rapids are often formed where boulders are trapped on ledges and ribs in the river bed.

Suggested Reading:

Shelton, John S. *Geology Illustrated* (Freeman, 1966).

Hill, Mary. *Geology of the Sierra Nevada* (UC Press,1975).

Alt, David D. and Donald W. Hyndman. *Roadside Geology of Northern California* (Mountain Press, 1975).

Bailey, Edgar H. *Geology of Northern California* (Bulletin 190, California Division of Mines and Geology, 1966).

Oakeshott, Gordon B. *California's Changing Landscapes* (McGraw-Hill, 1971).

Wright, Terry. *Introduction to the Geology of the Sierra Foothills* (Wilderness Interpretation, PO Box 1194, Pollock Pines CA 95726, 1981; also reprinted in John Cassidy, ed., *A Guide to Three Rivers*).

Wright, Terry. *Guide to Geology and Rapids, South Fork American River* (Wilderness Interpretation, 1981).

Wright, Terry. *Rocks and Rapids of the Tuolumne River* (Wilderness Interpretation, 1982).

Ernst, W. G., ed. *The Geotectonic Development of California* (Prentice-Hall, 1981).

What's That on the Bank?

Plant Communities of the River Canyons

Let someone else watch for rapids. You can keep busy just looking at the trees, flowers, and bushes. From fog-drenched groves of coastal redwood to sun-baked foothill slopes dotted with oak, madrone, and chaparral, California's river canyons display some of the world's most varied and remarkable plants. Half a mile of river bank in the Sierra Nevada often hosts five or six plant communities containing hundreds of species. Springtime boaters will see entire green hillsides bedecked with the bright pinks, golds, and blues of redbud, poppy, lupine. Wild flower lovers will see an amazing array, from the familiar Indian paint brush and lush streamside clumps of monkey flowers to the delicate Clarkias and Mariposa lilies.

It's easy to be overwhelmed by the rich variety of California flora. Once you start looking at oaks, for example, you learn that there are sixteen species in the state, not to mention localized hybrids and sub-species, and some of them aren't easy to tell apart. California has twenty species of pines, more than any other region on earth. So the best way to organize your knowledge is to get acquainted with the basic plant communities and their most common members.

Plant communities occupy portions of the river canyons where environmental factors are favorable to the growth of their member species. Boundaries between the communities are often not entirely clear, and considerable overlapping occurs, but the basic patterns of plant growth are regular and predictable. Six major variables interact to create a mosaic of distinct environments where some plants thrive and others fail.

Basic Environmental Factors

1. **Climate:** *temperature, precipitation, humidity, wind.*
2. **Soil Type:** *particle size, depth, mineral content.*
3. **Topography:** *altitude, slope, drainage patterns, solar exposure.*
4. **Ecology:** *plant and animal communities.*
5. **Natural Events:** *wild fire, flood, drought.*
6. **Human Activity:** *fire, fire prevention, logging, hydraulic mining, grazing, farming, flood control, air and water pollution.*

This chapter was written in collaboration with Bill Cross and Dodge Ely.

The single most important factor for plant life in the river canyons is an area's solar orientation, or exposure to the sun, which determines the availability of sunlight from season to season. The sun, which always stays in the southern half of the California sky, strikes north-facing river banks and canyon walls at oblique angles, even in mid-summer. In contrast, banks and slopes facing south are bathed in direct light and heated to higher temperatures. Consequently, moisture evaporates more quickly from plants and soil on south-facing banks than on those with northern exposure.

Since most of the Sierra rivers run roughly from east to west, and since even the Coast Range rivers ultimately fall into a west-northwest pattern, plants on one side frequently contrast sharply with those on the other. But when rivers run from north to south—like the Kern— sunlight falls with nearly equal intensity on both banks, and vegetation is more uniform on the two sides.

Plant Communities of the California River Canyons

1. **Riparian Woodland.**
2. **Grassland.**
3. **Chaparral.**
4. **Oak Woodland.**
5. **Yellow Pine Forest.**
6. **Coastal Redwood Forest.**
7. **Mixed Northwestern Forest.**

1. Riparian Woodland. Water-loving plants of the riparian (riverside) community flourish in moist, fertile soils along the rivers and creeks. They require a year-round water supply rare in a California climate characterized by relentless summer drought that can extend to five months or more. While plants higher on the canyon walls fall dormant during the long summer in order to conserve water, riparian species are often in their peak growth stages.

Seasonal high-water cycles and periodic floods subject riparian vegetation to dramatic changes. Streamside plants reduce the rate of erosion, but the river still gnaws away at them, undercutting older, established trees on the outside of a bend while fresh vegetation colonizes the expanding gravel bar on the opposite bank.*

The largest streamside trees in the river canyons are black cottonwoods, sycamores, bigleaf maples, white alders, and Oregon ash. Riparian undergrowth is made up of plants like Indian rhubarb, wild grapevine, button bush, mock orange, willow, and the nearly ubiquitous poison oak. Pacific dogwood and azalea are relatively rare along Sierra rivers but appear more frequently as one moves north in the Coast Range. California bay laurel and tanoak (not a true oak) grow a bit higher up on the banks. Some non-native species introduced during the last century now thrive beside California streams, including broom, Himalayan blackberry, an occasional fig tree, and the Chinese tree of paradise.

Riparian woodlands are important wildlife habitats. The luxuriant foliage provides food, shelter, nesting sites, and summer shade for many animals. In addition, shade and erosion control play critical roles in maintaining the purity of the water and the quality of the underwater ecosystem. But as more and more rivers and streams are dammed and flooded, diverted and dried up, or confined in man-made channels, these environmental niches are fast disappearing. To cite one example, in a little more than a century (1850 to 1972), riparian woodlands and forests along the Sacramento River declined from 775,000 acres to fewer than 18,000.

*However, downstream from large dams which rarely or never permit periodic flooding of the river channel, fast-growing brush chokes the stream bed. The Lower Kern River below Isabella Dam provides a good example of this phenomenon. Until the Forest Service permitted river runners to clear some of the overgrowth in the late seventies and early eighties, miles of the Lower Kern were nearly impassable, especially to rafts. The run is still far more dangerous than it would be if the river were occasionally allowed to scour its stream bed. Not all dams are designed for flood control, though, and in these cases vegetation still grows in more normal patterns in downstream river canyons. The South Fork American below Chili Bar is a good example.

2. Grassland. California's natural grasslands once covered most of the swamps and meadows of the Central Valley and blended into the surrounding oak-dotted foothill savannahs. Soils too dry for shrubs and poorly drained soils too wet for trees support natural grasslands. Grasses often colonize areas that have recently been disturbed, either by natural events like wild fire or landslide, or by human activity—fire, logging, clearing land for grazing.

The species that now dominate California's grasslands are not native to the state. Their seeds were sometimes brought here deliberately by European immigrants, but other seeds arrived by accident, riding unnoticed in the hems, crevices, and folds of clothing, shoes, and baggage. Four European grasses now predominate: wild oats and soft chess (deliberate); red brome and foxtail fescue (accidental). They survive only as seeds through the dry summer months. Annual grasses are usually foreign in origin, while perennial bunchgrasses are usually native. California river runners can see native bunchgrasses on the steeper slopes where grazing cattle have not destroyed them.

3. Chaparral. This term, derived from the Spanish "chaparro," or scrub oak, applies to a number of shrub species that thrive where extreme summer drought is the norm—in many parts of California, in other words, but especially in the Sierra foothills, where in an average year only five per cent of the precipitation falls between June and

255

October. Look for chaparral on rocky canyon slopes with southern exposure, where few other plants can tolerate the parched heat of the long summer.

Chaparral shrubs are ideally suited to these harsh conditions. Unlike their shallow-rooted riparian cousins, they typically have deep, extensive root systems—often bigger than the portion of the plant above the ground—that suck almost every drop of moisture from the dry, rocky soil. They also fall dormant in the summer to reduce their need for water, and their foliage has evolved to minimize moisture loss. Small, thick leaves reduce the surface area exposed to the drying effects of sun and wind. Light-colored foliage reflects some of the sunlight away from the plant. Many chaparral leaves are covered with short, dense hairs which reflect additional sunlight and reduce the flow of drying air across the leaf surface. Some species of manzanita even orient their leaves vertically to limit exposure to the intense midday sun.

The chaparral community is highly adapted not only to drought but to fire. In the absence of human intervention, a typical stand of chaparral will be burned every fifteen to forty-five years by natural wild fire caused by lightning. Periodic burning is essential for a healthy chaparral community. The seeds of most species germinate best when heated by fire, and many annual species thrive only in the open environment of a recently burned area. Without periodic burns, chaparral stands become overgrown and so dense that the diversity of animal life declines. Deer, coyotes, bobcats, and other sizable animals find it difficult to move about. Indiscriminate fire prevention, like overzealous flood control, degrades ecosystems by eliminating natural renewal. In the end, it is often a self-defeating policy. Eventually, when fire finally strikes overgrown stands—as it inevitably does—it burns hotter and destroys plants, seeds, and animals that could survive a cooler fire.

The most common species of California chaparral is chamise or greasewood, with its small, bundled, needle-like leaves. When it blooms, white flower clusters form at the ends of its many branches. Other common shrubs are ceanothus (also called buckbrush), many types of manzanita, toyon, and scrub oak. Many chaparral plants bloom in the late winter and very early spring. Hillsides dotted with the white, blue, or purple sprays of flowering ceanothus and the delicate pink and white blossoms of manzanita are among the finest sights in California.

4. Oak Woodland. This plant community is found throughout California, sometimes as hot, dry open grassland dotted with trees (savannah), sometimes, on cooler and wetter sites, as dense groves of oak and pine. Along rivers in the foothills of the central and southern Sierra, the oak woodland community typically dominates slopes with a northern exposure, with chaparral on the opposite side of the canyon and riparian vegetation beside the water. Isolated fingers of oak woodland often interrupt chaparral or grassland on the hotter and drier southern exposures by occupying shady ravines and establishing themselves where moisture accumulates.

The larger members of this community are digger pine, an easy tree to identify because of its sparse, feathery gray foliage and crooked, branching trunk, and a spectrum of oaks, both deciduous (blue oak, black oak, valley oak) and evergreen (interior live oak, canyon live oak). Some, like black oak and valley oak, are easy to distinguish; others require close examination and, for most people, a handbook. The situation is made more complicated by free hybridizing among various species. Lesser additional species include the buckeye, a small tree that shows fragrant ivory flowers in the spring and soon fades to a distinctive golden brown while it lies dormant through the summer drought, and the redbud, whose bright pink blossoms enliven California river country every spring.

5. Yellow Pine Forest.   Yellow pine forest is western North America's most broadly adapted and successful coniferous forest. It is found from southern California to British Columbia and east to the Rockies at elevations ranging from 2000' to 8500'. This is the pine forest which most California river runners will encounter. Most other Sierra pines inhabit more severe regions at higher elevations where most rivers are too steep and rocky to be boated. On runnable rivers, yellow pine forests are usually seen along the upper sections of the run on north-facing slopes, immediately above the foothill woodland and riparian communities. They occasionally grow at lower elevations (down to 1000') where ravines offer shade and moisture, or where the conifers have mingled with the riverside vegetation in a cool crook of the stream bank.

Yellow pine—also called Ponderosa—is easily distinguished by its yellow-orange, jigsaw-puzzle bark, long needles in bunches of three, and spiky cones. Yellow pine tolerates shade poorly and grows in open stands, often alongside the aromatic incense cedar. Incense cedar (not a true cedar) tolerates shade when young and is therefore able to grow among taller pines. The third common species in this community, the black oak, prefers slightly drier conditions and is rarely seen near the river, though its distinctive top-heavy silhouette may be spotted atop some of the higher slopes.*

*Pines, one of the earliest and most primitive trees, generally grow in places where nothing else thrives. Over time, oak forests tend to replace pine by shading out their seedlings and by sprouting from stumps after a fire, which pines cannot do. This natural succession takes place gradually, with plenty of intermingling. In California black oak and Oregon white oak are common members of the invading forces. Like most oaks, neither tree likes wet soil, so they are generally restricted to areas too dry to support lush growth. Both trees are deciduous, adding green to the spring countryside and yellow, gold, and brown to the autumn.

6. Coastal Redwood Forest.   The coast redwoods cluster near the ocean in the wet, temperate fog belt of the North Coast Range, which affords considerable moisture and protection from the sun even in summer. Where fog often blocks direct sunlight, differences between vegetation patterns on north- and south-facing slopes are reduced, and redwoods are found on both. But toward the inland limits of their range, fog cover is reduced and the trees cluster in north-facing ravines. Redwoods are found from the Santa Lucia Mountains north of San Luis Obispo all the way into southwestern Oregon. The redwoods can withstand neither drought nor hard frost, yet they commonly live up to 1500 years, and the oldest known tree is 3000 years old.

The chief associate of the coast redwood is the Douglas fir (not a true fir). These two giant conifers form a dense forest canopy beneath which only shade-tolerant species can survive: smaller conifers such as Pacific yew and California nutmeg, rhododendron, hazelnut, huckleberries, ferns, mosses, and many members of the lily family.

Redwoods thrive in the flood plains of rivers and creeks. Periodic high water deposits fresh, nutrient-rich silt around their bases, and the shallow-rooted conifers use the accumulating layers for support by extending new roots as the deposits pile up. The world's tallest known tree grows in an area like this along Redwood Creek. But the redwood forest seldom extends all the way to the river's edge. The banks themselves are host to a distinctive riparian woodland much like the Sierra's, but lusher and denser. Trees often lean out over the river in search of sunlight, creating a tunnel-like effect. Springtime floats beneath flowering arches of Pacific dogwood are among California's best river experiences.

7. Mixed Northwestern Forest. Inland, the redwood forest soon disappears, giving way to a mixed and variable forest typical of the North Coast Range and the Klamath and Siskiyou Mountains. The mixed northwestern forest ranges from a conifer community dominated by Douglas fir, just east of the redwood forest, to oak woodlands on the driest slopes much farther inland. In wetter areas sugar pine may be found along with Douglas fir. Sugar pine, the largest pine species, is easily identified by the foot-long cones hanging from the ends of its branches. Douglas fir itself has twisted spiral needles and distinctive small cones. Several broadleaf trees—including Pacific madrone, tan-oak, golden chinquapin, and Cascara buckthorn—often mingle with the conifers.

In warmer and drier areas—for example, on slopes with southern exposure—Douglas fir is less common, and a non-coniferous forest flourishes. The trees making up the mixed areas of the Douglas fir forest become dominant here. Madrone is easily identified by its thin, peeling bark. Golden chinquapin has a peculiar spiny fruit midway between the beechnut and the acorn. Other common species on these drier sites include bay, canyon live oak, interior live oak, poison oak, buckeye, and manzanita.

Suggestions for Further Reading:

There are many useful field guides, including the comprehensive series *California Natural History Guides* published by the University of California Press. Several were written by Philip Munz, the acknowledged authority on California native plants. In addition, the following books might prove helpful.

Bakker, Elna S. *An Island Called California: An Ecological Introduction to its Natural Communities* (UC Press, 1971).

Munz, Philip A. *A California Flora and Supplement* (UC Press, 1959).

Storer, Tracy I. and Robert L. Usinger. *Sierra Nevada Natural History: An Illustrated Handbook* (UC Press, 1963).

Whitney, Stephen. *A Sierra Club Naturalist's Guide to the Sierra Nevada* (Sierra Club Books, 1979).

Try the Top of the Eddy

Fishing on California White Water Rivers

Anglers who also like white water boating have a double advantage. Rafts, kayaks, and canoes can take them where other fishermen cannot easily go. And even if the fish aren't biting, running the river makes the trip worth while. But the fish will be biting if you know where to go—and when.

California rivers offer fishing adventures for every season. The best time for trout fishing in the Sierra Nevada is the fall. Then the action moves to the rivers of the North Coast Range for rainy-season salmon and steelhead runs that last into the spring. Winter storms in the Coast Range and late spring snow melt in the Sierra Nevada sometimes produce flows too high or too cold for successful fishing. In the summer, fishing is good during the week on popular white water rivers, but on weekends boat traffic is often so heavy that fishing becomes an early morning and late evening affair.

Trout Fishing in the Sierra Nevada

Fall trout fishing in the Sierra is one of the best angling experiences anywhere. In late autumn, days are usually clear and bright, nights are crisp, and most other visitors are off the river. True, some streams are too low for boating in the fall. But others, including some dam-controlled rivers like the Tuolumne, still have sufficient flows for boating as well as fishing.

Native rainbow trout, easily distinguishable by a shimmering crimson lateral stripe, are the most common trout in California white water rivers. They are found mainly in the Sierra, as well as in a few protected reserves like the upper Middle Fork Eel. Other trout species include the California state fish, the golden trout, found at high elevations in the southern and central Sierra, and magnificent hybridized golden and rainbow in the same regions. Brown trout are European in origin. They were stocked in California streams by fishing enthusiasts around the turn of the century.

This chapter was written in collaboration with Michael McIntyre, a white water outfitter and licensed fishing guide. If you want additional information, contact him c/o Whitewater Angler, 1770 5th Avenue, Sacramento, CA 95818; phone (916) 442-3066.

Water temperatures in the fall often rise above 55°, promoting exciting action as trout rise to the surface to feed. Fishing is best at dawn or just before dark, since trout usually dive deep during the bright part of the day. Trout look for underwater micro-eddies where they can wait while the current sweeps past with its aquatic smorgasbord—so the tail waves of riffles, the heads of eddies and large pools, and pockets of calm water behind boulders are good spots to find them.

In recent years the state Department of Fish and Game (DFG) has opened a number of Sierra rivers to winter fishing under special restrictions—among them the South Fork American between Chili Bar and the Highway 49 bridge, which is easily accessible by paved roads throughout the year. Winter fishing has also been allowed on the Middle Fork American and the South Fork Yuba. Regulations change from year to year; check with the DFG.

Angling Tips

From mid-summer into fall, fly fishermen should work the eddies ("pocket water") with lifelike wet flies such as Wooly Worms and Montana Nymphs. When the water temperature rises above 52° in Sierra streams, surface action is about to begin. For this situation Western dry fly searching patterns like Royal Wulffs and Humpys (sizes 10–16) are good bets. Use barbless hooks, and release healthy trout.

Spin fishing is good in Sierra streams throughout the year. Mepps and Rooster Tails are proven spinners. Remember that our native rainbow trout are too scarce to be caught only once, so cut two of the three hooks off treble hooks, and pinch down the remaining barb. Gently return your catch to the stream. For live insect bait in the fall, look for grasshoppers, flying ants, and stonefly nymphs. Fish caught on bait will probably swallow the hook; if so, they should be taken.

Stoneflies are the principal aquatic insect on the menu of Sierra trout. Small golden stoneflies appear early in the year. Along some rivers a giant dark stonefly, or salmon fly, emerges in late April or early May. If you spot adult stoneflies shimmering in streamside willows, look for stonefly nymphs under rocks in bubbly, well-oxygenated riffles and use them for bait. Or try a wet fly that imitates a large stonefly nymph, or a dry fly resembling an adult. Locate the hatching nymphs in the river. Then let the bait or the lure tumble down the riffle and drift into an eddy behind a rock near the hatch. Get ready for furious action.

Basic Fly Patterns and Lures: Trout

Wet Flies	Dry Flies	Spinners
Gold-ribbed Hare's Ear	Elkhair Caddis	Mepps
Bomber (black or brown)	Royal Wulff	Rooster Tail
Girdle Bug	Adams	
Zug Bug	Humpy (red, yellow, or black)	
Wooly Worm (black and grizzly)		
Wooly Bugger (olive and black)		
Matuka Sculpin (olive or brown)		

North Coast Fishing

From November through March, the rivers of California's North Coast Range are the scene of fine salmon and steelhead fishing. Salmon begin swimming upstream between late September and late October in most years. Some of the biggest king (chinook) salmon in the world—40 to 60 pounds—are caught in the Smith River every winter.

Steelhead follow a few weeks later, feeding on newly deposited salmon roe (eggs). Steelhead are almost identical to rainbow trout except that they live most of their adult lives in the ocean. The fall and winter "half-pounder" steelhead migration as far up the Klamath as Happy Camp provides some of the best fishing in the world. In the last couple of years, since the federal governnment restored reasonable minimum flows to the Trinity River, an increasing number of these anadromous* fish have been turning right at Weitchpec and heading up the Trinity as well. Other North Coast streams, including boatable rivers like the Smith and the Middle and South Forks of the Eel, also have good steelhead runs.

The "half-pounders" actually range from one to five pounds, and they are hungry and full of fight. Seasoned sport fishermen who have never tried steelhead will be surprised by their strength and endurance. Steelhead are in short supply these days, so responsible anglers will use barbless hooks and gently release the fish after catching them. (Anyway, steelhead don't make very good eating in the winter; perhaps because of the high sediment load in the rivers, they have a mossy taste.) On the other hand, while adult steelhead migrate up the rivers for spawning every year, salmon swim upstream only once, to breed and die. It is therefore acceptable practice to harvest an occasional salmon for food.

*Anadromous fish like salmon, steelhead, and shad are ocean dwellers that were hatched in freshwater streams and return to their birthplaces for breeding and spawning.

Angling Tips

Successful rainy-season fishing depends on flow and water clarity. When the river is too high, the fish take cover. When the stream is too cloudy with silt, they can't see the bait or the lure. The best time is a couple of days after heavy rains, when the hungry fish come out to feed. Since water temperatures tend to remain in the 48° to 55° range from winter until mid-summer or later, most fish will be feeding below the surface. Bait fishermen should try bouncing natural bait (like stonefly nymphs or worms) along the river bottom and moving it behind boulders into the eddies where fish like to feed. Remember that a fish caught with bait will probably swallow the hook; if so, it should be taken.

In general, you can use the same gear for steelhead and salmon that you use for Sierra trout, though you might want slightly heavier line. Most North Coast fishing is done from the bank, but some anglers "back-troll" for salmon from boats, trailing Hot Shots lures as they row against the current. Salmon and steelhead go for roe—or roe imitations if you're not a bait fisherman. Yarn Flies are good spinners, and fly fishermen successfully use standard steelhead patterns, such as Winter's Hope and Comets, with a sunken fly.

Basic Fly Patterns and Lures

Steelhead		Salmon	
Wet Flies	**Spinners**	**Wet Flies**	**Spinners**
Skunk	Mepps	Comet	Crocodile
Comet	Rooster Tail	(silver or gold)	Daredevil
Mossback	Hot Shot	Boss	Hot Shot
Brindlebug	Yarn Flies	Winter's Hope	(large)
Fall Favorite		Purple Peril	Yarn Flies
Winter's Hope			

More Tips

- Pack your rods in metal or plastic tubes to avoid breaking them.
- Remember that waders can fill up with water and drag you downstream if you fall into the current. Consider putting on a life jacket. Or try wearing a wet suit, which is much safer than waders.
- For up-to-date regulations, check with the California Department of Fish and Game, 1416 9th St., Sacramento, CA 95814; phone (916) 445-3531.
- Get a valid California fishing license at a sporting goods store. Don't forget to buy a trout stamp. It's not required, but it supports programs aimed at protecting and increasing the wild trout population.

Brian Fessenden

Living river canyons are traded for reservoirs like this one.

Water Follies

A Guide to California Water Politics

River running is growing up in an era of instant nostalgia. We are beginning to appreciate our wild streams just as they are disappearing behind dams. In 1980, its last full boating season, 50,000 people floated the Stanislaus, and thousands more hiked and fished along its banks. Two years later, this unique wilderness river vanished beneath the waters of New Melones Reservoir—a federally-funded project that can scarcely be justified even on its own narrow economic terms.[1] A number of the other rivers featured in this book are threatened by plans for more dams. As we go to press, it is still anybody's guess whether the magnificent Tuolumne will also be sacrificed, or whether the river will receive the federal protection it deserves by being admitted to the National Wild and Scenic River System. Amazingly enough, there is even serious talk about reviving the potentially catastrophic Auburn Dam project on the American River.[2]

Not all dams are bad. It is hard to imagine our society without dams and hydroelectric installations. The point is that we now have enough dams—1200 in California alone. Some are useful, some are not so useful. There is only one river system in the state, the Smith in the far northwestern corner, left entirely undammed. From high in the mountains to the floor of the Central Valley, most Sierra rivers wear reservoirs and dams like beads on a string.

Unfortunately, some of the power and much of the water these dams make available is used unwisely. Part of the problem is heedless urban development, and part of the problem is our lack of systematic water and power conservation. But it is agriculture which consumes the lion's share of California's water. Cheap, subsidized irrigation water made available by federal and state dams and canals has artificially inflated the demand for water. Federal tax policies allowing easy write-offs have encouraged corporate speculation in big-time agriculture and have lined up powerful economic interests behind further expansion of the state's water system. Before more dams can be justified, Californians need to take a closer look at where our water is going now.

Portions of this chapter appeared under the same title in an article by Fryar Calhoun in *Sacramento Magazine* and are reprinted with permission.

Since the 1870's, a network of dams and canals to transport water from rivers to farms has been growing all over the Sierra foothills and the Central Valley. In recent decades the federal and state governments have greatly expanded the last century's work. California now has the world's largest plumbing system, stretching from the northern end of the Sacramento Valley to the Mexican border and from Arizona to the Pacific. We have so much water at our command that huge arid regions in the Imperial Valley and along the west side of the southern San Joaquin Valley have been made to bloom. The Los Angeles-San Diego megalopolis of 15 million people has grown up in an area that could support only a tiny fraction of that number with its own water.

Water made possible the rapid growth of urban southern California's population, and along with it the political clout to impose its vision on the rest of the state. A race for water in the early twentieth century determined the pattern of California's urban development. Around the turn of the century San Francisco, with its 350,000 inhabitants, was the great city of California. The semi-arid South Coast around Los Angeles accounted for only 30 per cent of the state's population. While San Francisco struggled with its Hetch Hetchy project on the upper Tuolumne until 1934, William Mulholland tapped the Owens River for L.A. in 1913 and set off a land boom in southern California that has continued to this day, dwarfing expansion in the north.

Developers believe in providing surplus water—room to grow. At several different stages southern California expanded its water supply. After the Owens River came the development of the the Mono Lake watershed in 1940 (expanded in 1970); the Colorado River Aqueduct (1941); and the California Water Project, which first pumped water across the Tehachapi Mountains in 1971. At each stage Los Angeles and the Metropolitan Water District of Southern California (MWD) acquired far more water than the South Coast needed.[3] Future urban expansion was assured. Meanwhile, enormous amounts of surplus water were sold to agricultural interests at low prices. Then more dams and canals were proposed to stave off the shortage that always seemed to be just around the corner but never materialized.

As a result, residents of the South Coast are better supplied with drinking water than Bay Area dwellers—despite the persistent and politically potent myth that the taps may one day run dry.[4] In the Bay Area, people still seethe about spoiled southerners in Burbank and Beverly Hills who went on sprinkling their gardens, hosing off their sidewalks, and changing the water in their swimming pools during the 1976-77 drought while strict conservation measures were in effect up north. But much of that righteous indignation is misplaced. The fact of the matter is that urban southern Californians scarcely reduced their consumption of water simply because they didn't have to.[5]

The real split is not between north and south, but between city and farm. All urban consumption—residential, business, industrial, and governmental—accounts for only 15 per cent of the water in California impounded for human use. The rest—85 per cent—goes to agriculture. Back in 1977, the second year of the drought, the number of acres in this state planted in water-intensive crops (such as fruit and nut orchards, melons, and vegetables) actually *increased*. Many of these fields were irrigated by surplus "urban" water pumped out of the Delta and down the California Aqueduct, where it was sold by the State Water Project to farms in the San Joaquin Valley and Kern County.

City dwellers along the South Coast—that is, most Californians— are subsidizing the growth of big corporate farming by paying for the construction of dams and canals whether they use the water or not. Over the years, urban southern Californians have paid 70 per cent of the cost of the California Water Project through higher water rates and property taxes, but they have consumed only 24 per cent of the water. Because the region is so well supplied with water from other sources, southern California does not need its full California Aqueduct allotment. The surplus is sold at bargain prices to big corporate farms in areas that were arid patches of waste land not long ago.[6]

Since the late sixties, when the California Aqueduct began to deliver water from the Sacramento Delta to the dry "West Side" of Kern County and the southern San Joaquin Valley, 850,000 formerly barren acres in this region have been brought under cultivation and irrigated with state and federal water. These fields and orchards consume as much water annually as the entire Los Angeles-San Diego area. The new farms aren't exactly growing food for the world's starving masses. Most traditional crops like cotton and alfalfa have long been in surplus. Still, during the big boom in the sixties, thousands of acres were planted in these crops as well as in grapes, olives, almonds, and pistachios. West Side land cost corporations and consortiums of individual investors $50 an acre around 1960. While the new water sources were developed and the young trees and vines grew into maturity, the investors took substantial tax write-offs.[7] By 1980 the land was worth $3000 an acre, and agribusiness was campaigning for still more water.

Irrigation water in California is so cheap that some of it is used neither wisely nor too well.[8] To cite the most flagrant example, a recent state report estimated that the farms of the Imperial Valley waste more than 400,000 acre-feet[9] of Colorado River water every year in evaporation and seepage—as much as a city of two million consumes. Farms in the Sacramento and San Joaquin Valleys have better records, but water is generally so inexpensive and plentiful that instances of overwatering are easy enough to find. Even a ten per cent saving in California irrigation water would increase the total supply available to urban areas by over 60 per cent. This would be more than enough to provide for population growth without building new reservoirs and digging more ditches.

If water cost more, farmers would be less likely to waste it, and speculation in desert agribusiness would be curtailed. Presently, farmers can buy water for a fraction of its true cost, while the federal taxpayer or the urban southern Californian covers the expense of building and maintaining the dams, reservoirs, and canals. The federal government sells its water to farmers for as little as $3.50 per acre-foot. Surplus state irrigation water costs slightly more, and regularly-contracted state water goes for about $30 per acre-foot near the Delta and more farther south.

As long as water is so cheap that there is little incentive to conserve it, as long as many water projects—especially federal—never pay for themselves, can it honestly be argued that California really needs more dams, reservoirs, and canals? Why shouldn't dams sell water and power at competitive market rates or at prices reflecting their true cost of construction—or, better yet, their replacement cost?[10]. Shouldn't alternatives less harmful to the environment be considered before more of our scarce river canyons are destroyed?

Some dams and diversion projects are built primarily to generate power, not to store water. In the last few years new federal subsidies, in the forms of tax credits and guaranteed high rates for electrical power, have touched off an unprecedented flurry of proposals for more hydroelectric installations. Projects have been proposed on almost every stream in the state, from boatable rivers to the smallest creeks. Unfortunately, the Federal Energy Regulatory Commission (FERC), which reviews these proposals, exists primarily to license power projects, not to reject them. The sheer number of applications makes it hard to separate the good from the bad, and the agency's procedures make it difficult for the public to intervene in order to protest unnecessary or harmful proposals. Ominously, out of more than a thousand applications submitted in the past, FERC has denied only one on grounds that it might damage the environment. Unless federal subsidies are removed from hydroelectric projects, this threat to California streams may prove a very serious one.[11]

California has 1200 reservoirs, yet dam builders, politicians, and union officials still argue the dubious benefits, recreational and economic, of more of these man-made lakes with their unnatural, sharply fluctuating shore lines. Building dams creates jobs, they say. But there is another side to these arguments. Scenic beauty is not the only defense available to river lovers. In 1980 commercial rafting outfitters generated some $1.5 million from their operations on the remaining upper nine miles of the Stanislaus. Thousands of other river lovers— private boaters, hikers, fishermen—also spent money in nearby towns like Sonora and Angel's Camp. Then, the benefits of building New Melones Dam turned out to be exaggerated. Most of the construction jobs went to skilled workers brought in from outside the area, and members of their families often competed with natives for local jobs. Unemployment in Sonora actually *rose* during the dam-building years.

Fighting off unnecessary dams is definitely a rear-guard action. When one unfeasible proposal is abandoned, another springs up to take its place. So in some cases legislative protection may well be the only answer. The Stanislaus never came close to receiving National Wild and Scenic status in time to prevent the construction of New Melones Dam. The Tuolumne has a better chance of being admitted to this exclusive, federally-protected club, but the outcome is still in doubt. There is also a state Wild and Scenic River system, created in 1972 by the California Legislature and consisting primarily of rivers of the northern Coast Ranges[12]. In January 1981, as one of his last acts in office, outgoing Secretary of the Interior Cecil Andrus accepted Governor Jerry Brown's proposal that the California Wild and Scenic Rivers be included in the national system. His decision has been the subject of litigation ever since. In May 1984 the U.S. Court of Appeals ruled that Andrus had acted within his powers, so at present these rivers also enjoy federal protection.

Even written guarantees cannot be expected to protect rivers forever. Unless we adopt a more reasonable approach to the use of our natural resources, state and federal protection may be only temporary stopgaps. The fate of California's superb natural fisheries provides an instructive example.[13] At least seven federal and state laws, not to mention some important state regulations, promise protection to the fisheries of the Sacramento Delta and San Francisco Bay. Yet the actual Delta catch has declined disastrously ever since the pumping plants of the California Water Project began exporting water south in the late sixties. Migratory fish, notably salmon, are confused by the strong currents running southward toward the pumps, and many fail to reach their upstream spawning grounds. Small fry—the next generations of fish—are sucked into the pumps and killed in spite of the elaborate and expensive screens designed to keep them out.

To cite another example, during the second year of the 1976-77 drought, the state government revised its Delta water standards downward and let flows in the Delta drop while San Joaquin farmers continued to receive substantial (though reduced) supplies of irrigation water via the California Aqueduct and the federal Delta-Mendota canal. Written guarantees go only so far. They can be brushed aside when the political climate permits. In the words of former State Senator Peter Behr, author of the California Wild and Scenic River Act, "You cannot contain a thirsty beast in a paper cage."

1. New Melones Dam has yet to find buyers for most of its water and sells its electricity so cheaply that if it ever pays for itself, it will take nearly a century.

2. For more information, see the chapters on the Stanislaus, Tuolumne, American, Mokelumne, Feather, Russian, Eel, Sacramento, Trinity, and Klamath.

3. The MWD has rarely taken its full allotment from either the California Aqueduct or the Colorado River.

4. Thanks to heavy support in southern California, the California Water Plan, which authorized construction of the California Aqueduct and a number of reservoirs, was approved in a 1960 statewide referendum by the narrow margin of 174,000 votes out of a total of 5.8 million cast. In contrast, the vote was unfavorable in every northern California county except Butte, where Oroville, the project's biggest dam, was to be built. Surprisingly, in 1982 the Peripheral Canal was rejected in a referendum by 62 to 38 per cent—not just because most northern California counties disapproved by huge majorities, but also because southern Californians voted less overwhelmingly for water development than usual.

5. Bay Area residents like to talk about "our" northern California rivers, but urban areas in both north and south import their water from distant rivers. San Francisco drinks the Tuolumne, and the East Bay bathes in the Mokelumne. Los Angeles washes its cars with the Owens River. When San Diego turns on the tap, part of the mighty Colorado flows out. All these coastal cities use water at about the same rate. San Francisco consumes about 140 gallons per capita per day—80 per cent of the Los Angeles rate of roughly 170. Valley towns like Fresno and Sacramento typically use nearly twice as much per capita—close to 300 gallons a day.

6. The roll of the largest landowners in the new agricultural sweepstakes reads like the Fortune 500: Chevron Oil, Getty Oil, Shell Oil, Tenneco West, Southern Pacific, McCarthy Joint Venture (owned largely by Prudential Insurance), the Blackwell Land Company, and the Tejon Ranch Company (owned in part by the publishers of the *Los Angeles Times*. It's not that huge corporate farms are more efficient. A University of California study examined farms of various sizes and was unable to demonstrate greater efficiency in production beyond the 640-acre level. But with their financial resources, they can survive crises of overproduction and depressed prices better than smaller traditional farms.

7. Too late, the federal government closed some of the tax loopholes that permitted this kind of speculation. When the huge new West Side orchards came into full production, small farmers in traditional olive- and almond-growing areas of the Sacramento Valley found themselves on the brink of ruin. Wholesale prices plummeted, indicating a worldwide glut in the making. Orchards in the Sacramento Valley were put up for sale. But almonds and olives became little if any cheaper at the retail level.

8. Arguments that more expensive irrigation water will increase the cost to the consumer of food and fiber do not stand up on closer inspection. First, the cost of water is a small component of the total cost of growing and marketing a crop. More important, most major crops are in surplus, agricultural commodity prices have been depressed for years, and farmers are in no position to command higher prices for their products.

9. As the term implies, an acre-foot of water would cover an acre of ground (43,560 sq. ft.) to a depth of one foot. It would fill a cube roughly 69 feet on a side. That amounts to 325,000 gallons, enough to supply a family of five for a year—if their lawn isn't too large. Forty per cent of the residential water consumed in California is applied to lawns. It has been estimated that nearly 300,000 acre-feet *too much* water is sprinkled onto lawns every year—enough for a city of more than a million.

10. Water and power production should be fully contracted for before construction is authorized. In addition, water contractors (primarily the MWD) should be allowed to sell surplus state water to the highest bidder. Presently, regulations force contractors to sell it to farmers for transportation costs only, and urban dwellers continue to pay the yearly installments on construction costs. Realistic requirements such as these would be likely to reduce the pace of dam building considerably.

11. In the late seventies and early eighties the federal government began to encourage alternative forms of renewable energy generation (wind, solar, co-generation) with tax credits and other incentives. Unfortunately, the final legislation also included "small"

hydroelectric projects—up to 80 megawatt capacity, hardly a small installation. Unlike wind or solar energy, hydroelectric projects are often harmful to the environment, and they hardly represent a new technology deserving subsidies for development.

12. The state system includes most of the Eel, Trinity, Klamath, Smith, and their major forks and tributaries, as well as a high-elevation stretch of the North Fork American and the lower American between Folsom and Sacramento. The gorge of the Middle Fork Feather is the only California charter member of the national system.

13. The fish populations in some rivers have been badly damaged by upstream dams which divert or drastically alter the rivers' natural flow. See the chapters on the Eel, Trinity, and Klamath.

Suggested Reading:

The California Water Atlas (State Government of California, 1978, 1979).

Dennis, Harry. *Water and Power* (Friends of the Earth Books, 1981).

Engelbert, Ernest A., ed. *Competition for California Water* (UC Press, 1982).

Kahrl, William. *Water and Power: The Conflict over Los Angeles' Water Supply in the Owens Valley* (UC Press, 1982).

Powledge, Fred. *Water* (Farrar, Strauss, and Giroux, 1982).

Walker, Richard and Michael Storper. "The California Water System: Another Round of Expansion?" *Public Affairs Report*, Vol. 20, No. 2.

River Conservation Organizations:

American Rivers Conservation Council (ARCC)
322 Fourth St. N.E.
Washington, DC 20002
(202) 547-6900

Friends of the River (FOR)
909 12th St., Suite 207
Sacramento, CA 95814
(916) 442-3155

Friends of the River (FOR)
Ft. Mason Center, Bldg. C
San Francisco, CA 94123
(415) 771-0400

Friends of the River has other local chapters around the state. Organizations dealing with specific rivers are mentioned in the individual river chapters in this book.

Whose Rivers Are They?

Legal Problems of River Running and River Access

On a bright April morning a couple of years ago, our small rafting party put in on the South Fork of the Eel just downstream from Branscomb. We launched from private property, but we had received the landowner's permission to put in there and even to camp on her land the previous night. A couple of miles downstream, all signs of civilization vanished. Or so we thought until we rounded a bend and saw first a new house, then a perplexed man standing on the bank. "Who gave you the right to run this river?" he demanded. We had only begun to answer by the time we were out of earshot. This chapter is what we might have said.

Freedom of navigation and the public's right to use rivers are guaranteed by the Commerce Clause of the U.S. Constitution, the Congressional act admitting California to the Union, and the California State Constitution. The act of admission requires "that all the navigable waters within said State shall be common highways and forever free." The state constitution forbids individual, joint, and corporate landowners from obstructing free navigation. It also provides that "the Legislature shall enact such laws as will give the most liberal construction to this provision, so that access to the navigable waters of this State shall be always attainable for the people thereof."[1]

In spite of these forthright statements, things aren't so simple. White water boating is a new sport and poses novel legal problems. The rights of private recreational boaters are still evolving, and they tend to come into conflict with the rights, interests, and traditional views of riverside landowners. According to Section 830 of the Califoria Civil Code, when property "borders upon a navigable lake or stream, where there is no tide, the owner takes to the edge of the lake or stream, at low-water mark; when it borders upon any other water, the owner takes to the middle of the lake or stream." Obviously, there is plenty of potential for conflict with the public right of navigation.

Usually, when such conflicts come to trial, courts are reluctant to do more than decide the facts and law of specific cases. Still, the general trend—especially at higher judicial levels—is to affirm the public's right to use the rivers. In several important decisions, California courts have

This chapter was written in collaboration with William Resneck, a Berkeley attorney and private river runner.

272

decided that property rights must yield to the constitutionally-guaranteed public right of passage on navigable waterways. In 1971 the California Court of Appeals heard a case involving the little Fall River, a tributary of the Pit. The court upheld the public's right to use the river, including banks, beaches, sand bars, and gravel bars below the normal high water mark (not the exceptional high water line created by occasional floods). The Court of Appeals also upheld the public's right to float the Russian River, even though the river was not historically navigable in summer and fall. (The diversion of Eel River water provides the Russian with an artificial year-round flow.) In this case the local trial court protected the public's right to portage around a dam over property owned by a local park district. Then, in 1979, a Court of Appeals decision invalidated El Dorado County's attempt to prohibit boating on the South Fork American, America's second most popular white water river.[2]

In other words, generally speaking, once the boater is legally on the river, use of the stream and the banks below the high water mark may be considered proper. But the right of access to the river itself is different. Normally, permission is required. The public has no right to cross private property to reach the river unless the landowner has agreed to allow such access or has failed to make a serious effort to prevent it for at least five years.[3]

On the other hand, the courts have tended to uphold the public's right to use easements where county roads cross the river for access to the banks. For example, in the seventies landowners along the Rio Bravo section of the Kern tried to prevent the public from reaching the river, even though the easement where the county road and bridge crossed the Kern was wide enough. Eventually, after a number of conflicting judicial rulings, the landowners abandoned their attempt. A similar situation arose in Imperial County, where landowners tried to stop the public from using a traditional access point to the Colorado River and were eventually overruled by the state Court of Appeals.[4]

Beyond the issues of navigability and access, who really owns our rivers, lakes, and streams? Do private individuals, or even large groups and powerful interests like irrigation districts and municipal water authorities have an unlimited right to lay claim to California's water? A 1983 California Supreme Court decision went a long way toward sketching out an answer to these questions. In its ruling on a Mono Lake case, the court affirmed that the lake is held in trust by the state for the benefit of the public. If this principle is extended to other bodies of navigable water, our rivers and lakes stand a much better chance of protection from unwise development in the future.[5]

Encouraging as these decisions have been, boaters should remember that the arm of the law is a long way away when they put in on wilderness rivers. The best way to deal with conflicts about river access is to be tactful and polite. Landowners or their caretakers may not be interested in citations of constitutional and legal principles. There have

273

been incidents where guns were brandished to reinforce a private notion of trespass. Assuming you survive, you can always appeal to the authorities, but don't expect instant satisfaction. Local sheriffs and judges are likely to be more sympathetic to their neighbor than to rafters or kayakers who show up on the river one day and start talking about their rights.

1. While the Commerce Clause of the U.S. Constitution refers to commercial navigation, the act of admission to statehood and the California constitution use broad language. Article 10, Section 4 of the state constitution, quoted in part above, also forbids landowners "to exclude the right of way to [navigable] water whenever it is required for any public purpose."

2. The Fall River question was decided in People v. Mack (1971), 19 Cal. App. 3d 1040. The distinction between the "normal" or seasonal high water line and the limit reached by flood waters was specifically defined by the California State Legislature in a revision of the Harbors and Navigation Code, Section 100. The Russian River case was Hitchings v. Del Rio Woods Recreation and Park District (1976) 55 Cal. App. 3d 560. Conceivably, the reasoning about the right to portage might be extended to apply to scouting as well. But this is uncharted legal territory. The American River case was People Ex Rel. Younger v. County of El Dorado (1979) 96 Cal. App. 3d 403.

3. Presently the legal principles by which courts decide these issues are (a) dedication implied in law and (b) dedication implied in fact. The former requires continuous "adverse" use of the property—that is, public use for access—for five years without substantial opposition by the owner. The latter involves acquiescence or affirmative acts by the owner. These principles have been applied both in cases involving access to California ocean beaches and recently in a case on river access. For the ocean beaches, see the California Supreme Court decision in Gion v. City of Santa Cruz (1970) 2 Cal. App. 3d 29. For the river, see the next footnote.

4. Brumbaugh v. County of Imperial (1982) 134 Cal. App. 3d 556. This decision discusses the questions of access rights implied in law and in fact.

5. For the Mono Lake decision, see National Audobon Society v. Superior Court (1983) 33 Cal. 3d 419. On development issues see the chapter "Water Follies."

Where To Get It and How To Do It

White Water Equipment, Instruction and Publications

Pacific River Supply
6044 Bernhard
Richmond, CA 94805
(415) 232-0822

Pacific River Supply South
955 E. Second St.,
Long Beach, CA 90802
(213) 432-0187

R.E.I.
9 City Boulevard West
Orange, CA 92668
(714) 634-2391

R.E.I.
405 W. Torrance Blvd.
Carson, CA 90745
(213) 538-2429

Real Cheap Sports
36 W. Santa Clara St.
Ventura, CA 93002
(805) 648-3803

Sequoia Outdoor Center
11316 Kernville Road
PO Box S--Sequoia
Kernville, CA 93238
(619) 376-3776

Robbins Mountain Shop
7257 North Abby Rd.
Fresno, CA 96350
(209) 431-7152

Western Mountaineering
931 Pacific Ave.
Santa Cruz, CA 95060
(408) 429-6300

Western Mountaineering
550 South First St.
San Jose, CA 95113
(408) 298-6300

Reg Lake Paddle Sports
341 Visitacion
Brisbane, CA 94005
(415) 467-2800

Outdoors Unlimited Coop
24 Kirkham St.
San Francisco, CA 94143
(415) 666-2078

R.E.I.
1338 San Pablo Ave.
Berkeley, CA 94702
(415) 527-4140

California Canoe and Kayak
2170 Redwood Highway
Greenbrae, CA 94904
(415) 461-1750

Clavey Equipment
30 Pamaron Way, Unit M
Novato, CA 94947
(415) 883-8826

American River Recreation
11257 Bridge St.
Rancho Cordova, CA 95670
(916) 635-4479

The River Store
PO Box 472
Lotus, CA 95651
(916) 626-3435

This is probably not a complete list. Our apologies to organizations which we inadvertently left out.

Outdoor Adventures
U.C. Davis
Davis, CA 95616
(916) 752-1995

National Outdoor College
11383 Pyrites Way #A
Rancho Cordova, CA 95670
(916) 638-7900

Alpine West
1021 R Street
Sacramento, CA 95814
(916) 441-1627

California Rivers
PO Box 468
Geyserville, CA 95441
(707) 857-3872

The Fifth Season
426 N. Mt. Shasta Blvd.
Mt. Shasta, CA 96067
(916) 926-2776

Adventure's Edge
650 10th St.
Arcata, CA 95521
(707) 822-4673

Mail Order Equipment

Blackadar Boating
PO Box 1170
Salmon, ID 83467

Cascade Outfitters
PO Box 209
Springfield, OR 97477

Northwest River Supplies
PO Box 9186
Moscow, ID 83843

Idaho Outdoor Equipment
PO Box 8005
Boise, ID 83707

Colorado Kayak Supply
PO Box 291
Buena Vista, CO 81211

Four Corners Marine
PO Box 379
Durango, CO 81302

For instruction you can also contact the River Touring Section of your local Sierra Club chapter.

River Running Books and Magazines

McGinnis, William.
Whitewater Rafting
(Quadrangle, 1975).

Urban, John.
Whitewater Handbook
(Appalachian Mountain Club, 1981).

Tejada-Flores, Lito.
Wildwater
(Sierra Club Books, 1978).

Foshee, John.
You Too Can Canoe
(Strode, 1977).

Holbek, Lars and Chuck Stanley.
A Guide to the Best Whitewater in the State of California
(FOR Books, 1984).

River Runner Magazine
PO Box 2047,
Vista, CA 92083.

Paddler's News Bulletin
Sierra Club
River Touring Section,
PO Box 384,
San Bruno, CA 94066.

Currents
National Organization of
River Sports,
PO Box 6847,
Colorado Springs, CO 80934.

American Whitewater
146 N. Brockway
Palatine, IL 60067

Canoe Magazine
PO Box 10748
Des Moines, IA 50349

EASY WHITE WATER

River Runs in this Guide of Class II–III Difficulty or Less
(Low and Moderate Flows Only)

RIVER	DIFFICULTY	LENGTH (miles)	SEASON	WILDERNESS	PAGE
Kern					
Powerhouse Run (part of Upper Kern)	II–III	2	April–July	No	28
Rancheria Road to Lake Ming (part of Rio Bravo Run)	II–III	2.2	All year	No	35
Merced					
Suspension Bridge to Briceburg	II	7	March–June	No	54
Mokelumne					
Electra Run	II	3	All year	No	82
East Fork Carson					
Wilderness Run	II	20	May–June	Yes	94
South Fork American					
Coloma to Lotus	II	3	All year	No	98
Middle Fork American					
Greenwood Bridge Site to Mammoth Bar	II	8	April–Sept	Yes	105
North Fork American					
Big Bend Run (below Chamberlain Falls Run)	II	4	March–early June	Yes	115
Truckee					
Squaw Creek to above Floriston	II–III	4	April–October	No	119
Bear					
Bear River Campground to Dog Bar	II	2	April–June	Yes	245
Russian					
Squaw Rock Run	II$_3$	8	December–August	No	139

RIVER	DIFFICULTY	LENGTH (miles)	SEASON	WILDERNESS	PAGE
Cache Creek					
Rumsey Run	II–III	8.5	December–August	No	143
Rancheria Creek					
Mountain View Road to Hendy Woods State Park	II+	13	December–early April	Yes	147
South Fork Eel					
Big Bend to Redwood Flat	II	9	December–April	Partial	173
Trinity					
Lewiston to Junction City	II	37	March–November	Partial	189
Big Flat Campground to Cedar Flat	II+	19	All year	No	191
Hawkins Bar to Weitchpec	II$_3$	39	All year	Partial	198
Salmon					
Forks of Salmon to Nordheimer	II–III	4.3	April–July	No	208
Wooley Creek to Highway 96	II–III	5	April–June	No	208
Scott					
Scott Bar to Klamath Confluence	II–III	3.5	April–June	No	213
Klamath					
Interstate 5 to Sarah Totten Campground	II	37	March–November	No	217
Sarah Totten Campground to above Ishi Pishi Falls	II–III	76	All year	Partial	224
Dolan's Bar to Weitchpec	II–III	17	All year	Partial	224
Smith					
Gasquet to above Oregon Hole Gorge	II–III	6	November–May or June	No	237

Index of Featured Rivers

RUN	DIFFICULTY	LENGTH (MILES)	SEASON	WILDERNESS	PAGE
1. Forks of the Kern	V	17	May–July	Yes	15
2. Upper Kern	II–Vp	19	April–July	No	21
3. Lower Kern	IVp	18	Summer	Partial	29
4. Rio Bravo Run	II–IVp	5	All year	Partial	35
5. Kaweah	III–Vp	10	April–June	No	39
6. Upper Kings	V+p	10	July	Yes	44
7. Kings	III	9.5	April–July	No	49
8. Merced	II–IVp	29	March–June	Partial	54
9. Upper Tuolumne	Vp	9	July–October	Yes	62
10. Tuolumne	IV+	18	March–October	Yes	69
11. Lower Stanislaus	III–V	4	All year ?	Yes	78
12. Mokelumne	II	3	All year	No	82
13. Cosumnes	II–Vp	20	March–May	Yes	86
14. Upper East Fork Carson	III	7	May–June	No	91
15. East Fork Carson Wilderness Run	II	20	May–June	Yes	94
16. South Fork American Chili Bar and Gorge Runs	III	20	All year	Partial	98
17. Middle Fork American	II–Vp	25	May–September	Yes	105
18. North Fork American Giant Gap Run	V	14	April–June	Yes	111
19. North Fork American Chamberlain Falls and Big Bend Runs	II–IV+	9	March–June	Yes	115
20. Truckee	II–III+	27	April–October	No	119
21. North Fork Yuba	III–V	19	April–June	No	123
22. Middle Fork Feather	V+p	32	June	Yes	128
23. Deer Creek	Vp	23	April–May	Yes	133

RUN	DIFFICULTY	LENGTH (MILES)	SEASON	WILDERNESS	PAGE
24. Russian River	II	8	All year	No	139
25. Cache Creek	II–III	8.5	December–August	No	143
26. Rancheria Creek	II+	13	December–April	Yes	147
27. Stony Creek	III–IV	5	December–April	Yes	151
28. Eel Pillsbury Run	III+	6	Most of year	Yes	158
29. Eel Dos Rios to Alderpoint	II–III	46	March–May	Yes	161
30. North Fork Eel	III	8	December–April	Yes	166
31. Middle Fork Eel	II–IV$_6$	30	March–May	Yes	168
32. South Fork Eel	IV–V	16	December–April	Yes	173
33. Redwood Creek	I–IVp	25	March–May	Yes	179
34. Upper Sacramento	III–IV$_5$	36	April–June	Partial	184
35. Trinity North Fork Confluence to China Slide	II+–III+	25	All year	No	191
36. Trinity Burnt Ranch Gorge	V	8.5	July–September	Yes	194
37. Trinity Hawkins Bar to Weitchpec	II$_3$	39	All year	Partial	198
38. South Fork Trinity	Vp	48	April–May	Yes	202
39. Salmon	II–V	19	April–July	Partial	208
40. Scott	III–V	21.5	April–June	Partial	213
41. Upper Klamath	IV+	17	April–October	Partial	219
42. Klamath Sarah Totten Campground to Weitchpec	II–IIIp	100	All year	Partial	224
43. North Fork Smith	IV	13	November–May	Yes	234
44. Smith Gasquet to South Fork Confluence	II–III$_5$	8	November–May	No	237
45. South Fork Smith	III$_5$	13	November–May	No	240

Class V Wilderness Runs

For teams of seasoned experts only

Forks of the Kern
Upper Kings
Upper Tuolumne
North Fork American: Giant Gap Run
Middle Fork Feather Gorge
Deer Creek
Trinity: Burnt Ranch Gorge
South Fork Trinity: Highway 36 to Bridge Site

Please protect the river environment

- **Pack it in, pack it out.** Leave nothing behind. Carry plenty of waterproof plastic trash bags and use them for litter.

- **Pack out solid human waste** unless toilet facilities are provided (rare along California rivers). Use watertight ammo boxes double-lined with heavy-duty plastic trash bags. Add Clorox II powder or lime to cut the odor. Never urinate into solid waste bags.

- **Wash only above the high water line.** Use biodegradable soap.

- **Be careful with fire.** Contain ashes and coals in a fire pan. Extinguish fires completely. Always have a shovel.

About the Authors

Jim Cassady, 38, a native of Maryland, first dug a paddle into white water as a canoeist on Eastern and Midwestern creeks and rivers. After he migrated to southern California, where he taught social science in a Long Beach high school, Cassady learned to kayak and later became a professional rafting guide. He now lives in the San Francisco Bay Area and owns Pacific River Supply in Richmond. He has also designed a new self-bailing raft produced by Whitewater Manufacturing of Grants Pass, Oregon. Cassady led pioneering trips down some of California's toughest white water rivers, including Burnt Ranch Gorge of the Trinity, the Upper Kings, the North Fork Mokelumne, Middle Fork of the Feather and the Forks of the Kern. He has boated more than 200 rivers in the U.S. and abroad, including the 45 featured in this guide book.

Fryar Calhoun, 41, grew up in the flat, dry West Texas Panhandle, far from white water rivers. Later he lived and studied on the East Coast and in Europe, then spent a number of years teaching history at U.C. Berkeley. Until 1976, when a friend took him on a raft trip down the Salmon River in Idaho, he thought the outdoors meant playing tennis. Since then he has run rivers throughout the Western U.S., organized a private white water rafting cooperative, worked as a professional rafting guide, and published articles on rivers and other subjects in *New West*, *California*, *Texas Monthly*, *Sacramento*, and *Motorland* magazines.

Also by Cassady and Calhoun: Detailed guides with shaded-relief river maps to five of California's best-known white water runs: the Tuolumne (Meral's Pool to Ward's Ferry), South Fork American, Forks of the Kern, Upper Kern, and Lower Kern.

Available at your local white water equipment dealer or bookstore, or from the authors, PO Box 3580, Berkeley, CA 94703.

Index of First-Person Stories

River	Contributor	Page
Forks of the Kern	Fryar Calhoun	20
Upper Kings	Jim Cassady	45
Upper San Joaquin*	Reg Lake	48
Upper Tuolumne	Marty McDonnell	67
Tuolumne	Fryar Calhoun	73
Middle Fork Feather	Jim Cassady	131
Eel	Spreck Rosekrans	172
Redwood Creek	Jim Cassady	183
South Fork Trinity	Jim Cassady	203
Los Angeles and others	Jim Cassady	247

*For reasons obvious to those who read Reg Lake's story on page 48, the Upper San Joaquin is not covered by this guide book. For the rest of the San Joaquin, see page 243.